ON THE HOUSE

On the House

An Inside Look
at the House of Commons

ROB WALSH

McGill-Queen's University Press
Montreal & Kingston • London • Chicago

© McGill-Queen's University Press 2017

ISBN 978-0-7735-5145-9 (cloth)
ISBN 978-0-7735-5223-4 (ePDF)
ISBN 978-0-7735-5224-1 (ePUB)

Legal deposit fourth quarter 2017
Bibliothèque nationale du Québec

Printed in Canada on acid-free paper that is 100% ancient forest free
(100% post-consumer recycled), processed chlorine free.

McGill-Queen's University Press acknowledges the support of the
Canada Council for the Arts for our publishing program. We also
acknowledge the financial support of the Government of Canada
through the Canada Book Fund for our publishing activities.

Library and Archives Canada Cataloguing in Publication

Walsh, Rob, 1946–, author
    On the House : an inside look at the House of Commons / Rob Walsh.

Includes bibliographical references and index.
Issued in print and electronic formats.
ISBN 978-0-7735-5145-9 (hardcover). – ISBN 978-0-7735-5223-4 (ePDF). –
ISBN 978-0-7735-5224-1 (ePUB)

    1. Canada. Parliament. House of Commons. 2. Democracy – Canada.
3. Canada – Politics and government. I. Title.

JL161.W35 2017   328.71'072   C2017-903966-0
                                            C2017-903967-9

This book was typeset by True to Type in 10.5/14 Sabon

For the

Institute of Parliamentary
and Political Law

Institut de Droit Parlementaire et Politique

Contents

Foreword

PETER MILLIKEN

A book about the workings of the House of Commons that is neither a procedural manual nor an academic critique of its functions is a rarity. Rob Walsh, the House's law clerk and parliamentary counsel from 1999 to 2012, has written a book about his experience as legislative counsel that provides us with an informative and useful review of both the role he played in helping the House function and the way the House deals with many of the things for which it is constitutionally responsible. Mr Walsh served the House for over twenty years and provided advice to members, committees, and staff on a huge variety of issues and questions. He has written a book that will be very helpful to members, advisors, students of Parliament, and professors in the political sphere as well as compiling a wonderful package of information for those interested in the functioning of our Parliament.

The law clerk provides advice on the legislative process to members, standing committees, procedural clerks, committee staff, the Speaker, and the Board of Internal Economy that governs the financial and administrative business of the House, as well as to others who request advice to ensure that bills introduced into the House will be lawful if adopted, are passed in accordance with the law and the rules of the House, and are within the legislative competence of the Parliament of Canada. His book sets out many details of how our system functions, how decisions are made in Parliament, and how the legislative role of the House operates in rendering decisions on many matters that are brought forward in government bills and private member's bills debated in the House and considered in committees.

Mr Walsh served during five majority parliaments and three minority parliaments so his book reflects events that varied greatly in different circumstances. The role of the House and its committees change with shifts in government and this makes the book a wonderful read for those interested in how our parliamentary system works. I had the pleasure of working with Mr Walsh for most of the time he worked at the House of Commons and much enjoyed his counsel and ideas, as did many of my colleagues. This book represents a very substantial contribution to information on how our legislative process operates and will be of considerable interest to those who are involved in it or who wish to learn more about it.

Hon. Peter Milliken, BA, MA, LLB, PC, OC, FRSC
MP, Kingston and the Islands (Ontario) (1988–2011)
34th Speaker of the House of Commons (2001–11)

Prologue

Imagine you've been elected to the House of Commons. You'd been politically active in your hometown but hadn't thought of running for Parliament until friends urged you to go for it. It was a long shot; you never thought you'd win but you did. You've packed your bags and found your way to Ottawa (which you had never visited before). And here you are.

You've had many tasks since election day. You've had to find a place to live in Ottawa during each session (something members from ridings around Ottawa don't need to worry about), move into the parliamentary office assigned to you, start recruiting staff, and establish a constituency office (unless you can take over the outgoing member's office).

House Administration organized a day-long orientation session that helped a bit, providing mostly administrative, financial, and legal details relating to the institutional organization of the House, staffing your offices, and managing your office budget as well as enlisting some veteran members to sit on panels to talk about the ups and downs of the parliamentary life you're about to begin. You may have found this somewhat overwhelming: too much information too soon. A House Administration staffer has been assigned to assist you in getting organized before the opening of Parliament in a few weeks. You attended your first party caucus – little more than a hello-how-are-you gathering – where you met fellow party members from parts of Canada you'd never visited. You're soon looking forward to getting back home and you hope to get back before returning to Ottawa for the opening of the new Parliament.

Somewhere in these weeks, before you make your first appearance in the Chamber, you must arrange with the Office of the Clerk to take your oath as a member of Parliament, since you cannot take your seat in the Chamber until you have sworn an oath of allegiance or loyalty to the Queen.[1] When the first Bloc Québécois members arrived, they were uncomfortable swearing allegiance to the Queen as they were committed to seeking Quebec independence and some observers agreed that it was hypocritical of them to take the oath. For my part, I didn't see any contradiction between the Bloc's pursuit of Quebec independence and loyalty to the Queen as they had always made it clear that they sought Quebec sovereignty through democratic means.

As a newcomer, you'll probably be seated in one of the back rows of the Chamber, perhaps in the second-to-last row, which has drop-down seats, not armchairs like the other rows, and was added in 2015 to accommodate the thirty additional seats needed to maintain proportional representation in the House following population changes reflected in the last decennial census (2011).[2]

As a member of Parliament, you are at the beginning of a new chapter in your life, probably unlike anything you have ever done before. You will learn and learn and never stop learning, developing parliamentary skills largely through trial and error. In addition to proceedings in the Chamber or in committees, there will be lots of meetings, private political consultations with constituents or constituency groups or with other members or your staff, and lots of travelling and many nights without enough sleep and frequently finding yourself eating on the run or not at all (be careful). In the meantime, your constituents back home will follow reports on the House in the media, particularly when you are featured, and will look forward to hearing your explanations of what goes on there.

I'd like to share with you how I experienced the House; as you become immersed in it, my observations may give you a sense of the place from the perspective of someone working "downstairs," supporting your parliamentary and political world "upstairs." It was quite a learning experience for me and likely will be for you, too.

When I came to the House in 1991, I thought I knew enough to deal with what I had been hired to do (draft private member's bills and amendments to bills). As it turned out, I didn't know how little I knew about the place or about the job I had taken on – my past professional experience as a lawyer had a very limited application in this environment. The House was like nothing I had ever experienced before. I was not without some political smarts but I had no idea what it meant to work as a non-partisan parliamentary lawyer in a partisan political workplace. By the time I left the House, over twenty years later, I had come to understand the place fairly well, I think, though each session brought changes as the players and the issues changed. I learned from watching and supporting the business of the House up close and at times on a quite personal level, making my share of mistakes along the way.

We'll look first at the main players you will often see on their feet in the Chamber or in your caucus and at the proceedings in the Chamber and in committees. However, any explanation of the House must include its historical evolution and its constitutional place today, the big picture. More than 800 years of political struggle against the powers of the Crown led to the parliamentary system of government as we know it today, including, eventually, the House of Commons as a vital part of this system with legal powers and privileges that support it in carrying out its constitutional functions.

Then we'll move closer and look at the various proceedings by which the House carries out its constitutional functions, particularly how it did this during the years I was there. Finally, we'll look at the administrative infrastructure – the officials you'll need to deal with in running your office and managing your office budget – that supports the House and gives institutional permanence to this otherwise transient place that will be your home away from home for at least a few years, if not longer. My focus will be on the House as an institution and not on the politicians who, with the greatest of respect, come and go.

At the end of the day, the business of the House is politics and politics is all about relationships: political, personal, and, importantly, constitutional. At the same time, conflict is fundamental to the parliamentary environment and your challenge will be to work effectively within the sometimes offensively hostile adversarial environment. The tiresome formalisms of House procedural rules and practices enable an assembly of over 330 members (albeit grouped according to political party) to consider the many-faceted business of the House (and its committees) in an orderly manner and to arrive at timely results through votes. Without procedural rules – which are difficult to understand and won't be discussed in depth here – this process would break down.

Perhaps after finishing this book you will want to look at the House even more closely. If you like reading history, the historical evolution of the parliamentary system of government is fascinating. If you are intrigued by law and legal rules in relation to politics, texts on the law of parliamentary privilege might interest you. In either case, a good start would be the encyclopedic text published by the House: *House of Commons Procedure and Practice.* The sources I identify in the footnotes and the bibliography might also be helpful.

When you are through, feel free to send me your thoughts: onthehouse8@gmail.com.

ON THE HOUSE

Take Your Seat.
Read the Program.

You arrive early for the first sitting of the House in the new Parliament and take your assigned seat in one of the back rows.[1] Each seat has a small desk in which you can keep papers or books or a laptop[2] and a backboard that contains the microphone light and a wooden ring to take a glass of water (and only water), which the pages will refill if you ask.

You see all (or most) of your fellow members together for the first time. As of 2015, the House has 338 members (up from 308), almost two-thirds of whom are new like you. Most are men (75%). Some are younger than you would have expected. Some look very professional, others are more casual.[3] Perhaps you're worried that you will not perform as well as you – or your colleagues – think you should. Don't worry; you'll get the hang of it soon enough.

The décor and furnishings of the Chamber date not from Confederation in 1867 but from 1920, when the building re-opened after a fire in 1916. From 1916 to 1919, while the Parliament Buildings were being reconstructed, the House sat in what is now the Canadian Museum of Nature at the southern end of Metcalfe Street in Ottawa, about a kilometre from Parliament Hill.[4] Further renovations were done in the 1970s.[5]

No doubt you are impressed by the size of the Chamber. It's a huge room, very ornate, with much history obvious in its décor. The ceiling is very high and the large opaque windows on the west wall bring in natural light, but not enough that artificial lighting isn't also required, including very bright (and warm) television lights. Elevated galleries run along the sides of the Chamber and there are large galleries at each end. The lower gallery above the Speaker's chair is reserved for the Parliamentary Press Gallery. The larger upper gallery is for the public. The lower gallery above the main entrance at the other end is reserved for members of the diplomatic corps while the larger gallery above it is for the public. The side galleries on the Government side (facing the opposition side seats) are reserved for guests of the opposition parties and those on the opposition side (facing the Government side seats) are divided between senators, official guests of the Speaker, and guests of the prime minister and cabinet.

Your attention is immediately drawn to the throne-like Speaker's chair, with its ornate wooden canopy, which is on an elevated platform to enable the Speaker to see to the end of the Chamber and to be seen easily by members.[6] The steps around it are where the pages sit while waiting to be called.[7] There are small audio speakers discreetly placed on either side of the chair at ear level to help the Speaker hear the debates. A button on the right arm allows the Speaker to summon the clerk and another button mutes the Speaker's microphone to enable private consultations with members, the clerk, or a table officer during proceedings. At the Speaker's feet, hidden from view by a nicely carved wooden screen, is a computer monitor connected to the computers on the clerk's table – a long table in the middle of the floor in front of the Speaker's chair – that shows the day's procedural program, particularly which member is scheduled to speak next.

Government ministers and members sit on the Speaker's right side while the opposition parties sit on the Speaker's left.[8] By parliamentary tradition originating in England, the front rows are supposed to be at least an inch more than two sword lengths apart (slightly less than four metres).

You may have noticed a shiny and rather ornate object sitting on a rack at the end of the clerk's table. This is the mace, described in the House text, *House of Commons Procedure and Practice*, as "a massive sceptre, heavy and ornate" symbolizing "the right conferred on the Commons by the Crown to meet and pass laws."[9] It is kept under lock and key in the Speaker's office and is brought into the Chamber at the start of each day on the shoulder of the sergeant-at-arms (who, during sittings of the House, is seated in front of the main entrance). When the House adjourns at the end of the day, the sergeant picks up the mace, puts it on his shoulder, and leaves the Chamber, with the Speaker following. (Members are expected to stand during this ceremony but often don't.) Once the mace has left the Chamber, the sitting of the House is officially over as, by tradition, no business may be conducted in the House without the mace in its place at the end of the clerk's table. The original mace was lost in the fire of 1916 and for over a year, until 1917 when a replacement mace was presented to Prime Minister Borden by King George V, the House used a wooden replica. Since the 1980s, whenever the House is sitting on 3 February, the date of the fire, the sergeant-at-arms uses the wooden replica in commemoration of the fire.

This is the stage on which you and your colleagues will carry out your parliamentary functions for the next four years (or perhaps less), the stage where our parliamentary democracy plays itself out between elections. Occasionally you'll be on your feet, on centre stage, but not as often as those with assigned roles.

THE PLAYERS

The members most often in the footlights are the Speaker, the deputy speaker, the other presiding officers[10] (known in the House as "chair occupants" because they sometimes occupy the Speaker's chair), the House officers (House leaders and whips), ministers (the prime minister is usually in the Chamber only for question period, votes, and other special occasions) and parliamentary secretaries. Not to be forgotten, however, though largely overlooked in media coverage of the House, are private members such as yourself, without whom the House would not be the House.

The Speaker

The Speaker opens the House each day and will usually be in the chair for Question Period and Routine Proceedings as well as to deliver rulings or for recorded votes. At other times the deputy speaker or one of the two other chair occupants sits in for the Speaker. Political neutrality is an essential feature of the Speaker's function as a parliamentary referee. The Speaker decides procedural questions in accordance with the House's Standing Orders and its established procedures and practices.[11] Above all, the Speaker is the "guardian of the rights and privileges of members and of the House as an institution."[12] Under the Standing Orders, the Speaker must "ensure that the right of members to free speech is protected and exercised to the fullest possible extent; this is accomplished in part by ensuring that the rules and practices of the House are applied and that order and decorum are maintained."[13] Rulings by the Speaker are not subject to appeal to the whole House (unlike rulings by committee chairs, which are subject to appeal to the whole committee).[14]

Whether inside or outside the House, the Speaker avoids commenting on any of the political matters of the day. The Speaker does not attend the caucus meetings of his or her political party and does not participate in debates or vote on motions, except in the case of a tie vote, in which case the Speaker has a "casting vote" to break the tie.[15] Between 2003 and 2011, Speaker Milliken cast a tie-breaking vote in the House six times.[16] (In the previous 136 years since Confederation, the Speaker had cast a tie-breaking vote only four times.[17]) In theory, the Speaker is free to vote for or against the motion. However, Speakers have recognized that doing so could involve them in partisan debates that might adversely affect the confidence of members in their impartiality. For this reason, conventions or informal rules have developed, both here and in England, that urge the Speaker to vote in a manner that upholds the *status quo ante* – that has the least effect on the existing state of affairs. For example, on a motion for second reading of a bill the Speaker would vote in the affirmative, which allows further debate and another vote at a later stage. If the Speaker were to vote in the negative, the bill would be defeated and there could be no more debate on it.

On 16 September 2003, there was a tie vote on an amendment to a motion. "Since the House has been unable to take a decision tonight," said Speaker Milliken "I will vote [against the amendment] so that members may be given another opportunity to pronounce themselves on the issue at some future time."[18] On 19 May 2005, a tie at the second reading of a money bill by the minister of Finance put the party in power at risk,[19] as the Government would have had to resign if the Speaker had voted against the motion. This was the first time a Speaker had had to cast a vote on a confidence matter; in keeping with tradition, he voted in favour, which allowed further debate. On 8 October 2009, the Speaker voted against a motion for the House to move from debate on a private member's bill to another item of business ("to proceed to Orders of the Day")[20] as the motion, if carried, would have effectively ended any debate on the bill. On a tie at a final vote on a private member's bill amending an Act of Parliament, the Speaker voted against the bill, explaining that his negative vote was consistent with the *status quo ante* rule, that is, for not changing the existing law (not amending the act, as proposed in the bill).[21]

The Speaker will not intervene in the proceedings in Chamber unless a member raises a procedural objection or there is disorder. If disorder arises in the course of a proceeding, the Speaker might rise to call for order. If the member who has the floor is causing the disorder, the Speaker may cut the offending member's speech short by giving the floor to another member, hoping that this will send a message to the member (and to other members watching). The Speaker might also send a private message to the offending member or to the member's party whip advising that the member's actions or comments were inappropriate and then await an acknowledgment from the member. Without an acknowledgment, the Speaker might fail to "see" the member (that is, to recognize the member when he or she wishes to speak) until an assurance of good behaviour is received.

In more serious cases, the Speaker might ask for an apology; usually the member apologizes and nothing more is done. If the member refuses to apologize, the Speaker can "name" the member, in which case the Speaker addresses the member using his or her personal name (not the riding name – the "member from X riding" – which is the usual way members are addressed when they stand to speak) and orders the member to leave the Chamber for the rest of the day.[22] A member's refusal to apologize is seen as an affront to the authority and dignity of the Speaker (and usually indicates that the member is seeking the notoriety of being named). Naming seldom happens.

There is not much a Speaker can do when the disorderly behaviour involves a large number of members who cannot be individually identified. In these situations, the Speaker rises (which stops the proceeding) and calls for order but this doesn't always end the disorder. The Speaker will then wait patiently for members to calm down before allowing the proceeding to continue.[23] If one side of the House or one of the recognized parties appears responsible for the disorder, as can happen in Question Period, the Speaker might penalize that side or that party by counting the period of disorder as part of their allowed time, in which case the question may not get asked or an answer not given for lack of time and the Speaker will move on to the next question.[24] In extreme cases, the Speaker can suspend the sitting of the House.

In addition to his duties in the Chamber, the Speaker chairs the House's governing administrative body, the Board of Internal Economy (see chapter 6), and engages in diplomatic functions internationally and nationally on behalf of the House.[25]

House Officers

The other players who manage the business of the Chamber are the House leaders and whips, collectively referred to as House officers. House leaders – the Government House leader, the official opposition House leader, and the House leaders of the remaining recognized parties – should not be confused with the leaders of particular parties but are appointed by them and are responsible for managing House business for their respective parties. Each of the recognized parties will also have a member acting as a whip who is responsible for managing the members, particularly for ensuring that members show up for debates when it's their turn to speak and in sufficient numbers for votes. Members with personal difficulties affecting their availability can go to the whip to see if they can be accommodated. At times whips have the unhappy task of taking disciplinary actions against members who are not following instructions appropriately. One might see the whips as personnel managers.[26]

Private Members

Members who are not also ministers are called private members, some-times referred to as "ordinary" members. Private members have no House functions other than participating in its proceedings and, of course, vot-ing.[27] Most private members are associated with a recognized party, that is, a party that has at least twelve members. If this is not the case, the member sits as an independent member, although identified in the tele-vised debates with the name of their party affiliation.[28] You won't see independent members on their feet in the Chamber very often and they do not sit on committees.[29] Nor are they represented on the House's gov-erning administrative board, the Board of Internal Economy.

Private members may propose substantive (non-procedural) mo-tions and introduce bills, known as private member's bills, perhaps without the express support or endorsement of their party leadership or caucus. Whether through a motion or a bill, the private member is supporting an issue – possibly an isolated issue – that is of particular importance to the member or the member's riding and may not have been part of the party platform in the last election. In theory, private member motions and bills are not supposed to be treated as partisan initiatives, though the party in power – the Government – is entitled to take a position on the motion or bill. A member on the Govern-ment side is sometimes seen as using Private Members' Business to advance Government policy.[30]

Members in the opposition parties are assigned positions as critics of government departments or subject areas. By tradition, official opposition party critics are seen as a "shadow cabinet," which parallels the Government's cabinet, composed of ministers. These private mem-bers generally handle questions at Question Period and lead their party in speaking on issues falling within their areas of responsibility.

As a private member, you will have committee work (discussed below) and the extra-parliamentary task of maintaining or increasing political support for your party in your riding – unless your seat is a safe one for your party, in which case you can do more in the House or on a House committee. You may find that you must get back to your riding on weekends for community events. This back and forth may be taxing for you and, if you have a family, for your partner and children, depending on whether they have moved to Ottawa.

Ministers of the Crown and Parliamentary Secretaries

Most private members hope to someday become a minister; if nothing else, the pay is better.[31] A large part of the attraction is the public profile enjoyed by ministers, which can be helpful at the next election. Under the leadership of the prime minister, ministers sit in cabinet, which is a committee within the Privy Council, and is known formally as the Governor in Council. Ministers, with the prime minister, are the highest level of government and are referred to in this book as the Government. Each minister is responsible for a government department or a subject area such as sports, heritage, or science. Parliamentary secretaries, who are members on the Government side, serve as parliamentary assistants to ministers, as well as acting as spokespersons for the minister in the House, a committee, or during question period.[32] They are not members of cabinet.

Caucuses

Caucuses are in camera meetings of party members held each Wednesday morning. Only the caucuses of recognized parties are administratively and financially supported by the House, under the direction of the Board of Internal Economy. In these closed caucus meetings members can air their views or grievances openly. Open "democratic" debates between members of a party take place, if ever, in caucus (not in public in the Chamber). The members hear from their leaders and determine their positions on issues that are or are about to come before the House – or are prominent in the media. Unfortunately, the party's need to appear unified often makes for predictable and rather boring debates in the Chamber as disagreements voiced in caucus are not heard on the floor of the House. Partisan politics, where political strategy, enforced by internal party discipline, governs the political agenda of each of the parties in their debates, makes this unavoidable, as you will find in your interventions in debates in the Chamber, in committee, or in public elsewhere.

THE PROGRAM

The Standing Orders set out the daily program of the House, which is dominated by the business of the Government as directed by the Government House Leader (perhaps on instructions from cabinet or a committee of cabinet or the prime minister) and known in the House's daily program as Government Orders or Government Business.[33] This is understandable when one remembers that historically (see next chapter) Parliament is called to meet when the Crown needs it. A limited amount of time is given to matters of interest to the opposition parties or to private members. The usual week has thirty-three and a half sitting hours, of which approximately twenty-two are for Government business and five for private members' business. The balance is taken up by routine matters and opposition supply day motions (more on these later).

On Mondays, the House sits from 11 a.m. to 6:30 p.m. (a late start to allow members to get back from their ridings after the week-end). On Tuesdays and Thursdays, it sits from 10 a.m. to 6:30 p.m., on Wednesday from 2 p.m. to 6:30 p.m. (allowing time for the caucuses to meet in the morning), and on Friday from 10 a.m. to 2:30 p.m. (allowing for early departures to ridings for the weekend). Tuesday, Wednesday, and Thursday are the major workdays of the week, with committees also meeting on Tuesdays and Thursdays. Question Period (QP) takes place for forty-five minutes every sitting day at 2:15 p.m., except on Fridays, when it moves to 11:15 a.m. Wednesday's QP is usually the most interesting, as members have met in caucus in the morning and are full of (partisan) beans, as it were. Each Thursday, following Question Period, the official opposition House leader, asks the Government House leader to indicate what items the Government will be putting forward in the next week (which could later change without notice, although that would be unusual).

Order Paper, Notice Paper, Journal, Hansard

In accordance with the Standing Orders, for each sitting day the House publishes an Order Paper and Notice Paper, a Journal (the official record), and verbatim Debates (or Hansard), in both official languages.[34] Copies will be placed on your desk in the Chamber each day. The Order Paper lists all the items of House business that might be called for debate or consideration in the House in the coming weeks or months. Government business, whether legislative or other, is listed under the subhead "Government Orders." The business of private members, whether legislative or other, is listed under "Private Members' Business."

The Notice Paper lists items that are on notice and in two days will be placed in the Order Paper. The Journal sets out the business transacted by the House on the previous day. The editors in the Printing Services Office publish a verbatim account of speeches in the House on the previous day. These documents, like the Standing Orders, are rather complicated in their format and not user friendly, to say the least. All of these publications are posted on the Parliament of Canada website.

Standing Orders

The Standing Orders set out the procedural rules for House business – there should be a copy in your desk.[35] If the Standing Orders do not provide a rule, established practice fills the gap. The *House of Commons Procedure and Practice*, with its thorough treatment of the procedural rules and practices of the House and its committees, is also a useful reference.[36] It is important to remember that the House sets its own procedural rules and may vary or suspend them at any time.

The Standing Orders are difficult to understand without training in parliamentary procedure. I found that members generally did not look to them for procedural information but instead depended on their staff or the procedural clerks at the clerk's table.[37] For my part, though I had been professionally trained with regard to legal rules and was experienced in drafting rules (legislation or regulations), I had as much trouble with the Standing Orders as I would have with the Income Tax Act. Moreover, it seemed to me that the procedural rules in the Standing Orders were often applied in ways that were unsupported by the wording of the rules. My colleagues at the table, procedural clerks, explained the rules according to past practices, often without paying particular attention to the wording used. The unwritten procedural practices had to be learned and these at times took priority over the written rules.[38]

Procedural clerks are careful when they advise members on procedure. Senior procedural clerks say they provide procedural *information* but not *advice*, a distinction designed to keep them out of strategic political discussions with members. They have to keep their procedural hands clean, as it were. For my part, as a table officer who was a lawyer, not a procedural clerk, this restraint didn't come easy. When a lawyer discusses legal rules with a client, the client's objectives are part of the discussion. Advice is always based on strategic considerations. In the House I had to keep my lawyerly instincts in check and treat consultations on procedure as hypothetical information exchanges without regard to the member's procedural objectives.

The Standing Orders require that the House have a one-day special debate on the Standing Orders and procedures of the House and its committees between the sixtieth and ninetieth day of Parliament.[39] The motion for debate is that the House "take note of the Standing Orders and procedure of the House and its Committees." No suggestions for changes to the procedural rules are put to a vote as it is only a "take note" debate. Any such suggestions are referred to the Standing Committee on Procedure and House Affairs (PROC). A procedural issue raised with PROC could be taken on by the committee and result in a recommendation for a procedural change, but this is unlikely.

For example, there was a special debate on 6 October 2016.[40] Members had a variety of suggestions for changes to House procedure or practice: cancelling Friday sittings, giving the Speaker more control of the daily program in the House, having a second chamber to allow more debates while other business is handled, having members write their own speeches, limiting the Government's use of closure and time-allocation, and requiring better answers from the Government during Question Period. That's about all you'll see on procedural reform – suggestions by private members in debate – unless the Government takes an active role. Remarkably, neither the Government House leader nor the responsible minister (whose mandate letter from the prime minister had charged her with producing a plan for reforming the operations of the House) participated in the debate.

In his mandate letter on the appointment of the Government House leader in November 2015, setting out his priorities, the prime minister included reforming Question Period so that all ministers and the prime minister "are held to greater account," there are more free votes, improper use of omnibus bills and prorogation is halted, and House committees are strengthened. It was not until March 2017 that the Government House leader proposed reforms, which met with fierce denunciation by the opposition parties.[41] Reforms of House procedural practices need to be negotiated between the parties and are best done privately, which can take time.

Quorum

Section 48 of the Constitution Act, 1867 (formerly British North America Act), affirmed by the Standing Orders,[42] stipulates that at least twenty members, including the Speaker, must be present in the Chamber for the House to meet and exercise its powers. If there is no quorum, the Standing Orders provide for the Speaker to adjourn the House to the next sitting day, but this never happens; the Speaker ignores the lack of quorum unless a member (usually an opposition member) rises on a point of order and draws the Speaker's attention to the lack of quorum in the Chamber. This action is usually a delaying tactic to slow down the Government's agenda; the Government then has to muster enough members to establish a quorum. (The opposition is probably keeping their members from attending.) At times, there may be only three or four members in the Chamber while a debate is underway and nothing is said about the lack of quorum. Given section 48, is the House acting unlawfully when it conducts proceedings without a quorum present in the Chamber? Technically, perhaps, but if the proceeding does not include a vote, the question is constitutionally pointless. Only House votes have constitutional importance and there is invariably a quorum present for these. As a matter of House practice, the Speaker does not open the House for the day if there are no opposition members present and forming part of the quorum, which means that the Speaker sometimes has to wait for a quorum before opening the House.

An interesting and rather unusual account relating to quorum came to my attention in the 1990s. I had been contacted by a representative of a committee of government officials who were determining the minimum requirements for the continuity of constitutional government in the event of a major disaster, such as an epidemic or nuclear attack. I was told that they had received a legal opinion that, as the constitutional quorum requirement of the House of Commons was only twenty members, if the Government had twenty members of the cabinet in the Chamber they could act as the House and could elect one of the cabinet ministers to act as the Speaker. I was quite taken aback – it was preposterous to suggest that this was a legitimate application of s. 48 of the Constitution Act, 1867. Technically it might be correct in terms of numbers, but it wouldn't have any legitimacy, constitutional or otherwise. How could it be said that the House of Commons had met when no members from the other recognized parties, particularly the official opposition, had been present?

Daily Prayer

Once quorum is found, the sitting day begins with the Speaker leading the House in a brief prayer, followed by a moment of reflection.[43] The Speaker then directs that the doors to the Chamber be opened and the day's proceedings get underway. The prayer remained the same from its inception in 1877 until 1994, when its Christian orientation was made non-sectarian.

National Anthem

In 1995 the House agreed to members singing the national anthem – a bilingual version – before the opening of the House on Wednesday. The Speaker calls upon a member (who has earlier volunteered) to lead off the singing of the anthem, which is televised, although the House is not yet open to the public. Singing the national anthem in the Chamber was first suggested by the newly elected Reform Party (as it then was). The idea was sent to a committee for study. The committee recommended that the public not be allowed to enter the

Chamber while members were singing the national anthem as this might create disorder. Really? Was this a dig at the vocal talents of members generally? Why would there be disorder?

What had not been mentioned in the committee's report was that the Bloc Québécois, also newly elected to the House and the official opposition at the time, had objected to singing the national anthem in the House. The committee – at least the federalist parties represented on the committee – were concerned that the Bloc or its supporters would use the singing of the national anthem as an occasion for a public demonstration in the Chamber in favour of Quebec sovereignty. In my time at the House, Bloc members never participated in the singing of the national anthem.

PROCEEDINGS

You, like most visitors in the galleries, will probably not fully understand what's going on and may need to look to experienced members or staff to explain. Don't be discouraged; this is quite common among members – and not only new members. Some practices may seem quaint if not odd. For example, why do members refer to each other by the names of their constituencies ("the member for Trinity-Spadina" or "member for Port Moody-Coquitlam") or as "the honourable member" and not by their own names? And why do they address their remarks to the Speaker and not to each other? The answer, I've been told, is that this helps to depersonalize exchanges and prevent members from making personal remarks. In question period, how can the prime minister be asked a question when not there? (The prime minister is always present in the sense that no member may say that a member is not present.) There may be other strange practices, such as a "Ways and Means" motion. And what is meant by "Supply"?

While QP may usually have your full attention, most other proceedings will bore you silly (unless you are scheduled to speak), especially when you're in the Chamber doing House duty (fulfilling your duty to be present in the House when it's in session). Some members use this time to get office work done, to deal with email or to text messages, or do research on the internet (or, at Christmas time, sign Christmas cards).

There's a microphone on your desk, directly in front of you. The microphones are controlled by the person you can see looking down on members from the "pulpit" at the front of the public gallery above the entrance to the Chamber. Your microphone is activated once the Speaker recognizes you to speak and is on when the microphone light on your desk lights up. When you are finished speaking and sit down, you should check that the microphone light has gone off before making any comments to members near you.

You know that House proceedings are televised, but at first you don't see any cameras. You soon spot one hanging from the underside of the gallery on the other side of the Chamber and when you turn around you see one hanging under the gallery above and behind you. You'll notice the very large, very bright, and very warm TV lights mounted high on the side walls. The cameras are operated by technicians located in a studio above the gallery behind the pulpit but hidden from the Chamber by a dark glass wall. The camera is directed only at the member who has the floor, although members sitting nearby may also be visible – something to remember.[44]

If only a few members of your party are in their seats when one of your colleagues rises to speak, you and the others may be expected to move into the seats around your colleague to give the impression on TV that members from your party are all there and supporting the member speaking. If this happens, pay, or appear to be paying, attention to what your colleague is saying, rather than looking bored, distracted or laughing inappropriately.

Unless the Speaker rises, the TV camera stays on the member speaking. If the Speaker stands up unexpectedly, the camera will immediately go to the Speaker and the member speaking is expected to sit down until the Speaker allows the member to resume speaking. Whenever the Speaker stands, and for as long as the Speaker is standing, the camera is on the Speaker. This rule assists the Speaker in managing debates and, especially, Question Period. For instance, if a member directs a comment (a heckle) to another member, the camera will not go to that member for a reaction shot but will remain on the first member or move to the Speaker if the Speaker rises. Wide screen shots are permitted only during Question Period and recorded votes, "in order to give viewers a better appreciation of 'the context and dynamic of the House.'"[45]

The Speaker will only give you the floor to speak when you are at your seat. You may, however, leave your seat and go to another part of the Chamber for a private chat with another member. If you want to go to the other side of the Chamber (and not take the longer route by the corridor behind the Speaker's chair), watch out that you don't walk into the line of sight of the TV camera on the member speaking and when you reach the middle of the floor be sure to pause and bow to the Speaker before continuing. Do not go into the narrow clearing between the back of the clerk's chair and the Speaker's chair: by tradition there must be no impediment to the Speaker's access to the clerk and vice versa. Also by tradition, an infraction will cost you a bottle of scotch.

Opening Parliament

As a new member, you're probably keen to attend the first sitting day of the new Parliament, your first Parliament, which has its set procedure. At the start, the clerk reads out a letter from the secretary to the governor general informing the House that the deputy governor general will be proceeding to the Senate Chamber at 1 p.m. to open the first session of the new Parliament (the 42nd Parliament since Confederation). Deputy governor general? Doesn't the governor general open a new Parliament? There's a loud knocking on the doors of the main entrance at the south end of the Chamber. The sergeant-at-arms opens the doors and turns to announce that the Senate's "Usher of the Black Rod" seeks entry. The usher marches ceremoniously up to the clerk's table, his black rod over his shoulder, and announces that it is "the desire" of the deputy governor general that members "attend her immediately in the chamber of the Senate." No explanation, just a summons.

Members start assembling behind the sergeant-at-arms and the clerk as they leave the Chamber by the main entrance. You notice that some members are not getting up – you'll understand why soon. It's a rather chatty and casual crowd of members that ambles down the corridor from the House, through the central rotunda at the Peace Tower entrance, to the Senate at the eastern end of Centre Block. The entourage gathers in front of the brass rod – known as the bar – at the front of the Senate Chamber (commoners – non-senators – cannot enter the Chamber) and the Senate Speaker announces that he has been told by the deputy governor general (usually a justice of the Supreme Court) that he "does not see fit to declare the causes of his summoning the present Parliament of Canada [the Speech from the Throne, discussed below] until a speaker of the House of Commons shall have been chosen, according to law" but that he will make his declaration tomorrow. That's it: a false start. You've got to retrace your steps back to the House to elect a Speaker. Now you understand why some members didn't come along with you.

Election of the Speaker

Now that you're back in the Chamber, the next proceeding is the election of a Speaker.[46] Since 1986 this has been done by secret ballot. The "dean" of the House – the most senior member – presides from the Speaker's chair. All members, other than ministers and party leaders, are assumed to be candidates unless they withdraw their names. Most members will have asked the clerk to withdraw their names, leaving only a small group of (presumably) serious candidates. In the weeks or months leading up to the opening of the new Parliament, the candidate members will have been lobbying fellow members for support.

The candidate members are each given five minutes to address the House before the voting begins. Members are given a ballot listing the candidates and are to vote their preferences – first choice for Speaker, second choice, etc.[47] Once the ballots are cast, the sergeant-at-arms takes the ballot box into the Speaker's dining room (across the corridor from the Chamber and reached from behind the Speaker's chair). The clerk, with the assistance of the deputy clerk, a clerk assistant, and the law clerk, counts the vote. The winning candidate must get more than fifty per cent of the votes cast. If there is no winner, a second vote is conducted. The results of each ballot are not given other than to announce a winner or that a further vote is required. Those of us assisting on the vote count, behind a locked door with House security guards standing outside, were expected to keep the vote count confidential, forever, which we have done if only because the results are very soon forgotten.

On the first election of a Speaker by secret ballot, on 30 September 1986, there were thirty-nine candidates. It took eleven ballots over eleven hours to elect the new speaker, John Fraser, a member from the Government side (and a former minister).[48] Subsequent elections were usually quite lengthy. You were lucky in 2015 when, with preferential voting, a Speaker was elected on the first ballot.[49]

In 1994, the final ballot, or so it seemed, came to a choice between two candidates. After they had voted, some members left the Chamber, assuming one of the candidates would be elected. However, a further ballot was required, effectively divulging the result of the vote: a tie. Those of us locked in the counting room were amazed that there could be a tie. We recounted to be sure, scrambling around under tables and chairs to see that no ballots had been overlooked but the count was correct. Candidate supporters tried to retrieve the members who had left the Chamber. Who knows whether the departures affected the result.[50]

In 2001, following the general election in 2000 the result didn't surprise anyone on either side of the House. The member – Peter Milliken – had served as deputy speaker in the previous Parliament and was known as a life-long student of parliamentary procedure and practices. He was re-elected Speaker by acclamation following the June 2004 general election and again in 2006 and 2008 when he was sitting as an opposition member. This was only the second time since Confederation that an opposition party member had served as Speaker.[51] Speaker Milliken retired from the House in 2011 as the longest-serving speaker in Canadian history.

Speech from the Throne

The next day, again following the sergeant-at-arms carrying the mace on his shoulder, the Speaker leads a parade of table officers and members to the Senate for the reading of the Speech from the Throne. Since it's your first time, you might try to get up close behind the Speaker and the table officers to see the ceremony over their shoulders (from under a temporary platform set up for TV cameras – there is no TV in the Senate). While you and your colleagues must stand through the lengthy ceremony, senators and their guests are seated comfortably. The Speaker stands on a pulpit-like platform at the bar, facing the governor general seated in front of the ornate regal thrones at the other end of the Senate Chamber.

The prime minister is seated on the right of the governor general, without saying or doing anything during the ceremony. The chief of the Defence Staff and the Royal Canadian Mounted Police commissioner, in their colourful and medal be-decked uniforms, stand in the wings to either side of the governor general. The judges of the Supreme Court of Canada, dressed in their formal ermine robes, are seated directly in front of the governor general in the place usually occupied by the Senate clerk's table. The Senate Speaker and clerk are temporarily displaced to seats in front of the first row of desks on the government side.

The ceremony includes an exchange that is an important reflection of the relationship between the House and the Crown (which we'll look at more closely in the next chapter). The House Speaker "humbly" claims on behalf of the House "all their undoubted rights and privileges" and "especially that they may have freedom of speech in their debates, access to Your Excellency's person at all seasonable times, and that their proceedings may receive from Your Excellency the most favourable construction."[52]

In response, the Senate Speaker, on behalf of the governor general, declares that the queen "grants, and upon all occasions will recognize and allow, [the Commons] their constitutional privileges," assures the Commons that "their proceedings, as well as your words and actions, will constantly receive from her the most favourable construction." Thus, the privileges of the House (discussed in chapter 3) are expressly affirmed at the opening of each Parliament (or parliamentary session).

Eventually, after the governor general has read the Speech from the Throne (for the most part written in the Privy Council Office) announcing what the Government intends to do in the new Parliament, the sergeant-at-arms turns and leads the Speaker, clerk, table officers, and members back to the House, where members commence a debate in response to the Speech from the Throne, although they will hear from only two members before adjourning for the day. By tradition a new member from the Government side is given the honour of making the first speech in debate in the new Parliament. The real debate will take place the next day.

Routine Proceedings

Each day, following Question Period, the House takes a few minutes (fifteen to thirty) for routine matters: "business of a basic nature" where members can bring a variety of matters to the attention of the House.[53] Ministers introduce Government bills, without any speech or debate on the bill. The table gives the bill a C- number (whichever number is next in the sequence of government bills) and soon after the bill is sent out for printing and is posted on the parliamentary website. A similar process applies to the introduction of private member's bills except that the sponsor is allowed to make a brief statement (around one minute) indicating the content of the bill.[54]

Committees and inter-parliamentary delegations table their reports during Routine Proceedings with a "succinct explanation" of the content of the report.[55] Motions for concurrence in a committee report are also considered under Routine Proceedings.[56] A minister may make an announcement or statement on Government policy or a matter of national interest. When this occurs, the opposition parties are allowed to respond for no longer than the time taken by the minister.[57] As an indication of the importance of time for the daily program, the time taken for a statement by a minister, including opposition responses, is added to the time allotted to Government business on that day. Motions pertaining to the business of the House may also be moved under Routine Proceedings.

Each day, toward the end of Routine Proceedings, the House goes to Questions on the Order Paper, that is, written questions that have been submitted by members.[58] Hundreds, if not thousands, of government employees in a variety of departments or agencies prepare answers to these questions. The parliamentary secretary to the Government House leader rises to table responses and these are printed in the Debates for the day. Where a Government response is lengthy, the parliamentary secretary may ask that the response be treated as an "order for return," which means that the response is tabled but is not printed in the Debates. The parliamentary secretary asks that remaining questions be allowed to stand, that is, remain on the order paper for a response later. At this time, a member may raise concerns about the status of his or her question.[59]

At the end of routine proceedings, members present petitions from their constituents. The petitions must relate to a matter within the jurisdiction of the House or the Government.[60] Petitions began as the tool that led to statutes (see chapter 2) and today provide citizens with a vehicle by which to try to influence government policy and legislation and bring public concerns to the attention of Parliament.[61] The member is given a minute or so to explain to the House what the petition is about. This explanation is done as a service to the member's constituents and is not to be taken as indicating the member's agreement with the petition (unless this was clearly indicated). Petitions are sent to the responsible government department and require a response within forty-five days of tabling.[62] Recently, the House approved the use of electronic petitions ("e-petitions").[63]

Members' Statements

For fifteen minutes before the start of every Question Period, members, other than ministers but including parliamentary secretaries, are given an opportunity to speak for not longer than one minute on any topic of their choosing.[64] The topics can vary but usually relate to a matter of particular interest to the member's constituency (the passing of a respected member of the community, an athletic or artistic achievement by a constituent, a notable local anniversary, or an upcoming community event) or perhaps support a charitable cause. Increasingly, however, members' statements are of a partisan political nature, which is permissible unless it is an attack on another member (because there is no opportunity for the other member to reply), on a senator, on a ruling of a court, or on a judge, in which case the Speaker will interrupt to caution the member or perhaps to stop the statement.[65] Criticism of a political party or the Government is permissible.

The list of members seeking to make a statement is prepared for the Speaker based on lists received from the whips. In 2013, a private member on the Government side rose in the House to complain of the Government's control over what its members say in Members'

Statements. "If at any time," said the member, "that right and privilege to make an S.O. 31 [a Member's Statement] on an equal basis in this House is removed, I believe I have lost my privilege of equal right that I have in this House. I was scheduled on March 20 from 2:00 to 2:15 to make an S.O. 31. Fifteen minutes prior to that time, I was notified that my turn to present the S.O. 31 had been removed. The reason I was given was that the topic was not approved."[66] The Government whip responded that House practice has been that members' statements are managed by the recognized parties and that the Speaker could not be expected to become involved. "Essentially," said the Government whip, addressing the Speaker, not the member, "you are being invited to become involved in adjudicating the internal affairs of party caucuses and their management. Under any reasonable and generous interpretation of your powers, it is not for the Speaker to assume such a novel and expansive power."[67] There are thus limits on the independence of individual private members on the Government side. Independent members are allowed a statement from time to time proportionate to their number in the House, which means not very often.

Oral Questions (Question Period)

The most noted (or notorious) of House proceedings is Oral Questions, better known as Question Period or simply QP. Canadians who see the House only on television news programs are probably seeing clips from Question Period, which takes place every sitting day and lasts for forty-five minutes. A member or minister's parliamentary profile often turns on their performance in QP – a minister who is ineffective in QP may soon be out of cabinet or moved to a lighter portfolio in the next shuffle. Question Period is where the Government is held accountable on each sitting day.

Asking questions of the Government was first allowed by written questions only. Later oral questions were allowed as an informal practice but this soon became an established daily practice, though not covered by House rules until 1964 when the Standing Orders stipulated that such questions be of an urgent nature,[68] not require lengthy and detailed answers, and not be related to statements made in newspapers or involve legal opinions or matters that were before the courts (the sub judice rule). Answers were to be as brief as possible and not provoke debate. In 1975, the Speaker articulated several principles that constrained questions in Question Period but these constraints were eventually lost. It is believed by many that the arrival of television in 1977 made QP what it is today, a highly partisan and at times unruly exchange.

Voting

Voting in the House is done by "a majority of voices" as required by section 49 of the Constitution Act 1867. When the voices are "equal," the Speaker has a tie-breaking vote. One might think that the louder voice vote meant more votes were on that side. Not so. Sometimes the negative side will make an extra effort to outshout the affirmative side but the Speaker can see that there are more members sitting on the side voting in the affirmative. The Speaker must exercise some judgment when announcing the result of a voice vote.

If, after a voice vote, five or more members rise, a recorded vote must be taken. Recorded votes list the members voting on each side. Members can use this information to political advantage in a later debate, whether in the House or off the Hill, or in an election campaign. A recorded vote is usually scheduled for later the same day or, by agreement of the parties, on another day. Bells are rung throughout the precincts to call members to the Chamber for the vote but stop when the Government whip and the official opposition whip enter the Chamber together. The two whips walk up to the clerk's table, bow to the Speaker, take their seats, and the recorded vote gets underway. A table officer calls out the names of the members as they rise to vote, row by row, starting on the Government side in the case of an item of Government business, on the opposition side in the case of opposition business, and on the side of the sponsoring private member in the case of private member business.

For several years, I had the dubious pleasure of calling out votes, which meant calling out as many as 200 to 250 members by name from memory. At times, it was difficult, particularly where a member had recently made a significant change in hairstyle or hair colour.

There was a time when a member named Black sat next to a member who was black. Such things could play tricks on memory recall.

A member may abstain from a recorded vote by remaining seated during the call of the vote but such an abstention is not recorded. The usual method of abstaining is through not showing up or by "pairing." Members absent with whip approval are "paired" with a member from the other side of the House who will also be absent. Pairing is done by private agreement between the parties in order to maintain their relative strengths on the vote and to accommodate a certain amount of inevitable absenteeism. The paired members are listed in the day's *Debates* along with the vote result.[69] Those members absent without their whip's approval, who simply fail to show up for a vote, are neither paired nor listed in the Debates as absent and may have some explaining to do to their whips.[70]

Sometimes members make mistakes on recorded votes and try to have the record corrected. To do this, they must ask for the correction immediately. In 2012, a member rose to point out that he had voted twice on a private member's bill, once for the yeas and once for the nays. The member apologized for his "bipolar voting condition" and indicated that he had meant to vote against the bill. The tally of votes was revised to reflect the member's intent.[71]

Debates

Debates happen on a motion by a minister during Government Orders or by a private member during Private Members' Business. In a legislative proceeding, the motion would be on a bill ("That Bill C-23 be given second reading and referred to the Standing Committee on ..."). In a deliberative proceeding, it would be on a topic such as the environment, the economy, etc. Debates are always launched by a motion that is usually amendable.

The Standing Orders do not limit the total time for debates but each member can speak only once in a debate and the maximum time for a speech is reduced from twenty minutes to ten once there have been five hours of debate.[72] If the motion being debated is amended, the debate on the amendment becomes a separate debate and the clock starts running again. The Government can move a non-debatable motion that limits the amount of debate on a bill by allocating the days allowed for debate.[73] Time allocation motions are used when the Government wants to ensure timely consideration of its bills by reducing the amount of delay that the opposition parties can cause with sub-debates on amendment and sub-amendment motions.

Speeches

It used to be that members were expected to speak without relying on a written text – it was thought that this would make them better able to respond to the arguments of other members. In 1947, Speaker Fauteux commented that, "if the rule were otherwise members might read speeches written by other people and the time of the house [would] be taken up considering the arguments of persons who are not properly elected representatives of the people."[74] Regrettably, members today often deliver prepared speeches that reflect the views of their party more than their own. The parties, understandably, want their members to speak from the same page, as it were, and not disagree publicly. You may find yourself being told what you ought not to say and this may annoy you, perhaps at some point seriously, in which case you may have a problem that needs to be raised in caucus.

On Government bills or motions, the first round of speakers – the sponsoring minister or parliamentary secretary followed by the critics for the opposition parties – will make their party positions clear and members rising afterwards will likely add little new. Sometimes members from the same party will split the twenty-minute time limit for each slot on the speakers list. Usually the rules allow ten minutes for questions or comments following a speech. These exchanges may be used by a fellow member for a friendly question or comment designed to extend the member's speech.

Members are not allowed to use "props" during their speeches, that is, posters, banners, badges, insignia, or other visual aids designed to convey a message. However, red ribbons in support of AIDS victims or a similar white or pink ribbon in support of victims of other medical conditions as well as the Remembrance Day poppy are allowed.

Points of Order

Members can rise in the House at any time on a "point of order" alleging a procedural irregularity. The Speaker hears submissions and provides a ruling based on established House procedural rules and practices. The Speaker does not intervene on a procedural point unless a member raises a point of order. In cases where an immediate ruling is not required, the Speaker may take the point of order under advisement and deliver a ruling later, perhaps several days or weeks later depending on the complexity of the issue raised. Sometimes the Speaker recognizes that the member's point of order does not relate to procedure – and sometimes this is patently obvious – but is a way to take the floor for a few minutes to publicly object to something another member said or did.

Committees

The Standing Orders provide for twenty-four standing committees and two joint standing committees.[75] The membership on a committee is usually around sixteen members and is proportionate to the representation in the House: that is, the party with a majority in the House will have a majority on each committee. The parties select the members they assign to committees. If you are lucky, you will be assigned to a committee whose mandate interests you. Independent members may participate in committee proceedings if the committee permits.

The mandates of each of the standing committees are set out in the Standing Orders and most relate to a department of government, such as the Standing Committee on Finance, or the Standing Committee on Agriculture and Agri-food, or the Standing Committee on Health. Most committees must have a member from the Government side as their chair.[76] Five of the twenty-four committees have non-departmental mandates, such as the Standing Committee on Public Accounts or the Standing Committee on Access to Information, Privacy, and Ethics, and, given the nature of their mandates, are chaired by a member from the official opposition.[77] There are two joint committees (Commons-Senate), one that deals with the Library of Parliament and the other with the scrutiny of regulations (to ensure that government regulations are permitted by the governing Act of Parliament). The House can create special committees at any time, as it did with the Special Committee on the Canadian Mission in Afghanistan, the Special Committee on Co-operatives, or the Special Committee on Violence Against Indigenous Women.[78] The House may also create a legislative committee to review a bill, although bills are usually sent to the standing committee whose mandate relates to the content of the bill.[79]

In my view, committees are – and should be – the place where individual Canadians can make their views known to the political players, especially the Government, and ought to be valued for providing a platform to outsiders. While some see committees as mere sideshows to what goes on in the Chamber, often the reverse is the case. Committee meetings are far more interesting than proceedings in the Chamber (apart perhaps from QP) and if the matter under consideration interests you, you will find yourself more engaged by what goes on at a committee meeting than by proceedings in the Chamber.

Committees are at liberty to initiate proceedings on any matter that falls within their mandate.[80] The relationship between the House and its committees is, in theory, one of master and servant but at arm's length; the House treats committees as "masters of their own proceedings." If a member rises in the House to object to actions taken by a committee, the Speaker will remind the member that committees are the masters of their own proceedings, a rule that enables committees to organize their business as they see fit. In a majority Parliament, the Government majority on a committee can use that majority to control the committee agenda and no appeal to the Speaker is possible. An opposition with a majority in a minority Parliament can do the same thing and did on occasion in the minority years 2004–11, but this is less likely as the opposition parties often cannot work together.

A Government member on a committee once asked me about the tyranny of the majority. It was a minority Parliament, which meant that the opposition parties had a majority in the committee. "At what point," the member asked, "does the tyranny of the majority run roughshod over the ability of parliamentarians from all parties to do

the job they were sent here to do?,"[81] inferring that the members
of opposition parties were tyrannizing the Government members. I
reminded the member that in majority parliaments there are complaints of tyranny by the Government over the opposition. "Minorities always feel majorities are tyrannies, to some degree," I said. I did-
n't think the opposition majority was any more tyrannical in the
current Parliament than Government majorities had been in past
parliaments. "It's the nature of the beast [parliamentary democracy]
and it's the nature of the numbers. If you've got the numbers, you
win; if you don't have the numbers, you don't win" – a response bor-
dering on insolence, something a law clerk should avoid. In parliamentary terms, the majority has the right to prevail simply because it
is the majority.

The House can give instructions to a committee, though this is rare.
Usually, the House considers committee business only once it has a
report from the committee. A committee sets its own business agenda, although it must deal with whatever matters the House may send
it. Committees can vote to sit in camera, although public or open proceedings are the parliamentary rule. In a majority Parliament, however, the Government side can use its majority to force the committee to
go in camera on a matter that the Government doesn't want discussed
in public.

Proceedings in committees can be quite partisan and at times
rather nasty. As a result, they can sometimes be quite disorderly and
an embarrassment to most observers (unless they, too, have a partisan
interest). On occasion, when the business before a committee does
not excite partisan differences, committee meetings can be quite col-
legial, even productive. The media don't give such meetings much
attention, which enables committee members to put partisan show-
boating aside.

A House committee is neither a commission of inquiry nor a court
of law. Committees are part of the House's accountability function
(see chapter 5) with respect to Government policies and actions. A
committee is not responsible for finding solutions for the problems
that it identifies, though it can make recommendations.

Neither justice nor truth, it must be said, is the dominant priority
for House committees. Instead, they attempt to propose better public

policy or call the Government (or the government bureaucracy) to account, based on testimony that is a mix of facts and opinions, allegations and arguments. Their work is a political exercise done in the public interest. A House committee has no powers that it can use to enforce anything on anyone – the only action it can take is to table a report in the House. Committee hearings provide a platform where issues can be aired for public consumption by those directly involved without having to deal with legal jeopardy, the limitations of strict evidentiary rules, or intimidation by legalistic arguments from opposing lawyers. Members of Parliament need to hear testimony, uncensored, if they are to understand the issues presented to them within the limited time and resources available to them. A vigilant committee system serves the public interest by enabling public disclosures that otherwise might never happen.

Committee Witnesses

One of the first tasks for a committee is to draw up a list of witnesses. The parties negotiate the list, with the Government side wanting to call witnesses supportive of the Government and the opposition parties wanting to call witnesses they believe will be critical of the Government. An individual or interest group may ask to appear before a committee. Most witnesses appear voluntarily when invited by the committee.[82] If a person declines an invitation, a summons may be sent, in which case the person – with the exception of the governor general, senators, members, ministers, and judges – is obliged to appear: failure to appear could result in a citation for contempt of Parliament. As a rule, committees try to accommodate witnesses as to the time or date of an appearance.

Most witnesses are professionals in the subject matter under study, either public servants, public officials, or seasoned representatives of interest groups. Some witnesses – not many – are private citizens with a personal interest in the matter before the committee. Such people have no institutional, professional, or political agenda and only want to assist the committee in the matter under consideration. Sometimes a witness would rather not appear – perhaps having had to be served with a summons – and is very nervous about getting caught up in a political process or revealing something they would rather not talk about publicly.

The usual committee practice is for a witness to make a brief opening statement and then to allow questions or comments by members. A specific period of time is allocated to each party for questions or comments. In my time, seven or eight minutes was usually allowed on the first round and five minutes on subsequent rounds. Each party chooses the issues that its members will address in its questions so there may be little or no continuity in questions from one party to the next. In my view, where the committee is conducting what is actually more like an investigation, such as occurred with the sponsoring program or RCMP pension administration (discussed later), exchanges with witnesses are often not very effective, given the time allowed: once the time is up, the member's line of questioning must be resumed in the next round of questions, but by that time, other issues may have emerged and a new line of questions may need to be adopted. Members can also use their allotted time for partisan comments without allowing time for the witness to respond. A witness who hopes to avoid responding to some topics only needs to wait until the member's minutes expire, as the next member will probably pursue a different line of questions. A savvy witness may give lengthy (and perhaps unresponsive) answers to use up an unfriendly member's allotted time. And so it goes.

Witnesses are expected to speak truthfully but the demands for truthfulness may vary between witnesses, depending on the issue. For instance, a committee might insist on a higher standard of truthfulness for a minister, an officer of Parliament, or a public official than it would for a private citizen or a lower level public servant. Committees recognize that some witnesses – particularly high level public officials who have been before committees before – are sophisticated players who know how to "stick handle" a committee and avoid being fully responsive in their answers.

Committees generally don't require witnesses to take an oath on the Bible (or other religious text) or to make a solemn affirmation before testifying. Some feel it is offensive to require a witness to swear a formal oath before testifying as this suggests doubts about the truthfulness of a witness before any testimony has been heard. Legally, it's not clear whether swearing a formal oath before giving testimony is required for perjury charges against an untruthful witness.[83] However, an untruthful witness risks being found in contempt of Parliament. When a committee feels that a witness has misled the committee, it is usually considered sufficient punishment for the House to find the witness in contempt of Parliament with no further action taken.

For example, in March 2003, the Standing Committee on Government Operations and Estimates concluded that it had received false testimony from the privacy commissioner: in the course of reviewing the estimates of the Office of the Privacy Commissioner, testimony from the commissioner was contradicted by testimony from office staff. The committee tabled a unanimous report in the House saying that it had lost confidence in the privacy commissioner. "Absolute honesty in reporting to Parliament and its committees is a central requirement for all Officers of Parliament," said the committee, "Unconditional confidence in that honesty on the part of parliamentarians is essential if Parliament is to support its officers in their important duties."[84] The Speaker had to decide whether the committee report revealed a breach of the privileges of the House, albeit by a witness before a committee.

The Government House leader urged the Speaker to provide a "comprehensive" ruling that would include a "clear statement" of the responsibilities Canadians have for providing House committees with full and truthful information and the consequences that may follow from a failure to do so. An opposition member asked, "How bad do things have to be before democracy will be defended? In the contents of the report itself it very clearly outlines how Parliament has been offended. Here is the test case for the Government and for members of this House as a whole to ensure that democracy itself is defended."[85] Parliament has to defend its independent role, said the member. "Parliament is not the Government, and in the face of Parliament, the highest court of the land, this House has to defend itself, not only for its own convenience but for future generations. That is why 20 or 30 years from now, when perhaps a similar circumstance is looked at, it will be said, 'What was done?'"[86]

Then, unexpectedly, the chair of the committee rose to report that he had received a letter from the privacy commissioner (who resigned earlier that day) in which the commissioner apologized for his "mistakes" and "errors in judgment" and said he wanted to put the "very painful lessons" he had learned in the past months behind him. The member who had sought a comprehensive ruling from the Speaker allowed that in view of the apology the member did not want to proceed further. This was not good enough for some members. "Mr. Speaker," said one member, "I am somewhat distressed about this. I believe that if any individual were to commit perjury in one of the courts in our country, it is not very likely that the judge would say that since they were sorry, it was okay, and they should just carry on because it really did not matter. That would not happen."[87]

According to another member, "[The House] should be concerned with what kind of precedent we are setting. If in fact we are the highest court in the land, we have a person who has made misrepresentations, possibly stolen public funds, lied to a standing committee, falsified documents and records, and ultimately will walk away with nothing more than a stern talking to."[88] A few hours later, the member seeking a contempt ruling rose to report that there was unanimous agreement to find the privacy commissioner in contempt. This meant the House could find contempt without a debate or a vote, though it was still probably a painful experience for the commissioner.

A few years later, another committee also thought a witness had been untruthful. The auditor general had reported on questionable practices by the RCMP in administrating the RCMP pension and insurance plans. The committee then heard "far more troubling allegations" than had been in the auditor general's report.[89] Committee members developed a highly critical attitude toward RCMP higher management, including the RCMP deputy commissioner of human resources. It seemed to the committee that the deputy commissioner was not telling the whole truth in her testimony. The committee decided, out of fairness, that it should call her back to explain those parts of her testimony that concerned the committee.

The chair opened the meeting with a lengthy presentation of the committee's concerns. The deputy commissioner responded by attacking the committee for not being "truly interested" in what she would have to say. She insisted that she had answered all the questions put to her "to the best of my recollection and I stand by my answers again today."[90] The committee, in its report, said that the deputy commissioner's testimony, in view of other evidence it had received, was clearly false and she must have known it was false when she gave it. The professional position of the witness had played a part in the committee's finding: "Because [the deputy commissioner] is a senior, uniformed member of the RCMP, the Committee expected more from her as a witness. She is a professional who has been trained in the rules of evidence, conducting investigations, gathering evidence, and weighing testimony."[91]

This witness was not a private citizen who had made a mistake in her testimony – most committees are forgiving of this if the witness acknowledges the mistake. Here there was no acknowledgment of an error; instead there was defiance. The committee recommended – again unanimously – that the House find the deputy commissioner in contempt of Parliament "for providing false and misleading testimony" but that the House take no further action "as this finding of contempt is, in and of itself, a very serious sanction." The House unanimously accepted the recommendation of the committee and cited the deputy commissioner in contempt, without a debate or a vote.[92]

The witness felt she had been treated unjustly. In the next Parliament, she sought, through her member, to have the House's finding of contempt reversed. A later Parliament will not reverse the finding of a previous Parliament on something as sensitive as false testimony, any more than a different jury would reverse the findings of the jury that heard the evidence and rendered a verdict. The witness might have sought a pardon from the House (unprecedented), which would not have reversed the earlier finding of contempt but might have provided some sort of rehabilitation through forgiveness, but this was not what she had in mind.

If a person tries to discourage a witness from testifying or to influence the testimony of a witness or threatens repercussions if the witness testifies, this person could be found in contempt of Parliament. The issue of witness interference arose in 2010 with the Special Committee on the Canadian Mission in Afghanistan when it was alleged that government officials had tried to prevent a Canadian diplomat who had served in Afghanistan from appearing before the special committee by making threats that seemed designed to discourage the official from testifying. A legal opinion from the Department of Justice expressed the view that government officials appearing before House committees were not "absolved" from their legal obligation not to disclose sensitive information. The letter was cited in the House as an attempt to prevent the appearance of government officials as witnesses before the special committee. The Speaker ruled that the letter, as an expression of a legal opinion, could not be considered an attempt to interfere with committee witnesses, although the use made of the letter might be seen as an attempt to do so, that is, presenting this opinion to a government official about to appear before a House committee might be seen as an attempt to intimidate the official.[93]

Government officials are not expected to defend Government policies or the actions of the minister but they are expected to respond to committee questions pertaining to their administrative or operational actions. This is where the bureaucratic rubber hits the political road, as it were, and sometimes you can smell the rubber burning as the public official struggles to respond without causing problems for the minister or the department.[94]

Parliamentary Associations and Groups

And then there are the parliamentary associations and inter-parliamentary groups where private members (and senators) can become involved in parliamentary relations at the international level. They are voluntary and you can join as many or as few of them as you like. The aim of these groups, according to a Library of Parliament paper, "is to strengthen relations between Canadian parliamentarians and those in the countries concerned, fostering mutual cooperation and understanding between nations." To get funding from the Parliament of Canada (the House and Senate), an association must be recognized by the Joint Inter-parliamentary Council (JIC), a House-Senate administrative committee for inter-parliamentary activities.

Some parliamentary associations are multi-lateral and some are bilateral. The multi-lateral associations include, for example, the Canada-Africa Parliamentary Association, the Canada-Europe Parliamentary Association, the Canadian Branch of the Commonwealth Parliamentary Association, the Canadian Group of the Inter-Parliamentary Union, and the Canadian NATO Parliamentary Association while the bilateral associations include the Canada-China Legislative Association, the Canada-France Inter-parliamentary Association and the Canada-Japan, Canada-UK, and Canada-US parliamentary associations.

Inter-parliamentary groups, as distinct from associations, are not funded by Parliament or JIC but depend on membership fees from members and senators, which are payable from the office budgets of the members and senators. The aim of these groups, according to the same Library of Parliament paper, "is to strengthen relations between Canadian parliamentarians and those in the countries concerned, fostering mutual cooperation and understanding between nations." There are four such groups, namely, the Canada-Germany Inter-parliamentary Group and the Canada-Israel, the Canada-Italy, and the Canada-Ireland groups.

There are also other, smaller, inter-parliamentary groups, sometimes called "friendship groups," which are also not funded by JIC. Parliamentarians who have an interest in a specific international cause can engage with parliamentary colleagues elsewhere with a similar interest through these groups. Most of these are bilateral with another country but some are tied to a cause, such as the Parliamentarians for Global Action or the Parliamentary Friends of Falun Gong, Parliamentary Friends of the Kurds, Parliamentary Friends of Tibet, and the Save Darfur Parliamentary Coalition.

After any trip abroad, an association must table a report in the House, which is not debated or put to any review process or vote. In my years at the House, I never heard of much in the way of tangible product coming from these associations or groups though, as in diplomatic relations generally, much that is of intangible value might be achieved. In any event, for the private member who likes to travel, they can be fun and worth the time taken.

LET THE PLAY BEGIN

You've been waiting patiently to see the House in action. "Let the play begin!" you might say. But wait, you need some backstory to what you will see in the Chamber (and in committee), that is, some historical and constitutional context. The House, much like ourselves, is a product of its past: how did the House become the parliamentary institution that we have today? Where does the House stand, constitutionally, within our system of government? Also, perhaps some backstory will help you understand the seemingly odd procedural practices of the House.

2

The Backstory

The parliamentary system of government we have today in Canada did not begin as someone's good idea for a government. It evolved gradually during centuries of political conflict in England and then later in British North America before it became Canada. Basically, it was a struggle between the all-powerful king (or queen) and those who wanted to control the king (or queen).[1] In this chapter I look at the milestones in this struggle to see where the House of Commons sits constitutionally and where some of the practices and procedures of the House had their origins. The explanations and justifications for what the House does today are found in its past, the backstory to what you will be seeing and doing in the chamber and in committees.

In the beginning, the Crown had all the power; the people, including the wealthy barons and lords, had none. In time the Crown was brought to share its powers with the barons and lords and later with the people's representatives in Parliament. The driving force behind this change was the king's need for money. The Crown first depended on the barons and lords to provide funds or military resources but eventually the king began to look to the people's representatives in Parliament to provide funds through taxes.

The form of monarchical government in England and latter-day Canada may not have changed much but its substance has altered significantly in the move to parliamentary government. Getting there involved a long and winding road of political struggle; three steps forward, two steps back. We'll walk down that road to get a feel for our parliamentary system today, where many of the Crown's historic prerogative (discretionary) powers remain with the Crown but may be exercised only as the Government (through the prime minister) directs, with the Government accountable to Parliament, that is, the elected House of Commons. Ultimately, you and your colleagues in the House are in charge, although it may not seem that way.

HISTORICAL EVOLUTION

The parliamentary story began in 1215 when King John (1199–1216) signed the Magna Carta. The wealthy magnates of that time, fed up with the king's failures and abusive actions, compelled him to agree to consult the "Great Council" (the wealthy magnates) if he needed to raise funds through taxes and not to impose taxes by royal prerogative. The king remained the de jure and de facto ruler except that he could no longer unilaterally impose a tax. Although seen today as historic, the Magna Carta was largely ignored until the seventeenth century, when it was taken up as a rallying cry by those struggling against the arbitrary powers of the king. It became constitutional holy writ and has been revered ever since.[2]

Historians believe that the Magna Carta was the beginning of constitutional government in England as the monarch no longer had the right to unconditional loyalty from his or her subjects. It was also the beginning of legal rights for citizens when it imposed *legal* limitations on the powers of the king. The most notable legal limitation – which has remained part of the common law ever since – is the writ of habeas corpus, by which persons imprisoned by the king could seek their release in court if the imprisonment could not be shown to be lawful. According to one historian of the period, the Magna Carta "ended the primitive assumption that subjects owed their ruler absolute and unconditional obedience, and replaced it with two principles: that the king's government is itself subject to the law and that the king's law-making and tax-raising required the consent of the 'community of the realm.'"[3]

The struggles between the king and Parliament over money continued. In 1258, when Henry III (1216–72) requested funds, the barons insisted on reform of the kingdom's administration in exchange.[4] The king agreed to set up a joint committee comprised of the king's councillors and the barons that met in Oxford. This Oxford "parliament" produced a list of reforms that became known as the Provisions of Oxford. The most notable was the creation of an *elected* permanent King's Council that would oversee the actions of the king. Also, there were to be three parliaments each year.[5] Rule by the council was to replace personal rule by the king, but this provision was soon abandoned when the barons became divided. Henry recovered his powers and abandoned the Provisions of Oxford. While early days, nonetheless it was the start of a democratic basis for parliament.

In 1295, Edward I (1272–1307) summoned a Parliament that included representatives from the counties and cities "to consider, along with the magnates of our kingdom, the affairs of the said kingdom"; they were being asked to consider more than tax matters.[6] As there were no fixed rules about the composition of a parliament, it included whoever the king wanted.[7] While representatives from the "communities" (who would become the Commons) were not a necessary part of a parliament, they were sometimes included as economic expansion in England in the thirteenth century had led to the growth of towns and boroughs where knights and burgesses had influence along with the barons and nobles. Despite allowing for this broader representation, the king did not see himself bound by Parliament but accepted that on some matters he should consult it.

Legislation was initiated by the king and was usually adopted in Parliament without amendment. Although the representatives in the Commons seemed to be there only to witness the legislative process and perhaps offer some comments, formal assent was considered important.[8] At least some progress was being made toward a more democratic, parliamentary, system of government.

With the ascent to the throne of the misbehaving Edward II (1307–27), the nobles and prelates inserted a new oath into the coronation ceremony that required the king to promise to maintain and preserve the laws and customs that, it was said, the people had chosen. A group of bishops and nobles was appointed by Parliament (to which no commoners had been summoned) as "Lords Ordainers" to oversee the government of the kingdom. In 1311, the lords imposed forty-one "New Ordinances" on the king, one of which required that he confer with Parliament on matters of high policy (e.g., funding the military, royal finances), taxation, and the appointment of ministers.[9] Parliament was required to meet at least once a year, possibly twice, for judicial business. (Until the seventeenth century, Parliament also acted as a court of law – the highest court of the land.) A committee of lords was established to hear complaints against the king's ministers.[10] We can see here, in the early fourteenth century, the start of parliamentary oversight of the Government.

At the same time, Parliament asserted that the laws and customs must be amended when the people demand changes through petitions. There were two kinds of petition: private petitions from private citizens on private matters and common or public interest petitions that were non-political (in the sense that they posed no challenge to the king) and of common or public interest. Private petitions were made to the clerk of the Parliament and passed along to a panel of auditors consisting of barons, prelates, and justices who sent their findings to the king's officials for action. The Commons was not involved with these petitions. Common or public petitions were presented by the Commons in the general interests of the community and sought redress for unacceptable administrative or fiscal actions or for social grievances.[11] The petitions proposed responses and were recorded on the parliamentary roll as bills. Bills found acceptable by the king (and his council) were redrafted as statutes and entered on the statute rolls. For its part, the Commons insisted that its petitions be addressed before it would give any funds to the Crown. This was the start of the parliamentary principle, which still applies, that the Crown must hear the Commons' grievances before any of its spending plans are approved.[12] Today, this consideration takes place in the House on days designated for consideration of opposition motions (see chapter 4).

New parliaments were opened, as they are today, with the king, the lords, and the commoners, as well as the judges, assembling in one room to hear the "cause of summons" – that is, to hear the king explain why he summoned parliament.[13] The king's chief minister announced that the king would receive and answer petitions for the redress of grievances.[14] The "magnates and those of the commonalty" then moved into two separate rooms to debate and consider "how to meet the king's needs."[15] These separate gatherings would become the

House of Lords and the House of Commons and in Canada are the Senate and the House.

When the knights and burgesses – the commonalty – met, their first piece of business was an oath to keep secret what was discussed and to be loyal to one another. Secrecy was their only protection from reprisals by the king for what they might say in their debates. The right to absolute freedom of speech came much later. Before meeting with the king and the lords, the Commons agreed on what their Speaker would say on their behalf.[16] The role of the Speaker was to communicate the views of the Commons to the king, acting more as a representative of the Commons than its presiding official. The Speaker today, whether in England or Canada, does not have this spokesperson function between the House and the Crown (the Government), except occasionally as a matter of protocol; e.g,, in the opening of a parliamentary session (discussed in the previous chapter).

The independence of the Commons as a separate body began to grow. For example, in 1337, the Commons told Edward III (1327–77) that its members needed to confer with their constituents before granting him any funds. Also, to make sure that the next House did not include anyone working in the king's interest, the Commons insisted that none of the knights summoned to the next Parliament be sheriffs or other officials of the government. In Canada today, a person in the employ of the Crown – other than a minister – cannot be a member of parliament.[17]

In 1340, after Parliament refused to give him any funds, Edward accepted grievances from the Commons, one of which led to establishment of the rule that funds authorized by Parliament must be spent only on the purposes for which they were authorized. (This rule remains with us today.) In the following year, Edward allowed audits to ensure that the monies provided by Parliament had been used for the purposes for which they were provided; in Canada today this is done by the auditor general of Canada as this task is more than the House or Senate can manage, given the size and complexity of government today.[18]

Disputes arose between Parliament (the Commons) and the king over how, exactly, laws were to be made. The usual practice had been that the king enacted laws using his prerogative powers, sometimes on the advice of his council, although some were enacted in response to petitions from the Commons. The issue was whether the king could make laws solely through his prerogative powers or whether Parliament alone had the power to make laws. In 1399, Henry IV (1399–1413) agreed that on matters "to be done for the common profit of the realm" he would seek the "advice and assent" of the Commons before acting.[19] He didn't say anything about how he might use his prerogative powers, however.

In 1407 Henry acknowledged that proposed taxation or funding must first be sent to the House of Commons for approval.[20] (This rule was expressly included in the Canadian Constitution in 1867.[21]) His successor, Henry V (1413–22), promised that he would not make laws based on petitions from the Commons that differed from what the Commons had asked for in its petitions.[22] Here we see the start of the separation of the legislative function from the executive function, that is, law-making is vested in Parliament, which, as the legislative branch of government, is separate from the Crown as the executive branch of government.

Edward IV (1461–83) and Henry VII (1485–1509) didn't summon Parliament very often because they didn't need money very often – and there was no other reason for the king to summon a parliament. The lords, for their purposes, usually had sufficient access to the king through the King's Council, where many of them sat. The Commons was a junior partner and was consulted only as and when the king and/or the lords felt it was necessary.

In the late fifteenth century, the Commons' role as a political player, that is, in influencing public policy, was modest.[23] It still included a large number of "royal placemen," persons beholden or loyal to the king, which ensured that it co-operated with the His Majesty's Government on major issues.[24] (When you look at the Government's use of party discipline in majority parliaments, you may think we've returned to the fifteenth century.)

In 1523, Sir Thomas More, as Speaker of the House of Commons, went to Henry VIII (1509–47) with two petitions. The first was a personal request that the king not blame the House if he, as Speaker, should be mistaken in his report to the king on its proceedings. The second request, and a much more significant one, was that the Commons be allowed free speech with no fear of reprisals.[25] The king confirmed the right of members of Parliament to free speech in the House – although this right would not go unchallenged in the years to come.

In the forty-five-year reign of Elizabeth I (1558–1603), conflicts arose not only over demands for money but also over parliament's right to set its own agenda. As a demonstration of its independence from the Crown, in 1558 the House launched the practice of considering a bill on a topic of its choosing before it began any debate on the speech giving the queen's reasons for summoning Parliament (which today is the Speech from the Throne).[26] While this action was undertaken as a mere formality, it affirmed the House's right to deliberate on a matter of its own choosing without first turning to matters of concern to the king or queen. This practice was confirmed in 1604 by a resolution of the British House and has been the practice there ever since.

Similarly, in Canada today a bill entitled An Act Respecting the Administration of Oaths of Office, which becomes Bill C-1, is introduced by the prime minister on the first sitting day of the House after delivery of the Speech from the Throne opening the session. The bill is not printed and does not advance beyond introduction (first reading). The bill asserts the right of the "elected representatives of the people to act without the leave of the Crown" and "the right of the House of Commons to give precedence to matters not addressed in the Speech from the Throne." You may have wondered what the prime minister was doing on the opening day of the session when he rose to introduce this bill. Of course, with the Government's control of the House when it has a majority, the independence of the House asserted by this bill is largely symbolic.

When Elizabeth opened parliament, she affirmed that members had freedom of speech but added that there were limits to what Parliament (that is, the House of Commons) could do. On one occasion, she put the Commons in what she thought was its proper place when she told them: "It is in me and my power to call parliaments; it is in my power to end and determine the same; it is in my power to assent or dissent to anything done in parliament."[27]

The powers of the monarch – referred to as prerogative powers – remained a sore point between Parliament and the Crown, as they still are at times today. Through these powers the Crown acted with the force of law, separate and apart from Parliament. The classic eighteenth-century text on English common law, *Blackstone's Commentaries on the Laws of England*, defined the royal prerogative as "that special pre-eminence, which the King hath, over and above all other persons, and out of the ordinary course of the common law, in right of his regal dignity."[28] Prerogative powers put the monarch above the law and included a variety of discretionary powers that were seen as inherent in the monarch's authority as the sovereign.

Problems soon developed with Elizabeth's successor, James I (1603–25). James acknowledged parliament's right to make laws and grant taxation but otherwise didn't think much of the place: "The Commons is a body without a head," said James, "The members give their opinion in a disorderly manner. At their meetings, nothing is heard but cries, shouts and confusion. I am surprised that my ancestors should ever have allowed such an institution to come into existence."[29] James fought with the Commons over religion and foreign policy, which he felt were matters beyond its competence. The Commons insisted that such matters were "proper subjects and matter of counsel and debate in parliament."[30]

Relations between the king and the Commons went from bad to worse under Charles I (1625–49), who would eventually lose his head, literally, by order of the House of Commons. Charles put Parliament in its place much as Elizabeth and James had done before him. "Remember," said Charles, "parliaments are altogether in my power for the calling, sitting and continuance of them, therefore as I find the fruits of them good or evil, they are to continue or not to be."[31] He was referring to his prerogative powers to end a parliamentary session through prorogation or dissolution of parliament, powers that to this day remain with the Crown (as directed by the prime minister) in Canada and are the object of political comment from time to time (as they were in 2008 and 2009, discussed later).

Charles had the same problem as his predecessors: insufficient funds. His first Parliament gave him only a fraction of what he asked for and presented so many grievances that he lost patience and dissolved it. However, the war with France compelled him to call Parliament back and again he was refused funds. He sought funds elsewhere by various means, including forced loans to the Crown with imprisonment for refusing. His third Parliament again gave him only a fraction of what he needed and even that was subject to his confirming the rights that Parliament had earlier won against the Crown. He agreed not to levy taxes without parliamentary consent or to imprison people without cause.

However, when Parliament next met, the Commons was still unhappy with Charles: a member's goods had been seized and the member committed to the Star Chamber because he had refused to pay a certain tax. The Commons was offended by the king's action in creating a tax and particularly his failure to obtain its approval. The king directed the Speaker to adjourn the House, which the Speaker did, but as he was leaving the House two members stopped him and said: "By God's wounds, you shall sit till we please to rise!" It was the right of the House, these members felt, to decide when it would adjourn.[32] As if to make this abundantly clear, the House passed a resolution that there could be no tax without parliament's approval and that anyone who voluntarily paid a tax betrayed the liberties of England.[33] Unhappy with this, Charles dissolved Parliament (again) and declared that it had exceeded its function, blaming "the undutiful and seditious carriage of the lower house, provoked by 'some few vipers.'"[34] He didn't summon another parliament for eleven years.

The problem was not so much that Charles had prerogative powers but that the constitutional regime allowed him such powers – that "the existing constitution had ceased to correspond to reality."[35] Summoning and dissolving a parliament at will was despotic. The issue was whether supremacy in matters of public policy should remain with the king, with Parliament subject to his calling it into session and dissolving it when he didn't like what it was doing.

In late November 1641, the Commons, by a narrow majority, approved a petition entitled the "Grand Remonstrance."[36] The petition demanded that Charles replace his "evil counsellors" (Catholics) with "such persons … as your Parliament may have cause to confide in."[37] Charles denied that there was any need for reform of the government and refused to accept that Parliament should appoint his ministers.[38] He ordered the attorney-general to lay charges against the members that he thought were responsible for the Grand Remonstrance. Parliament thought this action was in breach of its privileges.[39]

In January 1642 Charles entered the Commons to arrest the members he thought were responsible for the Remonstrance. They, however, had left the chamber by a back door. He sat down in the Speaker's chair and, not seeing the members that he was looking for ("I see the birds have flown"), he asked the Speaker, William Lenthall, where they were. Lenthall made his historic response, which Speakers ever since have adopted as their own: "May it please your majesty," said Speaker Lenthall, "I have neither eyes to see nor tongue to speak in this place but as the House is pleased to direct me, whose servant I am here." Lenthal defied that the king had the authority over the House that he was claiming by taking the Speaker's chair. To this day, Lenthall's response defines the role of the Speaker as a servant of the House and not of the king (or the Government). Charles left the Commons empty-handed and since that time the monarch (including the governor general in Canada) has been unwelcome in the Commons. A week later, Charles and his family suddenly left London, which was taken as surrendering the City and the seat of government to Parliament. The members Charles had charged came out of hiding and returned in triumph to Parliament.[40]

In March, the Commons and the Lords passed a resolution that was tantamount to a declaration of parliamentary sovereignty: "That when the Lords and Commons in Parliament ... shall declare what the law of the land is, to have this not only questioned and controverted but contradicted and a command that it should not be obeyed, is a high breach of the privileges of Parliament."[41] Soon after, Parliament passed the Militia Bill, transferring command of the army from the king to Parliament. Charles refused to assent to the bill, whereupon Parliament approved it as an ordinance for safeguarding the realm. Parliament soon gained control of the Royal Navy as well. Of significance here is that Parliament had made the Militia Bill into law without having the king's assent.[42] Parliament, that is, the Lords and the Commons, had assumed legislative power unto itself alone.

In June, Parliament proposed "Nineteen Propositions," which included demands that members of the king's Privy Council be only persons approved by Parliament and that such matters as concern the public be debated and resolved only in Parliament. The king should exercise his powers only when his actions were approved by a majority of the Privy Council. His Majesty's Government would be answerable to Parliament (creating a seventeenth-century version of responsible government, which wouldn't arrive until the mid-nineteenth century.).

Charles saw these reforms as an attempt to cause "our just, ancient, regal power" to be "fetched down to the ground." Agreeing to this, said Charles, would be tantamount to deposing himself as king. While he might retain all the insignia of a king, "as to true and real power we should remain but the outside, but the picture, but the sign of a king."[43] As Elizabeth and James had done before him, Charles cautioned the houses of Parliament about debating matters that were not "proper to them." Government, said Charles, was entrusted to the king. Governmental powers, such as making treaties, choosing officers of state, appointing judges, and granting pardons, were historically vested in the king. He acknowledged that the Commons, as a check on the king or his councillors, was "solely entrusted" with powers of taxation and the impeachment of offenders. Said Charles, the Commons was "an excellent conserver of liberty but was never intended for any share in government or the choosing of them that govern."[44] This remains true to this day.

Soon after this, Parliament voted to raise an army of 10,000 and the United Kingdom descended into six years of civil wars between the king's royalist forces and parliament's army. By 1648, the royalist forces had lost the wars but the king was alive and well and a could not be ignored. A last effort was made to agree on the terms of a peace treaty. The political aspect was quickly settled: the king accepted that Parliament had been forced to wage war in its "just and lawful defence" and that his selection of ministers would be subject to parliamentary approval.[45] However, there were important religious or church-related issues that could not be settled. Charles felt he was being made into a puppet ruler. At the same time, the army and its supporters in Parliament were losing patience, with some parliamentarians fearing that if matters weren't resolved soon the army would take over. (The army was near the end of its patience over back pay.)

A new set of propositions – entitled Remonstrance of the Army – was presented to parliament. The Remonstrance urged that the monarchy be abolished and that Charles be "speedily brought to justice for the treason, blood and mischief he's therein guilty of."[46]

Charles didn't take the threat of a trial seriously – an accused can only be tried by his peers and he, as king, had no peers.[47] The army was brought in to forcibly remove those members who might vote against the Remonstrance and the remaining rump voted on New Year's Day 1649 to establish a High Court of Justice to put the king on trial.

A High Court of Justice was established by an act of the Commons (without the concurrence of the Lords) to put the king on trial.[48] Charles was convicted as a "Tyrant, Traitor, Murderer and a public enemy." Before passing a sentence of death, the president of the High Court said to the king, "There is a contract and a bargain made between the King and his people, and your oath is taken; certainly, Sir, the bond is reciprocal. The one tie, the one bond, is the bond of protection that is due from the Sovereign ... Sir, if this bond be once broken, farewell sovereignty."[49] Charles was beheaded on 30 January 1649.

Soon after, a member of the Commons, Oliver Cromwell, came into a leadership role and summoned a new Parliament. Questions arose about the legitimacy of such a Parliament as the summons had not been issued by the king but by a self-appointed official. Some of the members of the new Parliament challenged Cromwell's authority, to which he replied that they were "a free Parliament only so long as they accepted the authority that summoned them there."[50]

Displeased with this parliament, Cromwell, like Charles before him, dissolved it and governed England with a Council of Officers. This form of government was not well received, however. Cromwell summoned another parliament, the Second Protectorate Parliament, to ratify his actions. This Parliament offered Cromwell the throne, but he declined. They then offered to make him lord protector for life, with the power to name his own successor. On 26 June 1657, Cromwell was "crowned" as lord protector of the realm. Nothing changed much in the parliamentary world: bickering debates continued. Cromwell soon dissolved this Parliament as he had dissolved the earlier one. In the end, he had failed to establish a viable parliamentary system of government that functioned without a monarch on the throne.

When Cromwell died in 1658, his son, Richard, took over as lord protector but didn't do well at it. He summoned a Parliament in 1659 and the Council of Officers persuaded him to dissolve it a few months later. Richard soon resigned and a period of political chaos ensued. An army general occupied London and summoned back the Parliament of 1640, which was seen as the last legitimate Parliament because it was the last to have been summoned by the king. This Parliament dissolved itself in accordance with the Act Against Dissolution of 1641. The next Parliament met in April 1660 and began negotiations with Charles I's son, also a Charles, which led to restoration of the monarchy and the coronation of Charles II (1660–85). The monarchy was restored but only with the consent of parliament, establishing what might be called a parliamentary monarchy.

Unfortunately, James II (1685–1701) saw the king as the holder of absolute powers. It was as if he had learned nothing from history, whether as far back as the Magna Carta in 1215 or as recent as the beheading of his father. Parliamentary leaders took steps to replace James II with the Protestant Prince William of Orange and invited William to come to England, which he did with an army behind him. James fled the country and William took over His Majesty's Government.

William called for an assembly of the members of Parliament. This Parliament declared that the departure of James II had left the throne vacant and offered it to William and his wife, Mary, but first defined the powers of the king in a Declaration of Rights that was read aloud before William and Mary ascended the throne. The Declaration later became law as an Act of Parliament and has been known ever since as the Bill of Rights of 1689. Replacing James with William III (1689–1702) and enacting the Bill of Rights of 1689 has been known ever since as the Glorious Revolution.

The 1689 Bill of Rights gave the people of England, at least the male persons, certain immutable civil and political rights. Most important-ly for our purposes, it affirmed that the king could no longer make laws without Parliament's consent.[51] It established a constitutional relationship between the monarch and Parliament: a movement from rule by one person, the monarch, to the rule of laws made by Parliament. The Glorious Revolution established *parliamentary* sovereignty in England, with the House of Commons as the dominant house within Parliament.[52]

Articles 8 and 9 of the 1689 Bill of Rights remain of particular importance to the Houses of Commons in both England and Canada. Article 8 affirms that there will be free elections of members of parliament.[53] Article 9 assures freedom of speech in parliamentary debates and that proceedings in Parliament will be free of legal challenges in the courts.[54]

While the 1689 Bill of Rights may have established a constitutional relationship between Parliament and His Majesty, the same cannot be said about the relationship between Parliament and His Majesty's Government, at least not directly. The Government was not yet seen as separate and apart from the monarch as it is today in both England and Canada, where the monarch has become a constitutional figurehead. Ministers of the Crown were very much under the control of the monarch and took direction from the monarch. The prime minister of the day may have had influence but had neither control of the monarch nor political control of the Commons.

The Mutiny Act of 1689 required that military spending must be approved each year by parliament. This was the start of *annual* appropriations by parliament. Spending for non-military purposes was dealt with by an appropriation determined at the start of a monarch's reign and was payable each year without the need for further parliamentary approvals. By early in the nineteenth century, all government spending was subject to annual appropriation, as it is today both here and in England.

In 1739, Robert Walpole, first lord of the Treasury (the equivalent of prime minister), told the Commons that when he spoke in the House he spoke as one possessing powers from the king "but as being answerable to this House for the exercise of these powers."[55] The Government was moving from being accountable to the king to being accountable to parliament, in particular to the House of Commons.

By 1815, the convention of cabinet solidarity was established and by the time of the Reform Act of 1832, it was widely expected that a Government would resign if it lost a vote in the House on a major issue. In 1835, Prime Minister Peel resigned (and the Government with him), saying that, in his view, "the Government ought not to persist in carrying on public affairs ... in opposition to the decided opinion of a majority of the House of Commons."[56] Between the Reform Acts of 1832 and 1867, ten Governments resigned after losing a vote in the House.

In the meantime, the British Parliament passed the Constitutional Act of 1791, which created the colonies of Lower Canada (Quebec) and Upper Canada (Ontario).[57] In 1840, Lower Canada and Upper Canada were joined to create the Province of Canada. The Province struggled to get the colonial governor and the British government to accept the principle of responsible government in which the Crown's ministers would be collectively responsible to the elected colonial assembly, which would mean that the London-appointed governor would be accountable to the colonial assembly.[58]

Collective ministerial responsibility was the cornerstone of responsible government, a term first used in 1829 in a petition to England from Canada that asked for "a local and responsible ministry."[59] While the British understood collective ministerial responsibility, they did not seem aware of the idea of "responsible government." According to British Prime Minister Lord John Russell, in a message to the governor general of Canada in 1839: "It does not appear, indeed, that any very definite meaning is generally agreed upon by those who call themselves the advocates of this principle [of responsible government]," adding that "its very vagueness is a source of delusion." However, some in Britain must have felt they understood it as it appears in a report by Lord Durham in 1838. Durham had been sent to British North America to advise the British Government on the prospects for a parliamentary system of government in Canada and the resulting report describes responsible government as an "indisputable and essential part" of the British constitution.[60]

The Province of Canada was only a colony, so, in legal constitutional terms, its government – that is, the governor – was an official of Her Majesty's Government in Britain. The colony had an elected Legislative Assembly that provided representation for the people who paid taxes but it was the governor or governor general who ran the government of the colony and was responsible for implementing directions from the colonial secretary in London who acted on behalf of the British Government. The governor general could disallow an

act of the Legislative Assembly, which the governor general today cannot do. The governor general appointed members of the Legislative
Assembly to the Executive Council (cabinet) and was very much in
charge of the Government, much like the prime minister of Canada
is today. The Executive Council (cabinet) had only an advisory role.

The governor general was not, however, accountable to the elected
Legislative Assembly. In effect, the colonial government was owned
and operated by the British Government (which also provided funding for major capital projects such as railways and canals). And the
governor general reported or was accountable to the colonial secretary in London. From London's point of view, the Government of a
colony could not be accountable to local political interests. It was part
of an empire, after all.

In 1847, Lord Elgin was sent to the Province of Canada as its governor
general but with instructions from his superiors in London to support
and recognize the colonial executive's responsibility to the colonial legislature: Lord Durham's report must have won the day with the British
Government. The colonial government was to be vested in the political
party that controlled Parliament and would change only when that control changed.[61] The election of 1847–48 in the Province of Canada gave
a strong majority to a reform party led by Robert Baldwin in Canada
West (Ontario) and Louis-Hippolyte Lafontaine in Canada East (Quebec) and together they formed the new colonial Government, "a true
one-party cabinet, the first in the province of Canada."[62] There was no
doubt that the Baldwin-Lafontaine party had become the Government
because of its parliamentary majority and not as the result of personal
preference of the governor general. The installation of this new Government "indisputably" recognized "party cabinet rule" and established the
governor general's withdrawal from politics.[63]

The defining event for responsible government in Canada came in
1849 when governor general Lord Elgin gave his assent to the Rebellion Losses Bill, which provided compensation to persons in Lower
Canada (Quebec) who had suffered property losses in the rebellion of
1837.[64] (Compensation had been provided earlier in Upper Canada
(Ontario)). Critics thought it outrageous that the Crown would com-
pensate persons who had risen in rebellion against it. Opponents of

the bill questioned Lord Elgin's loyalty to the British Empire in giving his assent to the bill. Lord Elgin, however, felt he had to assent: the bill had been approved by the Legislative Assembly and his Executive Council (the cabinet) was asking for his assent. In his view, assent was the proper course of action. Self-government in the form of responsible government had arrived in Canada.

In 1867, the British Parliament enacted the British North America Act, which joined the British colonies in North America (Province of Canada, Nova Scotia, and New Brunswick) into a confederation, to be known as the Dominion of Canada.[65] The act acknowledged that the three colonies wanted to be "federally united" into one dominion under the Crown of England "with a constitution similar in principle to that of the United Kingdom."[66] Canada inherited the British parliamentary system of government as it was in 1867. The design and conventions of the British parliamentary system, though not mentioned in the Constitution Act 1867, would apply in Canada unless Canada should decide otherwise.

The last piece in the evolution of the parliamentary system of government as we have it today, whether in England or Canada, is the arrival in the late nineteenth century of organized political parties operating at the national level and outside parliament. Up to this time, beginning in the early seventeenth century, there had been broad political alliances within Parliament (which became informally known as Tories and Whigs), but these could shift from one issue to another and lacked organization outside parliament. As voting rights expanded and methods of communication improved, political parties developed and began presenting party platforms at elections.

Members of Parliament increasingly depended on support from their political parties to get elected or re-elected. This enabled the parties to develop internal discipline over their members, to the point that a Government with a majority of the seats in the House had effective control of the House, as is the case in Canada today. Some argue that the discipline imposed by the political parties over their members has taken us back to where we were before enactment of the Bill of Rights of 1689, when the king held all the power without being truly accountable to the House.

PARLIAMENTARY SYSTEM OF GOVERNMENT

And so we have in Canada today a parliamentary system of government that first developed in England. The operative word here is neither "parliamentary" nor "government" but "system," that is, a system of government comprised of three branches, each with its own constitutional function independent of the others, though not always acting separate and apart, and governed by constitutional rules and conventions. For Canada, the constitutional rules are found in the Constitution Acts of 1867 and 1982 and in a variety of unwritten conventions – or rules of practice – that developed over centuries as the parliamentary system evolved.

The three branches are the legislative (House of Commons and Senate), the executive (the prime minister and cabinet), and the judicial (the courts).[67] The critical aspects of this system of government are the relationships – the sharing of power – between the executive and the House of Commons (the dominant House of the legislative branch) and between each of these and the courts (the judicial branch). Power is shared between the executive and the House with respect to public finances (imposing taxes and spending public funds) and the making of laws (statutes and regulations). Power is also shared with the judicial branch insofar as the executive appoints the judges but the courts may declare executive policies or actions or House legislation unconstitutional and unenforceable. Thus, no branch has a completely free hand.

Parliamentary Supremacy and Parliamentary Sovereignty

In your time in the House, you will hear people mention parliamentary supremacy and parliamentary sovereignty. These terms are often used interchangeably to indicate that there is no authority higher than Parliament and that Parliament can do whatever it wants to do. While this may have been largely true in Britain, where these terms originated (until, that is, the United Kingdom joined the European Union in 1973), it is not true for Canada, at least not to the same extent.

The Parliament of Canada, unlike the UK Parliament, cannot do whatever it wants. It is subject to the requirements of the Constitution with respect to its legislative powers under the Constitution Act 1867 and to the protected rights of individual Canadians and minorities under the Constitution Act 1982 (the Charter of Rights and Freedoms). The so-called notwithstanding clause found in section 33 of the Charter, which permits Parliament to legislate contrary to sections 2 and 7 to 15 of the Charter, is a concession in favour of parliamentary sovereignty or supremacy but does not remove other constitutional limitations on parliament.

The only "supremacy" enjoyed by Canada's Parliament is that it can set its own internal procedures and can repeal whatever an earlier Parliament may have enacted. A recent example of its legislative "supremacy" are the amendments made in 2011 to the legislative regime governing the Canadian Wheat Board that ended the Wheat Board's monopoly over sales of wheat and barley in Canada.[68] A few days before The Marketing Freedom for Grain Farmers' Act became law, a Federal Court judge ruled that the Government had violated section 47 of the Canadian Wheat Board Act,[69] which stipulated that the Government could not introduce a bill in Parliament that would end the Wheat Board's control of wheat or barley sales without first consulting the Wheat Board and holding a vote among farmers to determine whether the farmers favoured the change. The judge decided that the principle of the rule of law as a "constitutional imperative" meant that the Government must respect the requirements of section 47 and the Government had not done this.[70] The court did not strike down the new act as illegal as it could not do this: a court can only strike down an act on the basis of lack of legislative jurisdiction or as a violation of the Charter, which are constitutional requirements. The new Marketing Freedom for Grain Farmers Act was not unconstitutional – the court had only decided that the Government's action in proposing the amendments was illegal, which may have been technically or literally correct. However, when the Government first proposed the amendments, it had intentionally ignored section 47 and sought legislative approval from the House: despite the court's ruling, the amendments were enacted as law. The Government was relying on the principle that a previous Parliament cannot bind a later parliament, meaning that the earlier Parliament that enacted section 47 could not bind the later Parliament on how it might legislate with respect to the Wheat Board. The court ruling therefore had no legal effect.[71] The Government didn't bother appealing the court's decision.

Relationships between Branches

The operations of the parliamentary system of government largely involve the relationship between the Government and the elected House. Fundamental to this relationship from the Government's point of view is that the Government, not the House, controls the financial and legislative agenda. From the House's point of view, however, there are two important countervailing principles here. First, House approval is required on any Government proposals for new taxes or tax increases and on the spending of public funds and, second, the Government is accountable to the House (it must sustain the House's confidence in the Government).

Each branch is expected to respect the functions of the other branches without interfering beyond what is permitted by their constitutional functions. One might say that the three branches are interrelated by "checks and balances" (to borrow a term used with the American congressional system). Most importantly, the Government must have the confidence of the House to stay in office. The Government decides who to prosecute for criminal offences (if they are under federal jurisdiction) but the courts run the trials and determine the guilt or innocence of the offender. The House legislates on financial matters but only as the Government may propose. The Government can collect only those taxes that have been approved by the House. The Government manages and spends public funds but only as the House authorizes. Judges of the courts are appointed by the Government but cannot be removed except through a parliamentary process. Parliament makes laws but does not apply or administer them. The Government administers the laws and in the event of a dispute the courts determine what the laws mean and how they apply. The courts make binding legal rulings on cases that are brought before them (that is, the courts cannot initiate a challenge to the laws) but enforcement of their rulings is left to government officials.

Prerogative Powers

Difficult relations between Parliament and the executive have usually been caused by use of a royal prerogative power. Most of the Crown's prerogative powers have been taken over by legislation and are exercised by ministers. Those powers not governed by statute – so-called residual powers – may only be exercised on the advice of the prime minister or the cabinet. With respect to foreign affairs, these residual powers include the power to make war or conclude a peace, to enter into treaties or other international agreements, to recognize foreign states, diplomatic relations generally, and the use of the armed forces. With respect to domestic matters, residual prerogative powers include the power to summon Parliament, to appoint a prime minister, to prorogue (or terminate) a session of Parliament, to dissolve Parliament and call a general election, to make appointments to public offices, and to bestow honours. To have legal effect, these actions are formally authorized by a proclamation signed by the governor general.

Three of these residual prerogative powers – the power to appoint a prime minister, the power to prorogue parliament, and the power to dissolve Parliament and call an election – can occasionally generate quite heated political debate. By constitutional convention, based on the principle of responsible government, the governor general is expected to exercise these powers only on the advice of the prime minister, possibly with an exception in the power to appoint a prime minister (discussed below).[72] There may be circumstances where the governor general must exercise this power without or contrary to advice from the prime minister.

Becoming Prime Minister

The governor general, without needing advice from the sitting prime minister, usually appoints the leader of the party that won the most seats in the last election as prime minister. This assumes that the incumbent prime minister has resigned. Where an opposition party has won the most seats (a plurality but not a majority), the incumbent prime minister is entitled to stay in office and meet the House in the new Parliament to see whether the prime minister's Government still has the confidence of the House. If the House votes non-confidence, constitutional convention requires that the prime minister resign and the governor general appoint a new prime minister, typically the leader of the opposition party that had won the most seats. When a

prime minister resigns for reasons other than an election, the governor general follows the advice of the outgoing prime minister on who
should be appointed.

Prorogation

The prerogative power to prorogue parliament, that is, to end a session, invites criticism insofar as it brings all business in the House in
that session to an end. Typically, a new session will be called, again by
the prerogative power, a few weeks later. Prorogations often draw
complaints from the opposition parties as prorogations enable the
Government to start a new agenda and get rid of any parliamentary
or political problems that were developing. Is this ok? Should a prime
minister be able to use prorogations for self-serving political purposes? Are there limits on the governor general's duty to follow the advice
of the prime minister?

In December 2008, a non-confidence motion was put on notice in
the House by the official opposition and was to be put to a vote in
about a week. The Government did not have a majority of the seats in
the House and was expected to lose the vote. If this happened, two of
the three opposition parties had agreed to form a coalition Government and had the support of the third opposition party. If this coalition had formed a Government, it would probably have had the confidence of the House, although some doubted that the confidence
would last very long. But the prime minister asked the governor
general to prorogue parliament, which prevented the non-confidence
motion from coming to a vote. Some observers thought that the governor general should have refused the prime minister's request for
prorogation – that is, acted contrary to the prime minister's advice –
and when the Government lost the confidence vote should have
appointed the leader of the official opposition as prime minister and
asked him to form a new Government.

In my view, the governor general had to grant prorogation, if only
as the lesser of two evils. If she had refused the prime minister's
advice, she would have breached the constitutional convention that
the governor general follows the prime minister's advice in the exercise of prerogative powers and would have faced demands that she

explain her decision, something the governor general never does. When the non-confidence motion was approved in the House, which seemed likely, she would have had to either follow the probable advice from the prime minister to dissolve Parliament and call another election (only three months after the previous election) or disregard his advice and call upon the leader of the official opposition to form a Government, refusing the prime minister's advice for a second time. She would then have been met with accusations (from the prime minister, among others) that she had again breached the constitutional convention of acting only on the prime minister's advice.

As well, the new coalition Government might have fallen apart fairly soon and lost the confidence of the House. The coalition prime minister would then have requested dissolution and the calling of an election. If the governor general followed this advice, abiding by the convention, many would probably have demanded to know why she had followed the prime minister's advice this time and not earlier. It would be a messy situation all round.

Most importantly, in my view, the governor general would have been forced into playing a political role that is beyond – and offends against – her constitutional role. When the governor general follows the prime minister's advice and grants prorogation, she is following the established constitutional convention that places political responsibility for prorogations – and for the exercise of all prerogative powers – with the prime minister, where it belongs.

On the other hand, one might argue that the governor general ought to have treated the request for prorogation as an abuse of her office by the prime minister and a wrongful obstruction of the parliamentary process – constitutional contempt, as it were – coming so soon after she had opened the new Parliament and read the Speech from the Throne setting out the Government's plans for the first session of Parliament and before the Government had done anything in the new Parliament. There seemed no plausible explanation for the prime minister's request for prorogation except that it served his partisan political purposes. Arguably, the governor general's constitutional position was being abused and she should not have allowed this lest the constitutional credibility of her office be undermined; she owed it to her office to defend her position against such abuse.

Given that she was aware that prorogation was being sought to prevent a non-confidence vote in the House, that is, to frustrate the business of the House, one might further argue that the governor general
made herself party to obstructing the House in the exercise of its constitutional function of holding the Government to account.

In March 2010, the House approved (this was a minority parliament) an opposition motion that, "in the opinion of the House, the
prime minister shall not advise the governor general to prorogue any
session of any Parliament for longer than seven calendar days without
a specific resolution of this House of Commons to support such a
prorogation." As the motion, like all such motions, was merely "in the
opinion of the House," it had no binding effect.[73] The House cannot,
by motion, determine how the Crown may exercise its prerogative
powers, though it could do something by legislation, as it has already
done in respect of many prerogative powers. The Standing Committee on Procedure and House Affairs held nine meetings on prorogation, hearing fourteen experts explain the law and the constitutional
conventions surrounding prorogation but did not table a report in
the House before Parliament was dissolved for an election on 26
March 2011.[74]

Many constitutional experts say that removing prorogation from
the hands of the prime minister requires a constitutional amendment,
which would require the consent of the provinces because it would,
contrary to section 41 of the Constitution Act 1982, affect the office
of the governor general. It seems to me, however, that if one considers
the prime minister's advisory power on prorogation as distinct from
the governor general's power to prorogue, ordinary legislation might
impose terms on the prime minister's advisory power without touching the powers, and thus the office, of the governor general. A legislative model for such action is provided in the so-called fixed-date elections legislation enacted in 2007.[75] In third reading debate on the bill,
the minister of justice said that "all parties agree with the principle
that the timing of elections should not be left to the prime minister
but should be set in advance so all Canadians know when the next
election will occur." He went on to say that "what we have is a situation where the prime minister is able to choose the date of the general election, not based necessarily on what is in the best interests of the

country, but what is in the best interests of his or her political party." One could say the same for the prime minister's power to seek prorogation. However, the bill expressly left untouched the governor general's power to dissolve Parliament and call an election (a power that is under the control of the prime minister).[76] This was likely seen as necessary for two reasons. First, there is the argument mentioned above that a constitutional amendment would require consent from the provinces. Second, the legislation had to allow for the governor general to dissolve Parliament and call an election whenever the Government lost the confidence of the House.

Despite this legislation, the prime minister called an election on 4 September 2008. This was challenged in the courts as illegal in view of the fixed-date legislation but the court dismissed the action, saying it could not rule on the calling of elections by the governor general.[77] A court cannot make an order affecting the prerogative powers of the governor general. How, then, was the legislation to be enforced? All legislation is expected to be enforceable.

The only possible enforceable meaning that can be given to the fixed-date election legislation is that it curtailed the prime minister's advisory role: he must advise the governor general to call an election, as the Act stipulates, for no later than the third Monday in October in the fourth year following the previous election. Might not the same sort of legislation be enacted with regard to the prime minister's advisory role in prorogation?

Perhaps the prime minister's advisory role in respect of prorogation could be shared, if not curtailed, by using legislation to amend the Parliament of Canada Act to include a provision mandating that the prime minister make a debateable motion for a prorogation in the House. As with all House motions, the motion would not be legally binding on the prime minister: the prime minister could seek prorogation from the governor general once the motion on prorogation was voted on in the House, regardless of the result. With a majority Government, the prime minister would likely get his way in the House but at least there would have been a debate in which the prime minister would have had to publicly defend seeking a prorogation. This procedure could be established through ordinary legislation, or more easily by changing the Standing Orders, and would not need a

constitutional amendment. The governor general's power to prorogue would be left unaffected, as in the so-called fixed date elections
legislation. This arrangement would, in my view, be as constitutionally valid as the fixed-date election legislation but, alas, no more
enforceable by the courts.[78]

Exercising Prerogative Powers

Constitutional experts differ on whether the governor general's prerogative powers may – or in some circumstances should – be exercised
without or against the advice of the prime minister.[79] A good example is the power to appoint a prime minister when the office is suddenly vacated and the preceding prime minister has not recommended a successor or if the prime minister is suddenly incapacitated.[80] In
these circumstances, the governor general must act without receiving
advice from the prime minister and, in keeping with the principle of
responsible government, appoint someone who will have the confidence of the House.

Here's another example where the governor general's prerogative
powers may need to be exercised without any advice from the prime
minister: the constitution requires the House to meet at least once
every twelve months. Suppose a prime minister, nearly twelve months
after a session ended through prorogation, refuses to recommend that
the governor general call a new session of Parliament or suppose a sitting of the House has been adjourned on a motion supported by the
Government's majority and it's been close to twelve months since the
House last met. Should the governor general act without receiving
advice from the prime minister? Must the governor general stand quietly back while the prime minister disregards the requirements of the
Constitution? What if a prime minister were to refuse to recommend
the appointment of senators and this left some provinces without representation in the Senate; or vacancies accumulated to a level where
the Senate could not form a quorum and so could not meet? Should
the governor general, without any advice from the prime minister,
appoint senators to fill the vacancies?

If a prime minister recommends that the governor general dissolve
Parliament and call an election within a few months of the previous

election, must the governor general follow this advice? Yes, according to the usual interpretation of the constitutional convention. However, there are some who believe the governor general could refuse to follow the prime minister's advice so soon after the previous election as another election would likely not bring a different result and would be an unwarranted expense on the public purse.

The Government and the House

The Government – in the persons of the prime minister and the ministers – sits in the House.[81] Government business is the primary concern of the House, as it was in the past when parliaments sat only when the Crown summoned them, usually because the king or queen needed money. For some observers, the presence of the Government in the House compromises the House's independence. The parliamentary system of government, however, does not have a complete separation of the legislative and executive branches of government (unlike the American congressional system of government). The Government, not parliament, governs but the houses of parliament, particularly the House of Commons, have the constitutional function of holding the Government to account. Some see Parliament as balancing the legislative and executive functions within an "executive legislature" that debates and passes legislation desired by the Government but at the same time acts as a political check on the Government.[82] Accountability is the "price" that the Government pays to maintain the confidence of the House.

Some consider this fusion of the executive and the legislative in the House of Commons to be the "genius" of the British parliamentary system as it allows for a Government that is strong because it can usually obtain the legislative approvals it seeks but is accountable on a daily basis. Others complain that the House, when the Government has a majority, is little more than a committee of the Government.[83]

Some observers seem to think, wrongly, that the House is a higher authority than the Government and should at times be able to tell the Government what to do. However, while the House may be the dominant legislative authority, it does not govern. The House has the power to approve proposed taxes and public spending and to make laws, which it does through its legislative powers, but these are the limits of its powers. House committees sometimes need reminding that they review Government business only in their function of holding the Government to account; that is, they should avoid acting as if they had any management authority over government departments or agencies. The House has no authority to direct the Government to take any particular action, any more than it could direct a court to deliver a particular decision. As political philosopher John Stuart Mill once said, "There is a radical distinction between controlling the business of government and actually doing it."[84] The House leaves the business of government to the Government because, in the absence of a situation that gives rise to a non-confidence vote or a Government defeat on a major item such as the budget, the Government has – or is assumed to have – the confidence of the House.

Financial Initiative of the Crown

While the House has primary authority for authorizing the spending of public funds (appropriations) and for the imposition of a new tax or an increase to an existing tax, the new tax, tax increase, or public spending must first be proposed by the Government; that is, the Government and not the House has the financial initiative.[85] This is fundamental to the constitutional relationship between the House and the Government.

Placing the financial initiative with the Government has its origins in Lord Durham's report in 1838, mentioned earlier. Durham felt that legislative assemblies invariably abused the public purse when they had the power to appropriate public funds. He urged London to ensure that the Crown maintained control of the public purse in colonial Canada. "I consider," said Lord Durham, "good government not to be attainable while the present unrestricted powers of voting public money and of managing the local expenditure of the community are lodged in the hands of the Assembly." As with his support for responsible government, Lord Durham seems again to have caught the ear of the British Government. His recommendation became section 54 of the British North America Act of 1867 (now renamed Constitution

Act 1867). The Crown's financial initiative in public spending is protected by the royal recommendation required under s. 54.

The Judicial Branch

Before late in the seventeenth century, the parliamentary system did not have what we would call an independent judicial branch. Judges were appointed and controlled by the Crown. This changed with the Bill of Rights of 1689: after it the monarch could remove a judge only following a resolution of both Houses of parliament. While the Crown continued to appoint judges, it could no longer influence or control the judges through threats of removal. In Canada, superior court judges (not provincial court judges) are appointed by the federal government: by the governor general on the recommendation of the prime minister in the case of Supreme Court judges and by the minister of justice for the other courts.[86] Judges cannot be removed except by resolution of both the House and the Senate.[87]

It is also expected that the prime minister or any minister or government official – or member of Parliament or senator – will not make public comments criticizing a judge personally. In 2014, the Prime Minister's Office issued a statement saying that the Chief Justice of Canada had acted "inappropriately" with respect to a recent nomination to the Supreme Court by the prime minister – there had been published reports alleging that the chief justice had "lobbied" against the nomination. According to the Geneva-based International Commission of Jurists, "the prime minister and minister of justice could best remedy their encroachment upon the independence and integrity of the judiciary by publicly withdrawing or apologize for their public criticism of the chief justice." No apologies were offered, however, at least not publicly.

In the House, there is an informal rule, called the sub judice ("before the court") rule, that members, out of respect for the independence of the judicial branch and to avoid appearing to be trying to influence a judicial outcome, must avoid commenting on issues that are before the courts. At the same time, judges must not allow political considerations to influence their judgments: a judge does not comment on a public issue except to the extent necessary for deciding a case. Judges must not express political opinions, ever. Public confidence in the political impartiality of judges is essential to the credibility and independence of the courts.

While the courts must wait until an issue comes before them in a legal action initiated by a private citizen or by the Government, they may be asked to give an advisory ruling on matters that have not yet come to them in a legal action.[88] For example, in 1996 the Government asked the Supreme Court whether Quebec could unilaterally leave Canada.[89] The Court had to interpret the Constitution and the system of government it supported, which meant attempting to discern the unwritten principles on which the constitution and our system of government relied. "Behind the written word," said the court, "is an historical lineage stretching back through the ages, which aids in the consideration of the underlying constitutional principles. These principles inform and sustain the constitutional text: they are vital unstated assumptions upon which the text is based."[90] In the court's opinion, a province could not unilaterally leave Canada. It based this opinion on four "foundational constitutional principles": federalism, democracy, constitutionalism, and the rule of law and respect for minority rights. This may only be an opinion but it bears great weight.

Some argue that under the Charter of Rights and Freedoms the courts enter into the political domain in many of their decisions on matters that should be left to Parliament to decide.[91] By tradition the courts stay out of political issues but the role of the courts changed with the Charter. Courts are now required to apply the Charter on matters that touch public policy questions that before the Charter would have been left to Parliament. To add fuel to these fires, the courts have relied on unwritten legal or constitutional principles that some consider political in nature. Critics of the courts have argued that they go beyond their judicial function when they invoke unwritten principles, effectively rewriting the law as if they were legislators. This "political" role, these critics argue, has led persons seeking political change to go to the courts with a claim under the Charter rather than seek change through the political process. In defence of her court, Chief Justice McLachlin has argued that "fundamental norms of justice so basic that they form part of the legal structure of governance" must be upheld whether or not they are expressed in the written constitution.[92] She acknowledged that some saw this as "a barely concealed power grab by activist judges."

A House committee would never call upon a judge to appear before a committee as a witness in relation to a decision by that judge or on a matter dealing with the internal business of a court. Judges are not accountable to Parliament or to the Government for their decisions. If a judge has made a decision that is wrong in law, the decision may be appealed to a higher court, although there is no appeal from a decision of the Supreme Court of Canada (hence the political interest in appointments to this court). On matters of personal conduct, complaints can be made to the Canadian Judicial Council, which is mandated "to promote efficiency, uniformity, and accountability, and to improve the quality of judicial service in the superior courts of Canada."[93]

Constitutional Conventions

Constitutional conventions are practices that have developed over the many years of parliamentary evolution and are now accepted as operative rules, although they are not written in law and are not enforceable in the courts. Most of the conventions are well known; I have already mentioned some of them. For example, the prime minister as head of the Government: this position was first that of the king's senior advisor or chief minister and leading representative in the Commons, who eventually became known as the prime minister. It is by convention that a committee of ministers (who on appointment become members of the Privy Council and therefore privy councillors), chaired by the prime minister, meets as the cabinet and advises on Government matters. It is expected, by convention, that most if not all ministers will be members of the House, although this is not constitutionally required. It is convention that the Government must resign if it loses the confidence of the House. As discussed earlier, it is convention that the governor general shall not exercise a prerogative power except on the advice of the prime minister. There are, as discussed earlier, conventions that govern naming a prime minister after an election. There is also the unwritten rule that the queen shall not appoint a governor general for Canada except on the recommendation of the prime minister.[94]

In 1981, the Supreme Court of Canada was asked whether there was a constitutional convention that required the Government to have the consent of the provinces before it went to London to request that the British Parliament "patriate" the Canadian Constitution – which at the time was a British statute, the British North America Act, 1867. It was argued that this convention was so well established that it had become a rule of law and enforceable by the courts. The court disagreed: "The very nature of a convention, as political in inception and depending on a consistent course of political recognition ... is inconsistent with its legal enforcement [by the court]."[95] Conventions, said the court, "ensure that the legal framework of the constitution will be operated in accordance with the prevailing constitutional values or principles of the period."[96] The court recognized, as part of Canada's parliamentary system of government, the convention that required a "substantial degree" or "substantive measure" of provincial consent to constitutional amendments affecting the provinces.[97] (The court was not suggesting the use of a referendum to determine a province's consent.) In this case, as in the others mentioned earlier, the court was being asked for an advisory ruling (a non-binding opinion). Needless to say, the Government considered itself *politically* bound by the ruling of the court.

In 1998, the Supreme Court affirmed that the Constitution was more than the written text, that it embraced "the entire global system of rules and principles which govern the exercise of constitutional authority."[98] The court reiterated the distinction it had made in 1981 between "the law of the constitution, which generally speaking will be enforced by the courts, and other constitutional rules, such as the conventions of the constitution, which carry only political sanctions."[99] While failure to respect a convention may not *legally* invalidate an action by the Government, it might cause the action to lack constitutional legitimacy but this would be a *political*, not a *legal*, question.

Schmidt v Attorney General of Canada

In 2016, a judge of the Federal Court of Canada looked at the Canadian parliamentary system of government and its three branches.[100] A

Department of Justice lawyer had charged that the minister of justice was not properly examining government bills before they were introduced into the House, as she was legally obliged to do under the Canadian Bill of Rights[101] and the Department of Justice Act. Under these acts, the minister must advise the House if a government bill is inconsistent with the Bill of Rights and the Charter, respectively.[102] The court decided that the minister was appropriately examining government bills. Then the court's judgment gets interesting for our purposes.

The judge felt he ought to "place this examination process [by the minister] into proper perspective by describing the exact role each branch of our constitution has to play and how each of them have to assume their respective responsibilities." The judge examined the larger constitutional context, both in Canada and elsewhere. "The examination provisions [in the two statutes] must be assessed [in] light of what they represent within the founding principles of constitutional monarchy and of democracy. The roles and duties of each branch cannot be treated as separate statutory schemes operating disjointedly from each other. Our constitution provides for the creation of three institutions that are, in essence, the expression of our Canadian democracy at play."[103] The judge needed to look at the roles of the three branches in order "to give a certain colouring, a certain perspective, to the role of the Minister of Justice." He found that all three branches had a "vital role to assume in identifying potential inconsistencies in draft legislation" as it was the "collectivity of our three constitutional institutions that are the ultimate protectors of our guaranteed rights."[104] In other words no branch operates in complete isolation – as I said earlier, the key word in "parliamentary system of government" is "system."

The court noted that Parliament, that is, the legislative branch, must do its job with legislation. "And herein lies a key aspect of this case," said the judge, "to each its own responsibilities. Parliament is expected to assume its obligations to examine bills and debate issues that may affect guaranteed rights. Parliament must not place its duties on the shoulders of the other branches, notably on those of the Minister of Justice."[105] The Minister of Justice is not Atlas, said the judge, "carrying the world of guaranteed rights on her shoulders. It is true that the Minister of Justice reports an inconsistency to parliament, but this duty does not make her a legal advisor to the House of Commons; others assume this role. Her loyalties remain to the Executive. Parliament has many other means by which it can acquire more than sufficient legal advice; it simply must make the effort to do so."[106] The judge concluded: "Guaranteed consistency with rights is not the sole purview of the Executive and of the Minister of Justice, it is an ideal to be strived for collectively and attained through the concerted efforts of the three branches of government working towards a common goal. Such is the way to ensure our laws are compliant with our guaranteed rights."[107]

Perhaps, at least in part, the minister of justice had the court's comments in *Schmidt* in mind when a few months later, on 13 June 2016, she took the unprecedented step of circulating to members an addendum to its legislative background paper on Bill C-14, An Act to amend the Criminal Code and to make related amendments to other Acts (medical assistance in dying), setting out the Government's analysis on the constitutionality of the bill.[108] The addendum discussed whether Bill C-14 complied with the ruling of the Supreme Court of Canada in *Carter v Canada*, where the court had ruled that the total prohibition of medically assisted suicide was unconstitutional. The court had suspended its ruling for a year to give Parliament time to come up with Charter-compliant legislation.[109] There were strong views on both sides of this question.

The details of Bill C-14 and the legal arguments made in the addendum in defence of the bill are not important here.[110] Rather, it is the unprecedented action of the Government in giving the opposition parties in the House (and the public) its assessment of the Charter compliance of one of its bills. The Government never shares its legal analysis of bills with the opposition (or the public) and, in my view, for good reason. The legislative process is about public policy and not legal issues. What was behind the minister's initiative? Was the new Government trying to live up to its campaign promise of more transparency?[111] If so, the gesture is less than convincing when one considers that the addendum was not distributed until after Bill C-14 had been debated and voted on in the House. It is also worth noting that in debate in the House the minister did not offer the analysis that she later provided in the addendum.[112]

The addendum discussed the relationship between Parliament and the courts, quoting a 1999 Supreme Court ruling where the court said that a judicial finding that an act was unconstitutional does not mean that Parliament must abide by the court's determination in every respect when producing new legislation. "To insist on slavish conformity," said the court in 1999, "would belie the mutual respect that underpins the relationship between the courts and legislature that is so essential to our constitutional democracy."[113] The addendum noted that the Supreme Court had described the relationship between Parliament and the courts as one of "dialogue," where Parliament had an important role in representing the interests of vulnerable groups, and that the courts did not hold a monopoly on the protection and promotion of rights and freedoms. The addendum also noted the Supreme Court's comment that "If constitutional democracy is meant to ensure that due regard is given to the voices of those vulnerable to being overlooked by the majority, then this court has an obligation to consider respectfully parliament's attempt to respond to such voices."[114] The constitutionality of legislation is a matter on which both Parliament and the courts may have views and both views need to be considered in any judicial determination; constitutionality is a shared responsibility. The difficult question is what the court meant by "consider respectfully."

Officers of Parliament

The working relationship between the House and the Government is supported by the work of officials known as officers of parliament (or sometimes referred to as agents of parliament). These officers support the House in holding the Government to account, ensuring that certain governmental functions are carried out properly and providing oversight beyond what is possible for the House itself. One parliamentary observer has described the officers of Parliament as "the integrity branch of government."[115]

The eight officers are the auditor general of Canada, the commissioner of official languages, the commissioner for access to information, the privacy commissioner, the conflicts of interest and ethics commissioner, the lobbying commissioner, the chief electoral officer, and the public service integrity commissioner.[116] The Government appoints the officers after consultations with the House and the Senate and in some cases the appointment is subject to their approval. As an exception, given the nature of the field, appointment of the chief electoral officer is made by the House alone.

Officers of Parliament have no constitutional status. They are creatures of statute and are governed by the terms of their respective statutes. They report to Parliament, not to the Government. Officers have an investigative function and, in some cases, legal powers to support their functions, such as the right to subpoena officials or to enter the premises of a department to access files. However, they do not have the power to make enforceable orders but can only make recommendations. Compliance with their recommendations depends on the good will of the Government, sometimes after pressure from the House committee to which the officer's report is referred.

The most prominent officer of Parliament is the auditor general of Canada (AG). The first independent auditor was appointed in 1878, with a mandate limited to examining the Government's financial transactions, much like most auditors. In 1977, the AG's job was expanded to include "performance audits" to determine whether the Government had obtained "value for money." Officers' reports are submitted to the House and are referred to the appropriate House committee: the auditor general's reports are usually referred to the Public Accounts Committee. This is particularly important with the AG's reports on Government spending programs – for instance, in November 2003, the AG's report on the Government's so-called sponsorship program led to committee hearings that arguably resulted in the Government losing its House majority in the 2004 election and losing office in the 2006 election.[117]

Federal officials sometimes feel caught between their professional duty to be loyal to the Government and the need to be responsive to inquiries by an officer of parliament, particularly when the House, to whom the officer reports, is looming in the background. One government study described relations between federal officials and officers of Parliament as resembling "the soft purr of a cat," provided their exchanges do not go beyond, "some well-rehearsed exchanges ... receipt and delivery of a complaint, a discreet inquiry, an apology from the department, a promise to correct the situation, announcement of a special study or audit, interview, informal consultations, information or awareness sessions ... Even an appearance before a parliamentary committee may only entail the loss of a few hours of sleep for officials responsible for preparing briefing books for their minister or deputy minister." However, if the issue becomes public and controversial and puts the minister on the defensive, "the relationship turns sour and the friendliness into accusations, recriminations, evasiveness and hostile words."[118]

The centrality of the reporting relationship officers of parliament have with Parliament, particularly the House, was made clear by the Supreme Court of Canada in a 1989 ruling where the auditor general had asked the court to compel the Government to provide information required for an audit. The court told the auditor general that he had to take his problem to the House and seek help there.[119] According to Chief Justice Dickson, "Where Parliament has indicated in the *Auditor General Act* that it wishes its own servant to report to it on denials of access to information needed to carry out his functions on parliament's behalf, it would not be appropriate for this court to consider granting remedies for such denials, if they, in fact, exist."

While officers of Parliament are meant to operate independent of the Government, they depend on it for their operating funds. Some observers feel that, given their financial dependence on the Government and their need to appear neutral between the Government and the House, most officers act more as managers than champions of their respective fields. They are caught between their policing role and their promotional or advocacy role, between coming down hard on a department or agency and losing the ability to promote or encourage change in departmental practices, that is, between playing friend or foe.

The duties of the ethics commissioner are directly involved with members as that office is responsible for administering the Conflict of Interest Code for Members of the House of Commons as well as the Conflict of Interest and Post-Employment Code for Public Office Holders. The Conflict of Interest Code for Members, in keeping with the independence of the House from the Government, is an appendix to the Standing Orders of the House and is enforceable only by the

House, based on reports from the ethics commissioner. The code for public office holders relating to ministers and government officials is found in the Conflict of Interest Act.[120] The ethics commissioner reports to the Speaker about matters concerning members and to the prime minister about ministers and government officials.

SUMMARY

So there you have it: a parliamentary system of government that evolved over many centuries to become what it is today – a system of government with three distinct branches that work both separately and jointly. The most powerful player may be the prime minister, particularly with a majority in the House, but the prime minister is not all-powerful. In the House, the opposition parties can publicly challenge the Government on each sitting day. The courts hold the Government to the requirements of the Constitution but stay away from questioning proceedings of the House.

Before we look at how the House carried out its constitutional functions when I was there, we look at the legal framework within which the House functions – the law of parliamentary privilege that supports the House in carrying out its constitutional functions.

3

Privilege

You might think you are privileged to be sitting in the House of Commons. And you are, perhaps even more than you realize, as you now have legal constitutional privileges. Most of us don't think of ourselves as "privileged" – as enjoying rights or benefits that others don't or as blessed with some favour or advantage, some special status. We don't like others seeing us this way as it might cause resentment. When a privilege or special status is claimed, the usual response, though not always voiced, is to question the claim: either we don't understand the reason for the privilege claimed or we understand but don't like it.

Yet the law allows for privileges or special status. Some of us are privileged by the law. For example, persons under seventeen are not subject to the criminal law in the same way as those over seventeen. Posted speed limits must be respected, except by persons driving emergency vehicles, particularly the police. We can be sued or arrested for breaking the law, but foreign diplomats are exempt from such sanctions. Lawyers are exempt from jury duty (you certainly wouldn't want a lawyer sitting on a jury!). Under solicitor-client privilege, a lawyer can never be required to disclose information received from the client, a privilege that ensures that the client can speak freely and receive legal advice that responds fully to his or her situation. The legal privileges and exemptions you enjoy as a member of Parliament are collectively referred to as parliamentary privilege.

In my years as the House's lawyer, I was frequently asked to explain – and many times needed to defend – parliamentary privilege to members or House committees who were surprised by it or objected to what a committee of the House was doing. Lawyers who believed that the actions of a committee violated rights guaranteed under the Charter, particularly due process, found it hard to accept that parliamentary privilege exempted the House and its committees from the strictures of the Charter. "What happened to the rule of law?" they would ask. "Nothing," I replied, "parliamentary privilege is part of the law. What you want is the rule of laws (such as the Charter and the Privacy Act)." I couldn't fault them, however. In my early days at the House, after more than twelve years as a practising lawyer, I was surprised by the extent of parliamentary privilege and how it seemed to allow the House to act unlawfully.

The *locus classicus* on parliamentary privilege is found in an 1844 British parliamentary text, Erskine May's *Treatise on the Law, Privileges, Proceedings and Usage of Parliament*: "Parliamentary privilege is the sum of the peculiar rights enjoyed by each House collectively ... and by members of each House individually, without which they could not discharge their functions, and which exceed those possessed by other bodies or individuals. Thus, privilege, though part of the law of the land, is to a certain extent an exemption from the general law."[1] Parliamentary privilege applies to the House as a whole and to individual members of Parliament. However, as the Erskine May text indicates, the privileges of individual members are derived from those of the House: that is, members have privileges in support of their parliamentary functions as members and not for other purposes.

The British statute that created Canada in 1867, the British North America Act (now the Constitution Act, 1867), provided that the Parliament of Canada could give itself such "privileges, immunities and powers" as it needed as long as these weren't greater than those enjoyed by the British Parliament.[2] Soon after Confederation, Parliament did just that: it gave itself the privileges, immunities, and powers of the British Parliament (without specifying those privileges, immunities, and powers) and declared that these were part of the general and public law of Canada and that the courts must take judicial notice of parliamentary privilege.[3] In 1704 the British House of Lords and the House of Commons agreed that neither house can "create to themselves new privileges, not warranted by the known laws and customs of parliament."[4] In 1867 the British Parliament must have been satisfied that the powers, immunities, and privileges that it had acquired by that time were sufficient as it stipulated in the 1867 Act that the new Canadian Parliament might not create new privileges for itself.[5]

Parliamentary privilege, that is, the legal powers, privileges, and immunities vested in Parliament, enables Parliament, in particular the House of Commons and the Senate, to carry out its constitutional functions effectively and without interference, at least interference of a legal nature. Similarly, the Government can use the Crown's residual prerogative powers and privileges in support of its executive functions without legal interference. The protection provided by parliamentary privilege is essential to the constitutional independence of the House. Without this protection, the business of Parliament could be constrained or needlessly delayed, if not defeated, by legal proceedings brought against it. Parliamentary privilege enables members to carry out their parliamentary functions freely as democratically elected representatives of the people.

What are these powers, immunities, and privileges and why are they not listed in the 1867 Act? The drafters of the 1867 Act may have felt that they were sufficiently well known as parts of the unwritten conventions and traditions of the parliamentary system that they did not need to be specified. After all, the 1867 Act was legislated in England, a country that has never felt the need for a written constitution. At a more practical level, if new privileges were created in the future, the 1867 Act would need to be amended. To see what these powers, immunities, and privileges are, we must look to parliamentary tradition. To determine what legal status parliamentary privilege has, we need to look at court cases where parliamentary privilege was an issue. The courts may not be able to interfere with the use of parliamentary privilege but they can determine whether the privilege claimed is recognized in law.

THE PRIVILEGES

The generally accepted privileges of the House are:

- No judicial or other legal review of its proceedings (Article 9, Bill of Rights of 1689), which gives it immunity from defamation and

other laws with respect to what is said in the course of a House or
committee proceeding or in authorized publications of debates or
other parliamentary papers.

- No interference with members' attendance at proceedings in the
  House or in committee.
- Ability to discipline members and "strangers."
- Regulation of its internal affairs.
- Power to punish members or others for breaches of House privi-
  leges or for contempt.
- Power to conduct inquiries and to summon witnesses and obtain
  documents.

FREEDOM OF SPEECH

Freedom of speech in the House, based on Article 9 of the UK Bill of
Rights of 1689, is perhaps the only well-known parliamentary privilege and it is absolute (though subject to House rules). A member cannot be taken to court for what is said in debates in the House or in a
committee. Speaking out publicly is everything to a member. "Speaking is what we do here," a member once said in the House, "In a
democracy, we do not solve our debates or disagreements through
the tip of a sword or through violence. We solve them through words:
words of praise, words of caution, words of criticism … We settle
debates in a democracy through words, and the ability of members to
express those words on this floor is the heart of the matter."[6]

Members are generally mindful of the benefits and hazards of this
freedom and seek to act responsibly in its exercise. The underlying
principle is that the public interest is best served if parliamentarians
are able to speak freely in debates. To claim this privilege, the speech
must occur in the course of a proceeding in parliament: statements
made when the member does not have the floor and that do not
relate to the matter under debate may not be protected. For example,
in 1976 a Quebec court held that the privilege of free speech did not
extend to words spoken to a journalist outside the chamber as the
privilege enjoyed by members of Parliament is intended to protect the
functions of Parliament, not statements by members in a press conference. "Absolute privilege," said the court, "is a drastic denial of the

right of every citizen who believes himself wronged to have access to the courts for redress and should not be lightly or easily extended. It is not the precinct of Parliament that is sacred but the function and that function has never required that press conferences given by members should be regarded as absolutely protected from legal liability."[7] Members need to be careful that they do not repeat what they said a few minutes earlier in the House or in committee as someone offended by their remarks could bring a legal action for defamation and parliamentary privilege would not be a defence.

The privilege of free speech may be absolute in relation to outside interference but there are limits to free speech within the House or a committee. First, there is the sub judice rule that members should not comment on matters that are before the courts, a rule designed to ensure respect for the role of the courts. It is expected that members will not use "unparliamentary" language, though unacceptable language is not defined anywhere. Language that is personally insulting to another member is considered unparliamentary. To describe a member as stupid, illegitimate, a hypocrite, or dishonest would be unparliamentary and the member would be asked to withdraw the remark. However, a member may use the same language to describe an action taken by a member or minister as long as the words are not applied to the member or minister personally: a minister's action may be stupid but the minister should not be described as stupid. A member may not accuse another member or a minister of telling a lie or "deliberately misleading" the House; "misleading" is all right but not "deliberately" misleading. It may seem artificial, if not also misleading at times, but a member is usually referred to as an "honourable member."

Occasionally a member may rise before an objection is made from the floor and apologize for the language used and revise or withdraw what was said, usually because the member has learned that another member will object unless there is an immediate apology. For example, on 6 June 2012, a Newfoundland member, speaking critically about the budget, said that the prime minister "doesn't know his arse from a hole in the ground." Before any objection was made, the member rose to explain that in his province language can be quite colourful though not appropriate in some places (such as the House) and apologized.

While infractions of rules about parliamentary language and sub judice comments may be enforceable, the Speaker has no rules to enforce general behaviour – the Speaker can deal with disorder involving one or a few members but not if it involves large numbers of members acting out. The notion that the flip side of free speech is civility can at times seem a foreign notion in the House or a committee. Debates driven by partisan political rivalry can become quite heated.

DISCIPLINING MEMBERS AND OTHERS

The House can discipline its members for breaches of its practices and privileges as well as anyone ("strangers") who interferes "with the conduct of parliamentary business [which it considers a breach of privilege or contempt]."[8] In 1991 and again in 2002, a member was called before the bar of the House (located at the south end of the chamber) to apologize for unacceptable behaviour in the course of a House proceeding.[9] Another disciplinary action might be "naming" a member (as mentioned in chapter 1). The House may permanently expel a member for conduct that, in the opinion of the House, renders the member unfit to sit in the House, in which case the member's seat becomes vacant.[10] Members can also be disciplined under the Conflict of Interest Code for Members, although this has not happened yet.

An unexpected situation that could have led to disciplinary action by the House arose in late 2014 when two members complained to their party leader about being sexually harassed by members from another party. The complaints were reported in the media, making them a matter of public interest, which meant they needed proper handling. The offending members were expelled from their party caucus, although there had been no independent assessment of the allegations. (A caucus is free to expel a member whenever it chooses and for whatever reason.) Given the seriousness of the accusations (and the public interest), many members felt the House could not leave the matter there, although, in my view, they could have and should have. The House was publicly embarrassed by the fact that it had no established policy or practice with respect to sexual harassment between members.[11] There was no available framework for determining whether the allegations were true or what kind of disciplinary action might be taken. The Standing Committee on Procedure and House Affairs (PROC) was instructed to develop a policy and process for handling sexual harassment complaints between members and in June 2015 the committee recommended and the House adopted a code of conduct pertaining to sexual harassment.[12] Under the code, members are required to pledge, in writing, that the member will "contribute to a work environment free of sexual harassment." It's not indicated whether members will take this pledge in some formal manner or whether all members are presumed to have taken the pledge. In my view, this initiative reflects the way in which House actions can sometimes be driven more by optics than substance.

The code that was developed applies only to "non-criminal" sexual harassment (whatever this means)[13] and defines sexual harassment as "unwanted conduct of a sexual nature that detrimentally affects the work environment" (leaving unanswered how the "demonstrable detrimental effect" is to be proved and how such an effect would be measured). Members making or facing allegations of sexual harassment must agree to respect confidentiality "throughout the process" and to respect the privacy of all participants. The code allows for resolution of complaints by the party whips if the complaining member consents, which means that they would be resolved privately, behind closed doors (the usual way of dealing with members' personal issues). Otherwise the complaint will be considered in an internal mediation process. If the mediation process does not lead to a result acceptable to both sides, either can take the allegations to the PROC committee, where it will be reviewed behind closed doors with a report tabled in the house recommending whether and, if so, what disciplinary action should be taken.

Whether or not the PROC committee upholds the complaint, the complaining member shall not be identified in the committee's report to the House. The committee report will provide "a summary of the investigation report that will be anonymized [sic] and will respect the privacy of the complainant and other individuals who provided evidence." Only the accused member will be identified. I suppose the thinking was that if the accused member is guilty, the member deserves to be publicly shamed. If innocent, the member deserves to have his name cleared (his identity will likely have become known).

How informative will such committee reports be when they provide only a summary? How likely is it that these committee reports will remain confidential?

After a PROC committee report upholding a complaint is tabled in the House (and thereby becomes public) and before the House votes to accept or not accept the report, the offending member named in the report has ten days in which to make a statement in the House. There seem to be no limitations of confidentiality or privacy placed on the offending member's statement. Presumably, the offending member will either seek exoneration or make an abject apology. Following this statement, any member may move a motion for the House to concur in the committee's report and this motion, like any concurrence motion, would be subject to debate, during which, says the code, members "should respect the confidentiality of the resolution process and the privacy of the members involved." Frankly, this all seems artificial, like something out of *Alice in Wonderland*. It presents a good example of how difficult, if not also inappropriate, it is for the House as a public political institution to try to formalize its disciplinary proceedings with respect to behaviour that is not political in nature.

The House's sexual harassment policy fails in both its process and its likely outcome. How can there be a meaningful and fair public debate in the House about whether to discipline a member when only a summary of the facts is made known? The outcome will be predictable unless the offending member can present facts that were not considered by the committee, which is unlikely, though the member would probably attempt to refute (again) the allegations, and then what does the House do with the member's counter-allegations, now made in public? And if, at the end, the complaining member remains unsatisfied with the disciplinary action taken, or lack thereof, the complaining member could rise in the House and go public about what happened despite the stipulation of confidentiality. Remember, free speech in the House means no legal action can be taken against a member for statements made in the House.

In all likelihood, members of all parties have quietly accepted the code because they are confident it will never be applied. It's not that sexual harassment won't happen but that invocation of the PROC committee trial process and the subsequent House proceeding borders on the absurd in a partisan political workplace where there are so many other ways to deal with sexual harassment and to do so effectively. As it always has been, should have been in this case, and will be in the future: the whips will quietly resolve such matters. In this case, the complaining members conveyed their allegations to the leader of the offending members' party and they became public. The leader had to do something to protect the party's "brand" and the House had to do something to protect its reputation as a public institution. It's all about public perception. They say everything is fair in love and war. The same can be said of politics, where the political interests of a member's party will always be given priority over the interests of the member. In this case, there was no formal finding that convicted or acquitted the offending members but their political careers were destroyed when they were expelled from caucus. This may be acceptable to some, given the nature of the allegations, but it lacks fairness. (I want to use the legal term "due process" but such a legal notion cannot be applied to proceedings in the House.)

CONTEMPT OF PARLIAMENT

Contempt of Parliament can be disobeying an order of the House, an offence against the privileges of the House or, more broadly, an offence against the dignity of the House. Contempt can be any action that the House considers offensive to its dignity as "the highest court in the land." Essentially, contempt is whatever the House says it is. A committee cannot cite for contempt but only recommend a contempt citation to the House. Erskine May described the contempt power as "the keystone of parliamentary privilege."[14] The House must have this power if it is to defend its proceedings against abuse or defend itself against otherwise offensive behaviour. In 1817, Lord Erskine, sitting on an appeal relating to the contempt powers of the British House, said that the House of Commons "whether a court or not, must like every other tribunal, have the power to protect itself from obstruction and insult, and to maintain its dignity and character."[15] In my years at the House, there were six contempt citations by the House. Two were against members (mentioned below), one against an officer of Parliament (the privacy commissioner), two against private corporations (meat packers), and one against a committee witness (RCMP deputy commissioner). The privacy commissioner was found to have been untruthful in his dealings with a House Committee.[16] The meat packers had refused to provide information to a House Committee (discussed below). The RCMP deputy commissioner was found to have deliberately misled the Public Accounts Committee.[17] There was also a contempt citation against the Government, brought by a committee of the House, based on the prime minister and cabinet having failed to provide documents to the Finance Committee.[18]

Before taking any action for contempt, the House calls upon those involved to explain their actions or to apologize, in the hope that this will "purge" the contempt. If this does not happen, the House could direct the Speaker to issue a warrant directing the sergeant at arms to take an individual into custody and to bring him or her before the bar of the House.[19] In Erskine May's view, if a Speaker's warrant states that the person arrested is guilty of a breach of privilege (or contempt), "the courts of law cannot inquire into the grounds of the judgment; but must leave him to suffer the punishment awarded by the High Court of Parliament by which he stands condemned."[20]

If the offender is defiant and refuses to explain or apologize, the House has the choice of either public chastisement or directing the sergeant at arms to hold the person in custody awaiting a further order of the House. This was last done in 1913 when Mr R.C. Miller refused to answer questions from a House committee about alleged payments made to the prime minister and cabinet in order to obtain contracts.[21] Today, imprisonment for contempt seems unlikely, which means that in some cases the House may be unable to credibly enforce a contempt citation, unless it applies a lesser penalty, such as a fine.

The House will publicly and formally discipline a member for contempt of Parliament if the offence is held to be a public insult to the honour and dignity of the House. This has happened twice, once in 1991 and again in 2002. In both cases the offence took place in the House during House proceedings. In each case, the member interfered with the mace, the symbol of the House's authority. In 1991, the member was called before the bar and reprimanded by the Speaker. In 2002, the member was suspended until he appeared before the bar and apologized, which he did (there was no reprimand by the Speaker).[22] In both cases the discipline was imposed by order of the House: the Speaker did not act on his own initiative but only after the House had deliberated and voted on the disciplinary action to be taken. In the 1991 case, before reprimanding the member, the Speaker had a few words for members generally: "The special privileges that members of the House of Commons enjoy are part of the constitutional law of Canada. Freedom of speech is one of the most revered of those privileges. However, with that privilege comes the responsibility to use it wisely and for the good of Canada. It is not a licence to say whatever one wishes under all the circumstances, or permission to disregard the rules of the House or the common practices of civility."[23] The Speaker reminded members that it was "essential that you always respect this institution and its rules and practices." With respect to the action by the member, the Speaker noted that the member had disregarded "the rules and practices of this place and the authority of the Speaker," which was a matter of "grave concern to this House and to all who cherish and respect this institution" and reprimanded him for this.

The House has never imposed a fine. In fact, the last time a fine was imposed by a parliament was in 1666 by the British House, which leads many to conclude that this power has lapsed. The legal authority usually cited is a 1762 court case where one of the judges made a passing comment that he thought the House did not have the power to impose fines.[24] But this was not a court ruling but merely an expression of opinion by a sitting judge. In my view, the House should have the power to impose fines, if it doesn't already have it. The fact that the House of Commons in Britain has not imposed a fine for a very long time or that the House here has never done so ought not to mean that the power to fine for contempt is no longer available. In 2004, a House committee recommended to the House that a fine be imposed against witnesses who were refusing to provide information to the committee. The Standing Committee on Agriculture and Agri-food was holding hearings into recent reports of mad cow disease in a herd of cattle in Alberta and on the pricing of beef at the slaughter, wholesale, and retail levels.[25] Beef farmers were being paid less by the meatpackers, yet the retail prices on beef had remained the same. The committee asked the five major meatpacking companies to produce financial statements and pricing documents. One complied with the request while a second said it feared that the information would get into the hands of its competitors but suggested the committee appoint an independent auditor who would review the information but keep specifics confidential. Another thought its information wouldn't be helpful to the committee. A fourth said it did not provide such information to "government bodies" and that its records were not organized into the segments that the committee sought; besides, such information was confidential. The fifth explained that it was a private company and a wholly owned subsidiary of an American corporation and that the financial information that the committee sought was "not available in a public forum." It was also concerned about disclosure of its financial information to its competitors and wanted to know how the committee would keep the information confidential.

The Agriculture Committee instructed its analysts to review the meatpackers' information and in their report "to protect the specific sensitive business information." The meatpackers were advised of this arrangement but none supplied the information requested by the committee. One of the meatpackers argued that, as the committee had no statutory obligation to provide confidentiality, it could not give the meatpackers "adequate protection." The committee tabled a report in the House recommending that two of the meatpackers be held in contempt if they did not provide the information requested by the committee by a certain date. The House concurred in this recommendation, immediately making the committee's recommendation an Order of the House.[26]

When the meatpackers were notified of the order of the House, three responded by providing information but two did not. The committee recommended to the House that the two meatpackers not complying with the House's direction be given until 20 May to comply, failing which each would pay a fine of $250,000 for each day thereafter until they complied.[27] However, before the House looked at the committee's recommendation, Parliament was dissolved for an election. In the next Parliament the committee reported to the House that by 3 December 2004 the meatpackers had provided the information sought by the committee. There was no mention of collecting the fine of $250,000 per day for the period from 20 May to 3 December.

It seems to me the mad cow case provides a good example of how compliance could only have been effected through a fine. How else is the House to ensure co-operation to fulfill its functions or to defend itself against contempt? If the House has the power to imprison for contempt, which is generally accepted (though it seems out-dated and if ever used may be challenged under the Charter), surely it also has the lesser power of imposing a fine, especially with respect to corporations.

PARLIAMENTARY PRIVILEGE IN THE COURTS

Article 9 of the Bill of Rights (1689), as mentioned earlier, is the basis for the free speech privilege of members in House or committee proceedings. However, Article 9 is not about free speech directly but about the jurisdiction of the courts with respect to House proceedings: the courts cannot exercise their powers of judicial review with respect to House proceedings. The courts cannot review or in any way question House or committee proceedings regardless of how irregular or unfair those proceedings may seem. The constitutional validity of House proceedings is beyond legal challenge. If the House accepts or approves a proceeding in the House or a committee, however irregular it might be under House rules, this is sufficient to establish the constitutional validity of the proceeding.

Some might question the constitutional validity of a House proceeding that took place when, contrary to section 48 of the Constitution Act, 1867, fewer than twenty members were present. In my view, the proceeding would not automatically be unconstitutional or invalid insofar as a court could not be asked to say it was. Section 48 would seem to have been included in the 1867 Act without taking Article 9 – which prevents any court from questioning House proceedings – into account.

From my position as law clerk and parliamentary counsel, I felt that the House should be ready and willing to defend its privileges in court cases where parliamentary privilege was an issue. When I came to the House in the early 1990s, the leading judicial authorities for parliamentary privilege were, with one notable exception, nineteenth-century British decisions. I felt that the House should seek Canadian judicial affirmation of its privileges whenever possible. Senior management at the House were fearful of testing such ideas in the courts, afraid of what the House might lose. Nonetheless, I looked for opportunities and we had several wins.

The Supreme Court of Canada has considered parliamentary privilege on three occasions. In 1878, the court affirmed that the courts have jurisdiction to determine whether a claimed privilege exists in law.[28] In 1993, two years after I joined the House, it affirmed that the law of parliamentary privilege was part of the constitutional law of Canada and not subordinated to the requirements of the Charter. In other words, one part of the constitution cannot be given priority over another part.[29] In 2005, after several decisions in lower courts, the Supreme Court gave parliamentary privilege – its content and its limits – comprehensive consideration. The court affirmed the principles established in 1878 and 1993 and made clear, and this is important, that statute laws may apply to the House where a matter is outside parliamentary privilege.[30] The issue was clear: legally, what was beyond and what was within the ambit of parliamentary privilege?

New Brunswick Broadcasting Co v Nova Scotia
(Speaker of the House of Assembly) (1993)

In *New Brunswick Broadcasting*, the issue was whether the Speaker of the Nova Scotia Legislative Assembly had the right to exclude television cameras from the legislative chamber. The New Brunswick Broadcasting Company, an affiliate of the Canadian Broadcasting Corporation (CBC), relied on the right of freedom of speech and freedom of the press under the Charter, arguing that to exclude television cameras was to deny to television media the ability to comment publicly on the legislative proceedings of the Assembly. The Nova Scotia Speaker took the view that the presence of television cameras would interfere with the decorum and orderly proceedings of the Legislative Assembly and denied them entry to the chamber. The Speaker lost in the Nova Scotia courts and appealed to the Supreme Court of Canada.

The House of Commons, the Senate, the other nine provincial legislative assemblies, and the two territories intervened in the Nova Scotia Legislative Assembly's appeal to the Supreme Court. The lower court decisions in Nova Scotia had put the power of a parliamentary house to control its proceedings in serious doubt. The House and the other assemblies argued that the Nova Scotia Legislative Assembly's order excluding the television cameras was based on its power to exclude persons ("strangers") from the chamber, a well-established privilege related to control of its proceedings. The broadcasting company, New Brunswick Broadcasting, argued that the Nova Scotia Legislative Assembly was governed by the Charter with respect to freedom of the press and that this freedom had been violated by the Speaker's order excluding the TV cameras from the chamber.

Madam Justice McLachlin (as she then was), writing with the support of a majority of the judges, described parliamentary privilege as a "legal exemption" from some duty, burden, attendance, or liability to which others would be subject. "It has long been accepted," she said, "that in order to perform their functions, legislative bodies require certain privileges relating to the conduct of their business. It has also long been accepted that these privileges must be held absolutely and constitutionally if they are to be effective; the legislative branch of our government must enjoy a certain autonomy which even the Crown and the courts cannot touch." Relying on the preamble to the Constitution Act, 1867 which states that the Dominion of Canada is to have a "Constitution similar in principle to that of the United Kingdom," she concluded that the privileges of the British House of Commons applied to the Nova Scotia Legislative Assembly and were constitutional in nature. Moreover, they were not subject to the Charter. The Speaker's action in excluding the TV cameras was, "an action taken pursuant to a right which enjoys constitutional status. Having constitutional status, this right is not one that can be abrogated by the *Charter*."[31] The Court may have been divided in its ruling but a win is a win: the law of parliamentary privilege was part of the constitutional law of Canada.

Vaid v House of Commons (2005)

My desire for Canadian judicial affirmation of parliamentary privilege was more than satisfied in *Vaid*. Of course, it took several years for this case to make its way up to the Supreme Court of Canada but the ruling – which was unanimous – will likely remain the leading authority on the law of parliamentary privilege in Canada for many years. The legal action arose from an internal administrative action by the House with respect to one of its employees, Mr Vaid. In the mid-1990s the House was reorganizing its administrative ranks as part of its plans to reduce its operating costs to assist Government plans to reduce the federal deficit. Many positions, including Mr Vaid's as the Speaker's chauffeur, were declared surplus and the incumbents were assigned to other duties temporarily until a vacancy arose in a position that had not been declared surplus. Mr Vaid, an Indo-Canadian, filed a complaint with the Canadian Human Rights Commission alleging that he had been the object of discrimination on the basis of race, colour, and national or ethnic origin. The Human Rights Commission notified the House of the complaint and it was forwarded to my office. I was authorized to write to the Commission denying that it had jurisdiction to hear the complaint, period, with no legal arguments included. I had in mind Article 9 of the Bill of Rights 1689: courts and tribunals cannot consider the privileged business of the House.

More specifically, the House felt that, due to parliamentary privilege, the Canadian Human Rights Act did not apply to the House and therefore the tribunal's jurisdiction did not include this complaint. The House argued that its power to hire, manage, and dismiss employees was within its privilege of exclusive control of its internal affairs. The human rights tribunal rejected the House's position. The House then sought judicial review of this ruling in the Federal Court.

The issue for the House was privileged control of its internal affairs, including management of its employees. In my view, the House had to argue parliamentary privilege and not respond to the allegations made in the complaint, as doing so could imply that the House accepted that House (and possibly members') staff could take employee grievances to the Human Rights Commission. If management of House and members' employees was made subject to external review by a tribunal or a court, there could be serious implications for the internal operations of the House: sensitive political business could be subject to review in a public legal process. It's important to remember the political nature of the business of the House.

It's hard to fight against an invocation of human rights: the House lost in the Federal Court and on its appeal to the Federal Court of

Appeal. We were seen as using parliamentary privilege to oppose human rights protection for House employees. To my mind, the extent of parliamentary privilege – not human rights – was the issue and this was important enough to seek a ruling from the Supreme Court of Canada.

In the Supreme Court the House succeeded in fending off the Human Rights Commission's tribunal – but not because the court upheld the privilege claimed. The court did not accept that the House's privileged control of its internal affairs applied to all its employees. According to Justice Binnie, speaking on behalf of the Court, the issue was whether the privilege claimed applied to "the ranks of service employees (such as catering staff) who support MPs in a general way, but play no role in the discharge of [the members'] constitutional functions."[32] Justice Binnie accepted that historically the House had the power to hire and fire employees but this was not proof that this power was immune from judicial review because it was covered by parliamentary privilege.[33] He did not say, however, whether Mr Vaid's position was one that was covered by privilege or indicate with any precision where the line should be drawn between those positions covered and those not, only that there was a line somewhere. The Court held that Mr Vaid should not have proceeded under the Canadian Human Rights Act but rather under the Parliamentary Employment and Staff Relations Act. The appeal was decided in the House's favour on a narrow legal procedural point and not on its claim of privilege but with a very helpful judicial disquisition on parliamentary privilege for future reference. I had a ruling from the highest court in Canada on parliamentary privilege. No more need to rely on old British cases.

Necessity

May's words on privilege – "without which they could not discharge their functions" – provide the underlying principle of necessity as the justification for privilege.[34] How the courts consider the element of necessity for parliamentary privilege may be problematic, however. According to Justice Binnie in *Vaid*, necessity is the "historical foundation" of every privilege of parliament. Relying on Madam Justice

McLachlin's ruling in *New Brunswick Broadcasting*, he said that when a matter fell within a sphere of matters necessary to the dignity and efficiency of the House, the courts have not inquired into questions concerning the privilege claimed. The references to dignity and efficiency were linked to autonomy, that a legislative assembly without control over its own procedure would "sink into utter contempt and inefficiency," a quote from an early nineteenth-century court case in England.

Necessity was needed to establish the existence and scope of "a *category* of privilege" being claimed and not to test the use made of a privilege. "Once the category (or sphere of activity) is established, it is for parliament, not the courts, to determine whether in a particular case the *exercise* of the privilege is necessary or appropriate. In other words, within categories of privilege, Parliament is the judge of the occasion and manner of its exercise and such exercise is not reviewable by the courts: Each specific instance of the exercise of a privilege need not be shown to be necessary" (italics and underlining in the original).[35] The role of the courts, said Justice Binnie, was "to ensure that a claim of privilege does not immunize from the ordinary law the consequences of conduct by Parliament or its officers and employees that exceed the necessary scope of the category of privilege." The necessity test was to be applied against the privilege claimed and not against the particular exercise or use made of the privilege. Once the privilege is established, based on the necessity test, a court should not question the particular use made of the privilege.

In my view, however, it may be difficult to apply the necessity test only to the scope of a privilege claimed. When a court considers scope, is it not, at least implicitly, also asking whether the action taken in the exercise of the privilege fell within the scope of the privilege? If so, isn't the court passing judgment on the use made of the privilege (under the guise of considering only scope), which it is not supposed to do? I suspect that the use made of the privilege will often lurk in the background, colouring the court's consideration of necessity, especially in *Vaid* where, in my view, the sacred principle of human rights coloured the way the case was seen by the Human Rights Commission tribunal and in the lower courts.

Twelve Propositions

The court in *Vaid* listed twelve propositions on parliamentary privilege that it felt were now accepted by the courts and parliamentary experts:[36]

(1) Legislative bodies are not "enclaves shielded from the ordinary law of the land."

(2) Parliamentary privilege is comprised of privileges, immunities, and powers without which Parliament could not discharge its functions.

(3) Parliamentary privilege does not create "a gap in the general public law of Canada but is an important part of it."

(4) Parliamentary privilege includes "the necessary immunity" that the law provides to enable members of Parliament "to do their legislative work." The idea of necessity is linked to the autonomy required by members to do their job.

(5) The historical foundation of every privilege is necessity. If a law can be applied to the House without interfering with the House's ability to carry out its constitutional functions, immunity is unnecessary and a claimed privilege would not exist.

(6) A court will also consider whether a privilege continues to be necessary. Parliamentary history, while highly relevant, is not conclusive.

(7) The time-honoured test for necessity is what "the dignity and efficiency of the House" require.

(8) The burden of proof of the existence of a privilege rests on the party asserting the privilege.

(9) Necessity applies to the existence or scope of a "category of privilege and not to the exercise or use made of a privilege."

(10) "Categories" of privilege include freedom of speech, control of House proceedings, power to exclude strangers, disciplinary authority over members and over non-members who interfere, and immunity of members from subpoenas during a session.

(11) The role of the courts is to ensure that privilege does not immunize consequences of conduct that exceeds the necessary scope of the category of privilege from the ordinary courts.

(12) Courts will look more closely where privilege has an impact on persons outside the House than where the privilege involves matters internal to the House.

On the last point, the court quoted with approval the English court case *Stockdale v Hansard* (1839), where the judge said: "All persons ought to be very tender in preserving to the House all privileges which may be necessary for their exercise, and to place the most implicit confidence in their representatives as to the due exercise of those privileges. But power, and especially the power of invading the rights of others, is a very different thing: it is to be regarded, not with tenderness, but with jealousy; and, unless the legality of it be clearly established, those who act under it must be answerable for the consequences.[37]

Vaid has provided a general rule for the application of parliamentary privilege in Canada, namely, that a claim for privilege, "must show that the sphere of activity for which privilege is claimed is *so closely and directly connected* with the fulfilment by the assembly or its members of their functions as a legislative and deliberative body, including the assembly's work in holding the government to account, that outside interference would undermine the level of autonomy required to enable the assembly and its members to do their work with dignity and efficiency" (italics added).[38] In future cases, much will depend on the meaning given to "so closely and directly connected." In the meantime, parliamentary privilege, as a matter of law, is not simply whatever the House may say it is. The courts will examine whether the privilege claimed exists in law. Once the privilege claimed is established, including its scope, the court will not (or ought not) question the particular use made of the privilege.

WITNESSES BEFORE HOUSE COMMITTEES

The parliamentary privilege of freedom of speech in parliamentary proceedings applies to statements made by witnesses who are appearing before a House committee. This protection is important to House committees if they are to receive full and frank testimony from those who appear before them as witnesses. People who appear before a House committee are sometimes concerned about the possible legal consequences of their testimony but are always assured that their testimony cannot be used in other legal proceedings. It's important that this protection is affirmed and defended when challenged. Any breach of this protection in other proceedings would forever undermine the credibility of assurances given to witnesses that their testimony was privileged. Sometimes, however, this assurance was not enough, particularly where the testimony involved possible criminal conduct and would be given at a televised meeting of the committee.

In 2004, one of the lawyers at the Gomery Commission of Inquiry into the sponsorship program wanted to cross-examine a witness with respect to testimony by the witness before a House committee.[39] The lawyer hoped to discredit the witness by showing inconsistencies between what had been said before the committee and what was later being said before the commission. I learned of the lawyer's plan through a phone call on a Sunday evening indicating that the lawyer would be using the committee testimony the next day. I felt strongly that the House had to intervene, even without my having instructions to do so, as the interests of my client (the House) would be adversely affected by the lawyer's action: assurances of protection given to future witnesses would be worthless if the lawyer was allowed to go through with his questioning. I immediately authorized sending legal counsel to the Gomery Commission to ask for time for the House to consider its position with respect to its privileges. Legal counsel advised Commissioner Gomery that the witness' testimony before the House committee was privileged and could not be used in the inquiry proceedings. Although seemingly taken aback by this intervention (judges may need to be reminded of parliamentary privilege, although they are supposed to consider it without being told), the commissioner gave us two weeks to get back to him with the House's decision on whether it wanted to assert its privileges.

Then I had to decide how would I go about getting the House to consider its position on this matter, given that its agenda was already taken up with other (pressing) matters. I decided to go first to the chair of the Public Accounts Committee (PAC), the committee the witness had testified before. Although privilege matters are handled under the mandate of the Standing Committee on Procedure and House Affairs (PROC), I figured PAC was where this process had to start as the House would want to hear from PAC before it decided whether PROC should consider the question, much as it takes a member to rise in the House and raise a point of privilege before the House refers the question to PROC.

The next day, Monday, I met with the PAC chair and was asked to appear before PAC at its next scheduled meeting, which was the next day. I appeared, explained the situation, and recommended that the committee defend the protection it gives to its witnesses. PAC debated the question and expedited a report to the House. The House considered PAC's report and referred it to PROC to handle within its mandate. PROC recommended that the House assert its privileges. Next, the House had to vote concurrence in the PROC report, which it did. We hustled back to the Gomery Commission to advise that the House wished to affirm its privilege. We had run this procedural gauntlet within the ten sitting days (two weeks) allowed by Justice Gomery.[40] It had been a hurried process fraught with uncertainty as there had been no precedent. The commissioner upheld the House's privilege of protected speech and disallowed use of the testimony,[41] averting any breach of the parliamentary protection afforded committee witnesses.[42]

I then learned through the grapevine that there had been raised eyebrows at the political level and among senior House managers that I had initiated this process without instructions. It is clearly understood that senior House officials, such as the clerk and certainly the law clerk, are mere servants of the House and do not take a pro-active role on behalf of the House. They must wait for instructions before acting. However, in the circumstances, I thought that sometimes one has to act without permission and hope for forgiveness later, provided everything turns out all right, which it had. Had it not, the repercussions for me might have been nasty. I also heard through the grapevine that the PAC chair's party leader, the leader of the official opposition at the time, did not like what PAC had done as it appeared to interfere with the Gomery Commission's work. Obviously, for his own partisan political purposes, the leader very much supported the commission's inquiry and didn't like its being constrained by the House for the sake of parliamentary privilege.

A former minister who had been involved in the sponsorship program went to the Federal Court for judicial review of the commissioner's decision respecting the House's privileges.[43] The court affirmed that the privilege pertaining to freedom of speech extended to testimony given before a House committee.[44] According to the judge, "it is important to Canadian democracy that a witness be able to speak openly before a parliamentary committee. This objective will be accomplished if the witness does not fear, while he is testifying before this committee, that his words may subsequently be used to discredit him in another proceeding, irrespective of whether or not it entails legal consequences. He is more likely to speak with confidence if he is given the assurance that he is fully protected by privilege and cannot be interrogated subsequently"[45] (underlining in original). Indeed.

A few years later, the Public Accounts Committee conducted an inquiry into matters raised in an Auditor-General's Report relating to the administration of the RCMP pension and insurance plans. Senior RCMP officials were called as witnesses. The committee came to the conclusion that a deputy commissioner who had testified before the committee had given false testimony and this led the RCMP to launch an internal disciplinary investigation to determine whether the deputy commissioner had breached the RCMP Code of Conduct. The deputy commissioner, relying on the law of parliamentary privilege, applied to the Federal Court for an order to stop the RCMP investigation.[46] The court ordered that the RCMP internal disciplinary investigation be stopped: the testimony before the committee could not be used in its disciplinary investigation.[47] The Federal Court affirmed the Supreme Court's comment in *Vaid* that parliamentary privilege is one of the ways by which the separation of powers is respected. Parliamentary privilege, said the judge, "is designed to prevent courts and other entities from interfering with parliament's legitimate sphere of activity."[48] The court upheld the application of privilege in support of the investigative function of Parliament to ensure that committee witnesses would speak freely before committees.[49]

STATUTE LAWS AND THE HOUSE

Notwithstanding the House's right to exclusive control of its proceedings, there is legislation that expressly applies to House proceedings and might seem to encroach on the House's privileged control of its proceedings. Can the House be taken to court for not complying with the requirements of the legislation? Yes, but when this happens the courts have respected the privileges of the House. For example, the Official Languages Act requires that all federal institutions provide their services in both official languages – and "federal institution" is defined as including the House of Commons. A committee witness went to court to complain that his rights under the act had been violated when a House committee refused to circulate his English-only brief to members of the committee.[50] The Federal Court held that the witness's complaint that his language rights had not been respected was really a complaint about committee procedure. The court said that the privilege claimed by the House, that is, exclusive control of its proceedings, had been "authoritatively established" and that the circulation or distribution of documents by the committee goes to "the very heart of 'control of process.'"[51] The court thus held that distribution and circulation of documents by a House committee was a necessary part of the privilege claimed and that the Official Languages Act, though it expressly applied to the House, was not allowed to override the House's control of its proceedings.

In another case under the Official Languages Act, the plaintiff complained that the Northwest Territories Legislative Assembly (NTLA) was not treating the two official languages equally when it broadcast its debates in French less often than in English and published its debates in English only.[52] NTLA argued that publication of its debates fell within its privileges and that this privilege cannot be circumscribed in a statute except by clear and express language. The trial judge did not accept this argument but on appeal NTLA's argument was upheld, notwithstanding the provision in the Northwest Territories Official Languages Act that required NTLA to publish its "records and journals" in both official languages.[53] The appeal court noted that the Supreme Court of Canada, in *New Brunswick Broadcasting*, had favourably cited the Erskine May text where it stated that parliamentary privilege "though part of the law of the land, is to a certain extent an exemption from the general law." Thus, "if even the *Charter* cannot cut down the exercise of legislative privilege, and if the courts are not empowered to review decisions made pursuant to privilege, it seems that more would be required than passage of a general statute (such as the Official Languages Act) to support the conclusion that a legislative privilege has been abrogated."[54] The language of the act, said the court, was "not sufficiently explicit to abrogate legislative privilege. Absent express language, abrogation of legislative privilege cannot be assumed."[55] Thus, a general application statute does not override parliamentary privilege.

It often happened (at least it seemed often to me) that a government department or agency, when asked by a committee to provide information to the committee, would invoke the Privacy Act and say the act obliged it to not disclose the information. I recall a committee meeting in 2009 that the chair had asked me to attend. Public Works Department officials, who were accompanied by their legal counsel, advised the Public Accounts Committee that Department of Justice lawyers had advised them that the information sought was subject to non-disclosure under the Privacy Act and that, based on this advice, they were not providing the information to the committee. I was asked by the chair to respond. I advised the committee that its request for information was not subject to the Privacy Act as this act, like any other act, did not override parliamentary privilege. The committee had the right to receive the information. Otherwise, legal advice from the Department of Justice would determine the rights of the committee. "Mr. Chairman," I said, "Clearly, this committee has constitutional status. The law of parliamentary privilege is clearly part of the constitutional law of the country. These committees are entitled to receive the information they ask for. If the practice of a given department, whether a legal practice or administrative, can trump this committee in its access to information, then Parliament becomes a joke. It's that simple."[56]

MEMBERS AND PARLIAMENTARY PRIVILEGE

Parliamentary privilege exempts members from court orders requiring them to attend court while Parliament is in session, based on the "paramount right of Parliament to the attendance and service of its members."[57] This exemption also applies during forty days before and after a session. Historically, these forty-day shoulder periods were meant to allow members time to make the trip from their ridings to Parliament and to prepare for the opening of a session or, at the end of a session, to wrap up their parliamentary affairs and get back to their ridings. In the days of horse and wagon, perhaps this was not an unreasonable amount of time for travel between the far reaches of the United Kingdom and Westminster.[58] The same cannot be said today either in England or Canada, where members can get to Parliament or back to their constituencies in a matter of hours.[59] Understandably, this privilege is not well received by persons trying to get a member (usually a minister) into court.[60] There have been court challenges to this privilege but to no avail, with two partial exceptions.

In 2003, the BC Court of Appeal said it did not find sufficient confirmation in the legal authorities on parliamentary privilege to confirm that the privilege of freedom from testifying in court included two forty-day shoulder periods.[61] The court allowed application of the privilege to House sessions but without any additional periods before or after. In another case in the same year the Federal Court amended the privilege by allowing only a fourteen-day period before and after a parliamentary session.[62] In both cases, the courts lacked proper understanding of the constitutional nature of parliamentary privilege, later provided by the Supreme Court in *Vaid*. In my view, the Federal Court mistakenly applied the necessity test to redefine the privilege claimed, which the Supreme Court said is not the purpose of the necessity test.[63] It is not for the courts to redefine a privilege according to what it may consider more appropriate in modern times. As the Supreme Court later confirmed in *Vaid*, once a court finds that the privilege claimed exists in law, the only issue for the court is its scope, that is, whether the matter before the court is within the category of matters to which the privilege applies – and determining scope does not mean updating the privilege as the court may consider appropriate.

An Ontario superior court judge also reduced the shoulder periods to fourteen days and held that the privilege applied only when the House was actually sitting.[64] If the House was adjourned for a break of a week or two weeks, which happens several times in a session, the judge ruled that a member could be summoned to court during that break. Again, this showed how ignorant judges (and legal counsel appearing before them, as I once was) can be about parliamentary matters. On appeal, the Ontario Court of Appeal affirmed that the privilege applied during a session and was not limited to actual sittings and included the forty-day extensions at each end.[65] Invoking *New Brunswick Broadcasting*, the Ontario court said necessity "is strictly limited to identifying whether a particular privilege exists. It does not permit a court to modify the privilege in light of changing social conditions."[66] According to the appellate judge, the "better view" was that the privilege included forty-day extensions, based on the scholarly literature that the court had reviewed and the two formal rulings of House of Commons Speakers where these extensions had been claimed.[67] Whether forty-day periods were still necessary for purposes of the privilege was for Parliament to decide and not the courts.[68]

The Ontario lower court decision and the BC ruling came to the attention of the Government House leader who, to his credit, rose in the House to complain of a breach of the privileges of the House by the courts. In his ruling, the Speaker took exception to the Ontario court appearing to think that members were on holiday when a sitting was adjourned. The House and its members had parliamentary privilege "to ensure that the other branches of government, the executive and the judicial, respect the independence of the legislative branch of government, which is the House and 'the other place' [the Senate].[69] This independence cannot be sustained if either of the other branches is able to redefine or reduce these privileges."[70] The rewriting of this privilege by the courts was seen as a breach of the privileges of the House and referred to PROC. The committee acknowledged that perhaps it was time for the House to review its privileges, particularly whether the forty-day extensions were still necessary.[71] Unfortunately, the House was dissolved for an election without the committee's recommendation being considered by the House and the matter has not been raised since.

PARLIAMENTARY PRECINCTS

In addition to House and committee proceedings, parliamentary privilege also applies to the place or precincts where the proceedings take place. The precincts of the House are comprised of the building, buildings, or rooms where the House, its committees, and individual members carry out their *parliamentary* functions, namely, the west half of the Centre Block, the West Block, or any place where a House committee meets. The grounds surrounding the parliamentary buildings on Parliament Hill are not part of the parliamentary precincts for purposes of parliamentary privilege nor are the members' constituency offices.

The law of parliamentary privilege gives the Speaker exclusive control of the parliamentary precincts. In 1916, when the parliamentary buildings were destroyed by fire and the two houses sat temporarily in a museum a few blocks away, the museum premises became the precincts of Parliament and enjoyed their privileges. Similarly, if a committee holds a meeting off the Hill, those premises have the privileges of parliamentary precincts while the committee is meeting there. The Speaker, through the sergeant-at-arms, is responsible for seeing that members can meet anywhere in the precincts without fear of interference by outsiders. The Speaker must ensure that the precincts are secure and will not be entered by unauthorized personnel.

Historically, unauthorized entry was particularly important in dealing with the Crown or its agents. It has been a long-standing constitutional convention, certainly since the time of King Charles I if not earlier, that the House must be able to meet without interference from the king or his officials. To this day, government officials may not exercise their legal powers in or within the precincts when Parliament is in session (plus forty days at either end) without the permission of the Speaker.[72] For example, a member cannot be served with a writ of summons or other legal papers nor can the police enter the precincts under a search warrant or to make an arrest. If the Speaker is satisfied that the legal papers are valid, which for a search warrant means determining only whether the warrant is valid "on its face," that is, in its form and content, approval is usually given, although on condition that it be done at a time of day and in a manner that least disturbs the parliamentary business of the House and its members. In the case of a search warrant pertaining to the office of a member, the Speaker does not give the member advance notice that there is a warrant as this would be an interference with the legal process. Entry into the precincts takes place under the supervision of the sergeant-at-arms and possibly the law clerk, acting on behalf of the Speaker. Government officials may, of course, enter the precincts to meet with members or House officials at any time.

The authority of the Speaker with respect to the precincts does not lessen the authority of the House over its precincts, though it generally leaves management of the precincts to the Speaker. The Ontario Court of Appeal has affirmed clearly that legal authority over the precincts belongs to the House: "it should be self-evident," said the court, "that control over the premises occupied by the House of Commons for the purpose of performing the members' parliamentary work is a necessary adjunct to the proper functioning of Parliament ... In my view, the courts would be overstepping legitimate constitutional bounds if they sought to interfere with the power of the House to control access to its own premises."[73]

The House has banned persons from entering the precincts on two occasions. In each case, the individual wanted to give a press conference in the room used for press conferences, the Centre Block's Charles Lynch Room. In 1998, it denied access to Ernst Zündel, a well-known Holocaust denier, and in 2007 to two free-speech activists. Zündel went to court to seek a ruling that his right to freedom of expression under the Charter had been wrongfully denied. The court held that the House had not denied Zündel the right to speak but only entry into the precincts of the House. Though the House didn't give any reasons for its action, the judge said "it [was] obvious to preserve the dignity and integrity of Parliament."[74] The two free-speech activists were well known for their anti-semitic and racist views and wanted to accuse the Canadian Human Rights Commission of engaging in spy activities against Canadians using the internet. The motion in the House, which was adopted unanimously without debate, used the language of the judge in the Zündel case to assert that banning these individuals was "to preserve the dignity and integrity of the House." Some thought the action of the House went against the right to freedom of speech. Moreover, it was noted that the House had banned the two individuals not for what they had said but for what they might say. After all, it was argued, there were laws against hate speech and if this was included in what they said, they could be prosecuted. However, the parties in the House apparently did not want the precincts of the House used as a platform for what they anticipated would be hate speech.

The Supreme Court of Canada has said that public access to the parliamentary precincts is not a right but a license that can be revoked at any time by the Speaker of the House.[75] Nor are the precincts a haven or sanctuary, like a church, where one might escape legal process. The privilege attached to the precincts is based on the parliamentary function of the House and its members. As a Canadian court once said, "It is not the precinct of Parliament that is sacred but the function."[76] As the House is in session most of the time, the protection against legal process within the precincts is virtually always in place.[77] It may be, however, that the courts would not set aside an action carried out within the precincts without the Speaker's approval unless it was the Speaker who was objecting to the action.

RULE OF LAW

In the minds of some, including lawyers, exemptions provided by parliamentary privilege put the House and its committees above the law, which seems contrary to the hallowed principle of the rule of law. Lawyers too often told me that legal issues between a private citizen (a committee witness) and a committee were governed by the Charter, particularly the Charter right of due process, seemingly unaware of the Supreme Court's 1993 decision in *New Brunswick Broadcasting* affirming that the Charter does not prevail over parliamentary privilege, which means that the proceedings of a committee are not subject to judicial review under the Charter.

In 2009, a senior Department of Justice lawyer wrote to me explaining why the Government could not disclose certain documents to a House committee. The lawyer invoked "several basic constitutional principles that must always be borne in mind."[78] The first of these principles, she wrote, was the rule of law: "No one is above the law and everyone – including government officials, the law officers of the Crown and the members of parliamentary committees – must abide by the law. All governmental authority must be exercised in accordance with the law." The second principle was parliamentary sovereignty. The third was responsible government and the fourth was the separation of powers. These principles, wrote the lawyer, were "essential to the functioning of parliamentary democracy in a state respectful of the rule of law." The letter did not explain how the second, third, or fourth principle affected the right of a parliamentary committee to receive information from the Government, which was the issue giving rise to the letter. The lawyer closed her letter affirming the obligation of the Government "to ensure respect for the national interest in accordance with the rule of law."

The government lawyer was invoking the rule of law to support the contention that statutory provisions, such as the non-disclosure provisions in the Privacy Act, the Access to Information Act, the Security of Information Act or, as in this case, the Canada Evidence Act, could be applied to proceedings of the House or its committees despite parliamentary privilege.[79] As mentioned above, the rule of law was being used to advance the rule of laws as set out in particular statute laws that do not, as a matter of law, apply to proceedings of the House or its committees, as confirmed by the Supreme Court of Canada in *Vaid*.

Parliamentary privilege was a frequent issue during the minority government years from 2004 to 2011. In some cases, parliamentary privilege became an issue where it would not have if the Government had had a majority. The situations that most often gave rise to questions of parliamentary privilege arose when a committee sought information from the Government that it didn't want to provide, committee witnesses needed assurance that their testimony could not be used against them in any subsequent proceeding or for any other purpose, or when a committee felt it had been given false testimony by a witness.

With the parliamentary backstory and parliamentary privilege in mind, it's time to look at how the House carries out its constitutional functions of legislating, deliberating, and holding the Government to account.

4

Legislating and Deliberating

In *Vaid v House of Commons* (2005), discussed in the previous chapter, the Supreme Court of Canada said that the House had three constitutional functions: legislating, deliberating, and holding the Government to account. We look at legislating and deliberating here and will look at holding the Government to account in the next chapter.

LEGISLATING

The legislative powers of the Parliament of Canada are limited by the Constitution Act 1867. Parliament may legislate only on matters listed in section 91 and not on the matters placed under the jurisdiction of the provinces in section 92. The legislative powers of Parliament and the provincial legislatures are, for the most part, exclusive. Section 91 also says that Parliament may legislate for the "peace, order and good government" of Canada on any matter not assigned to the provinces, which has allowed federal legislation on matters that, not envisioned in 1867, later became matters of significant national concern, such as radio communications, aeronautics, nuclear energy, and marine (ocean) pollution.[1]

The 1867 Act provides for shared legislative powers over education, agriculture, and immigration, giving both Parliament and the provincial legislatures legislative powers in these areas.[2] The act was amended in 1964 to provide shared powers over old age pensions and supplementary benefits and in 1982 over non-renewable natural resources, forestry, and electrical energy.[3] The environment is not mentioned in the Act but is generally accepted as an area of shared powers. One might say that, as a rule, Parliament's legislative powers apply to matters of national concern while provincial legislative powers apply to "all matters of a merely local or private nature in the province."

The legislative powers of the House are also limited by the Constitution Act 1982, in particular the Charter of Rights and Freedoms. The courts may declare legislation that violates the Charter to be unconstitutional and of no force and effect. The freedoms guaranteed under the Charter include freedom of conscience, religion, thought, belief, and expression, the media's right to free speech, and the right to peaceful assembly and association and freedom from unreasonable search and seizure, arbitrary detention, or imprisonment.[4] The Charter also guarantees the right to "life, liberty and security of the person" and other rights related to the criminal justice system.[5] Most importantly, the Charter guarantees the right to equal treatment under the law, including equal protection and benefit of the law without discrimination.[6]

However, the Charter's guarantee of these rights and freedoms is not absolute: the rights and freedoms are subject to "such reasonable limits prescribed by law as can be demonstrably justified in a free and democratic society."[7] Some have argued that this provision has led the courts to make political decisions that are beyond their judicial function and there can be no doubt that the Charter has greatly enhanced the judicial review powers of the courts with respect to legislation. Perhaps in anticipation of this complaint, the Charter allows Parliament to pass legislation that violates the Charter with respect to its freedoms, legal rights, and equality rights, provided the legislation declares that it recognizes it is violating the Charter. Such legislation must be re-enacted every five years.[8]

Government bills, the main area of legislative activity in the House and in committee, are usually very complicated, often hundreds of pages of highly technical and legalistic text. Fortunately, the Library of Parliament provides legislative summaries for each Government bill that make the bills more comprehensible. It's important to remember that government bills are the product of considerable research and study by policy and legal experts. Sometimes it can be several years before a government bill is ready for introduction in the House. Private member's bills, on the other hand, are much simpler, in most cases only three or four pages in length, although there are many more such bills in any session.[9]

Debates and votes on bills in the House focus on the public policy choices and objectives underlying the bills. With government bills, the opposition parties challenge the public policy choices of the Government, criticizing and sometimes suggesting amendments. Legal issues, particularly constitutionality (Charter compliance), are generally left for the courts to resolve. Members are usually not qualified to argue legal or constitutional issues and parliamentary debates are not the place to determine legal questions. This is not to say that the constitutionality of a bill might not be raised in debate and that members might not vote against a bill that they believed was unconstitutional. Legally, however, legislation is assumed to be constitutional until a court determines otherwise. The minister of justice is legally obliged to advise the House if a government bill is inconsistent with the Charter but, as we have seen, this doesn't mean what some might think it does.[10]

Items in lengthy government bills can easily be missed and fail to get the attention they deserve. For example, in 2007 the Budget Implementation bill amended the Financial Administration Act (FAA) to "modernize" it by allowing the Government to borrow money without first getting the approval of Parliament.[11] This was very simple to do: the amendment read: "The Governor in Council may authorize the Minister to borrow money on behalf of Her Majesty in right of Canada." No one in the House raised any questions. Private member's bills have tried to restore the need for parliamentary authority for Government borrowing but so far without success.[12] No longer needing approval before borrowing has enabled the Government to borrow funds to meet budgetary deficits (and to thereby increase the national debt[13]) without facing debate in the House that might draw public attention to the borrowing (and the increasing national debt).

As well, from time to time the Government introduces a Miscellaneous Statute Law Amendment Bill that proposes amendments to deal with the "anomalies, inconsistencies, archaisms and errors that can sometimes find their way into federal statutes."[14] The minister of justice is expected to rise in the House and assure members that there are no new legislative initiatives in the bill. These are legislative "housekeeping" bills that go through the House and Senate quickly.

So-called "omnibus" bills, which contain a large number of unrelated legislative changes, are another means by which important legislative changes – including new acts – can be enacted "covertly," that is, without the proper debate or vote they would get if they were presented in separate bills. These bills can overwhelm the opposition parties by the variety and quantity of their unrelated provisions.[15] Some years ago, the Speaker ruled that omnibus bills were supposed to have "one basic principle or purpose which ties together all the proposed enactments and thereby renders the bill intelligible for parliamentary purposes."[16] This rule seems to have been forgotten.

In my view, omnibus bills, particularly those seen in recent years, violate the legislative process. How can votes on such bills, including votes against the bill, have any meaning? For example, in 2012 the Government's Budget Implementation Bill contained 753 clauses, three or four times the number of clauses usually found.[17] Of these, three clauses proposed new acts (yes, three bills within one bill). As far as I could see, there was no governing principle to this bill. If new acts are needed, they should be proposed in separate bills. Moreover, the new acts seemed unrelated to implementation of the Government's 2012 budget (or to each other).[18] The opposition parties objected to the bill but there was no procedural rule that enabled the Speaker to require that the bill be divided into several bills. A former House Speaker said he would have split the bill into several bills: "I'm the Speaker and my responsibility is to the democratic process."[19]

A member who later became prime minister objected to omnibus government bills when he was on the opposition side some years earlier. "How can members represent their constituents on these various areas," he asked, "when they are forced to vote in a block on such legislation and on such concerns?" He went on to say,

> We can agree with some of the measures but oppose others. How do we express our views and the views of our constituents when the matters are so diverse? Dividing the bill into several components would allow members to represent views of their constituents on each of the different components in the bill.
>
> The bill contains many distinct proposals and principles and asking members to provide simple answers to such complex ques-

tions is in contradiction to the conventions and practices of
the House.[20]

When this member later became prime minister, his Government introduced omnibus bills that went beyond anything ever seen before.
What changed his mind? The current prime minister seems to have
had the same change of heart on omnibus bills once he left the opposition benches, introducing an omnibus budget bill that contained five
new acts.[21] And so it goes.

As a rule, the Government wants its bills to go through the House
as quickly as possible, while the opposition parties want them to go
through as slowly as possible. More time means more time for critics
to voice their opposition and, the opposition hopes, for public opinion
to be turned against the government bill.[22] Opposition members use
as much time as the rules permit (hence long and seemingly pointless
debates). The Government looks for procedural mechanisms to limit
debate, whether in the chamber or in committee. One mechanism,
used too often in the view of the opposition parties, is time-allocation.[23] When the Government feels a bill is taking too long to come to
a vote, it can use its majority to pass a time-allocation motion, which
imposes a limit on the number of hours allowed for further debate
before a vote must be taken. This dynamic of hurry up against slow
down underlies the House procedural reforms proposed by the Government on 10 March 2017.

The Legislative Process

Bills are given three "readings" in the House.[24] The first reading is a
formality at the time the bill is introduced in the House. There is no
debate. On second reading, the bill is debated "in principle" (and is
not subject to amendment). The minister sponsoring the bill leads off
the debate, giving the Government's reasons for the bill. If the bill is
approved at second reading, it is referred to committee (usually one of
the standing committees, though there could be a specially struck legislative committee) for study, clause by clause review, and possible
amendment. The bill returns to the House for "report stage," where
the committee's report on the bill is debated and further amendments

may be proposed. Finally, there is a third reading, where the bill, as amended if such is the case, is debated again with no further amendments allowed. The vote on third reading, if "the yea's have it," gives the House's final approval to the bill and it is sent to the Senate ("the other place").

At second reading, House procedural practice says that debate on the bill is on the overall principle of the bill and not on its details.[25] For example, with a bill restricting the ownership of guns, a later amendment in committee that would make it easier to own a gun would likely be inadmissible as going against the principle of the bill. Omnibus bills with many unrelated provisions can make a mockery of this procedural rule when such bills have no discernible overall principle. The minister sponsoring the bill begins the debate with a speech on the policy objectives of the bill, which may give an indication of the overall principle of the bill. The official opposition member who acts as critic for the subject matter of the bill responds, followed by the critics of the other parties in opposition. Speeches then continue, rotating between the recognized parties based on the number of members in each party: the more members, the more frequently a member from that party will be allowed to speak. There is a time limit of twenty minutes for each speech during the first five hours of a debate, with ten minutes for questions and comments, if any, after each speech. Thereafter a maximum of ten minutes is allowed for each speech until all members wishing to speak have done so, at which point the motion for second reading of the bill is put to a vote and, if passed, the bill goes to a committee.

While no amendments may be made to a bill during second reading, there can be amendments to the sponsoring minister's motion for second reading. The usual second reading motion proposes that the bill be given second reading and referred to a committee named in the motion. The opposition could move to amend the motion by changing the committee to which the bill is referred. Proposing such an amendment doubles the time available for debate on the bill at second reading because there are then two debates: a debate on the main motion and a debate on the proposed amendment. If a sub-amendment were proposed to the amendment, there would be a third debate on the sub-amendment.

Legislation in Committee

Once the House has approved a bill "in principle" at the second reading stage, a committee looks at the bill in detail, hears witnesses, if any, considers amendments, and votes on the bill's clauses before reporting back to the House. The first item of business for the committee might be agreeing on a list of witnesses, although a Government with a majority can prevent or greatly limit the hearing of witnesses. The Government's interest in moving its bills along as quickly as possible comes up against the wish of the opposition parties to have as many witnesses as possible to speak against the bill and delay the process. The first witness is usually the minister responsible for the bill, accompanied by a few departmental officials. Once all the scheduled witnesses have been heard, the committee goes through the bill clause by clause and considers any amendments that may be proposed.

With government bills, most amendments are proposed in committee and come from opposition members, as the Government usually does not want to amend its own bill. Amendments are the opposition's principal mechanism for procedurally opposing a government bill. Procedural rules on the admissibility of amendments can be frustrating for opposition members when their amendments, which propose changes that they think are important as a matter of public policy, are ruled inadmissible and denied a debate and a vote. A vote is particularly important because it puts the other parties on the parliamentary record (for use at the next election) as supporting or opposing what has been proposed.

As mentioned above, amendments may not go against the principle of a bill. Nor may they go beyond the scope of a bill. Such amendments are said to be introducing a "new idea" into the bill, that is, an idea that does not relate to anything proposed in the bill. For example, an amendment proposing environmental programs to protect fish would probably not be accepted on a bill proposing environmental protections for birds. This rule provides some discipline to the legislative process by not allowing unrelated items to be "tacked on" to a government bill.[26] Presumably, the Government has weighed the policy implications of what it is proposing and has decided to limit its proposal to what is set out in its bill. As the Government will be responsible for administering the bill when it becomes law – and for meeting administrative and enforcement costs – its proposals should be protected against extensions in a bill's scope.

An amendment to a bill amending an existing Act of Parliament, if passed, cannot amend a section in the "parent act" that may be implicated in the change but is not being amended in the bill. As a lawyer, I found this rule problematic at times. Occasionally it seemed clear that a section in the parent act, untouched in the amending bill, would need to be amended if the bill's amendments were passed. This is a "consequential" amendment, an amendment that is a consequence of another amendment. The lawyer drafting an amendment for a private member (virtually all amendments for private members are prepared in the Law Clerk's Office) might see that another section in the parent act would also need to be amended if the member's amendment is to work effectively, but the procedural rules won't allow the consequential amendment to be proposed.

These procedural rules, as with all procedural rules with respect to amendments to bills, apply even where the opposition parties have a majority on the committee in a minority parliament as they are based on the premise that the Government – whether in a majority or a minority parliament – has the right to govern (unless and until it loses the confidence of the House). If a committee were allowed, with House approval, to amend government bills in violation of the principle or scope limitation, the Government's ability to govern could be compromised.

Legislation Back from Committee (Report Stage)

The next stage in the legislative process occurs when the House takes up a committee's report on a bill and votes on whether it concurs with it, commonly referred to as report stage. The committee's report does not usually include a narrative presentation on the bill but simply confirms that the committee has reviewed the bill and approves it (or, rarely, does not), with or without amendments, as the case may be. Amendments approved by the committee are set out in the report. Additional amendments may be proposed at report stage[27] and these are reviewed for procedural admissibility largely in the same way as is done at committee stage.[28] Amendments proposed in committee and defeated there may not be proposed again at report stage. Also, an amendment that could have been proposed in committee will not be considered at report stage. To facilitate debate, proposed amendments are grouped according to common subject matter. Where this produces several groupings, there is often not enough time for debate beyond the first group before a vote must be taken in accordance with an earlier time allocation order. Despite this, the amendments in the groups that are not debated are still put to a vote at the end of the time allowed for the bill's report stage debate. To facilitate the process, a vote on an amendment can be applied to related or dependent amendments.

Report stage amendments may be subjected to a recorded vote, in which case the voting can go on into the late evening if there are a large number of amendments. To save time, the parties may apply their members' votes on a previous amendment to a later amendment rather than go through the process of a recorded vote that will produce the same result. In this case, the party's House leader rises to indicate that the party's vote on the last amendment will apply to the amendment before the House. In its early days (after the election of 1993), the Reform Party, wishing to show its commitment to the grassroots, would add something like "unless there are any members [of the Reform Party] who wish to vote otherwise." Veteran onlookers were amused by this and had no doubt that the practice wouldn't last, which it didn't.

Once voting on amendments is completed, the House votes on whether it concurs with the committee's report, which now may contain the further amendments made by the House in report stage, and the bill is set down for its third and final reading.

Third Reading

The Government, at such time as it chooses, will call the bill for its third and final reading where the bill is debated but no amendments may be proposed. The same procedural rules for debates apply. If the third reading motion is passed, the bill goes to the other place (the Senate).

Private Member's Bills

For one hour in each sitting day, during Private Members' Business, the House debates bills or motions sponsored by private members. This is where you might make a noticeable contribution as a new member. Many bills or motions by private members are introduced in the House but unfortunately only a few of them ever get debated and put to a vote. Such bills (or motions, discussed later) are taken up according to a random draw. The names of the first thirty members drawn are placed on an Order of Precedence that ranks their bills (and motions) for debate in the House.[29]

Given the rather limited amount of time allotted for Private Members' Business, the legislative process for a private member's bill, unlike a motion, can take quite a long time as the bill may need to ascend to the top of the Order of Precedence twice to receive second reading, which can include a maximum of two hour-long debates, and then go to committee. (First reading was when the bill was introduced during Routine Proceedings.) After the first hour of debate, if it has not been put to a vote, the bill drops down to the bottom of the Order of Precedence and must climb back up for its second hour and a vote.[30]

It used to be that referral to a committee (when there was a Government majority) was a sentence of quiet death for a private member's bill as it would probably never come back to the House. However, the rules were changed in 1997 and now the committee must report back within sixty sitting days or the bill is deemed reported back without amendment.[31] Once reported back to the House, the bill is placed at the bottom of the Order of Precedence and must ascend to the top for its report stage and third reading, for which a maximum of two hours is allotted. If this stage does not finish in the first hour, the bill must go (again) to the bottom of the Order of Precedence and climb back up to the top for its second and final hour of debate and a final vote. All private member's bills get a vote (this wasn't always the case) unless they are designated as non-votable because they concern questions that are outside the House's legislative jurisdiction, are unconstitutional, or raise questions that are "substantially the same" as questions that have already been decided by the House (in the same session) or that are already being presented in a bill or motion ahead of them in the Order of Precedence, or concern matters that are items of Government business.[32] Decisions on whether a bill is votable are made by a sub-committee of the Standing Committee on Procedure and House Affairs (PROC) after hearing submissions from the sponsoring member and perhaps some legal advice on the bill.

Before the long and winding legislative road begins, the private member usually has the bill drafted by professional legislative drafters in the Law Clerk's Office. The member could go elsewhere for drafting services but, for technical reasons related to the bilingual dual-column format of bills, the Law Clerk's Office must approve all bills before they are introduced in the House. The drafting of a bill may take anywhere from a few days to several weeks or months, depending on how many requests are already pending, the complexity of the member's legislative initiative, and whether the member is on the Order of Precedence following the draw.

If a private member's bill survives to the end of the legislative process – and this is a big "if" – it will have had to climb to the top of the Order of Precedence as many as four times over a period of twenty-four to thirty sitting weeks, usually a period of around twelve months when break weeks and the time taken at committee stage are included. If a Christmas break or summer break intervenes, the process could take well over a year. During that year, the member will be patiently lobbying other members for support. If the bill is passed by the House, the private member must find a sponsor in the Senate, where a similar process awaits.

As of 22 April 2015, in the session of Parliament that began on 16 October 2013, there were 464 private member's bills before the House, the vast majority of which had not advanced beyond first reading.[33] A bill that had been first introduced in the previous session on 22 June 2011 and had gone nowhere by the end of that session (a fifteen-month period) was reintroduced at the start of the next session and received final House approval over a year later. It had taken the private member three and a half years to get House approval. The bill went immediately to the Senate, where it took another six months to advance to final approval and royal assent after four years.[34] Another private member's bill introduced in the House around the same time

received final approval by the House four months later. It went immediately to the Senate where it advanced to second reading but no further before the parliamentary session was prorogued (a year later).
The private member reintroduced the bill in the House in the next
session. As it had been given final approval by the House in the previous session, the bill went immediately to the Senate where it
received final approval eight months later and royal assent the next
month, three years after it was first introduced in the House.[35] These
timelines are not unusual.

The Government may make its views known in the debates during
Private Members' Business but it is not supposed to control ("whip")
its members when the time comes to vote.[36] Private member's bills
are seen as initiatives of the sponsoring private member only and are
not, as a rule, initiatives of the Government or the sponsoring member's party or caucus, though in reality the contrary may sometimes
seem to be the case. The hope is that the initiatives of private members will not be treated as partisan.

For example, on a private member's bill related to citizenship introduced by a member on the Government side, the minister of citizenship had amendments to propose that went beyond the scope of the
bill.[37] The committee looking at the bill, on the initiative of the Government side in the committee (the majority), asked the House for
permission to expand the scope of the bill.[38] Several members objected to the committee's request.[39] Allowing the Government to expand
the scope of the bill to enable consideration of amendments that the
minister wanted to propose would, said the member who raised the
point of order, "completely expand the nature of private member's
bills, which deal with a specific subject, and in fact to change their
very nature from being private member's bills to being [government]
Bills." The member argued that if the request were allowed, "Governments could increasingly use private member's bills as a way of getting other issues in front of the House, bypassing ordinary debate [for
government bills] in second reading and the due consideration of this
House so that after only two hours of debate on one subject, which in
fact was what took place, the Government would then suddenly be
permitted to introduce other issues into the debate." The member further argued that allowing the amendment,

basically broadens entirely the scope of a private member's bill to include the rest of the Government's public agenda ... It is very simple. The effect will be that the Government could, by extrapolation, even add an omnibus feature to a private member's bill and say it is using its majority to add everything, the whole kitchen sink, into the measure.

Private member's bills are intended for private members to put forward issues, items, agendas and concerns that they have. They are not intended to be a way by which the Government skirts around the purposes of private member's bills and drives home its own agenda.

In his ruling, the Speaker acknowledged that there was "genuine disquiet about the impact of this attempted procedural course of action. The Chair is not deaf to those concerns and, in that light, wishes to reassure the House that this manner of proceedings does not obviate the need for committees to observe all the usual rules governing the admissibility of amendments to the clauses of a bill."[40]

The Speaker was unable to rule on the Government's role with respect to private member's bills because this question was not covered by a procedural rule that he could apply. The members' objections were based on their understanding of unwritten parliamentary tradition or practice regarding private member's bills, something the Speaker cannot deal with through a procedural ruling. In short, it was a political issue between the Government and private members about proper House practice. The Speaker ruled on the narrow procedural question of whether a committee could seek instructions from the House as this committee had done (which it could). As it happened, the House never gave the committee the instructions it sought so no worrisome precedent was set. The bill later came back to the House from committee without amendment.

Royal Recommendation

Perhaps the deadliest weapon against a private member's bill or a private member's amendment to a government bill is the royal recommendation. You need to be mindful of this requirement before sponsoring a bill or moving an amendment to a government bill.

Under section 54 of the Constitution Act 1867, the House cannot vote on spending public funds except where the proposed spending is recommended by the governor general (i.e., by the Government).[41] The recommendation is known as a royal recommendation and a bill that requires one cannot be introduced in the House without the recommendation attached. The underlying principle is that the Government must have control of the public purse (as Lord Durham urged in his report in 1838) and this means, in the parliamentary context, that only the Government may propose a new tax, tax increase, or new spending. The Government must have the financial initiative.

When I first arrived at the House, I was surprised to learn that it was my responsibility to obtain a royal recommendation from the governor general if a government bill required one. Sometimes we had very short notice that the Government intended to introduce the bill and had to scramble quickly to find the governor general and then race to get the bill to the GG for signature and then get back to the House in time to affix it to the bill before the minister introduced it in the House. On one occasion, we had to interrupt the governor general at lunch at Montebello, Quebec, a forty-minute drive from Ottawa; the governor general was taken aback by the interruption but allowed that he would do it this one time for his good friend, the minister. On another occasion, the governor general was at the airport waiting to greet Princess Diana.

My office's responsibility for obtaining royal recommendations was a holdover from the functions of the Law Clerk's Office in the distant past, when the office had much greater involvement in the preparation of government bills, including responsibility for deciding whether a bill required a royal recommendation and then getting one signed. In my view, this responsibility did not belong in my office. Since when did the governor general act on the advice of a lowly House official? The GG acts on the advice of the prime minister and cabinet. I complained to the clerk of the House and urged that we get rid of this task, arguing that it should be the responsibility of the Department of Justice, where government bills were drafted. The clerk agreed, admitting that he had been trying to get rid of the task for years. I called my counterpart in the Department of Justice and he, of course, said he doubted that it should be his department's responsibility. He suggested a meeting involving, if memory serves, the Privy Council Office and a few other offices. At the meeting, each agreed that seeking a royal recommendation from the governor general should not be the responsibility of the House's law clerk and then pointed to one of the others to take it on. Eventually the task was assigned to the Privy Council Office, where it belonged and has remained ever since.

As the governor general only acts as advised by the prime minister and cabinet, a private member can only obtain a royal recommendation through the Government. For private members generally, the absence of a royal recommendation is fatal to the success of a bill involving spending. Obtaining such a recommendation has happened only once that I can recall, in the mid-1990s, when a private member on the Government side (of course) obtained a royal recommendation for his bill to allow persons called for jury duty to qualify for employment insurance benefits.[42]

It was not always an easy task to determine whether a bill or amendment required a royal recommendation. The authoritative Erskine May text says that the test is whether the bill (or amendment) proposes a "new and distinct charge" upon the public purse. In this context, "charge" meant a fiscal burden on the Government. I interpreted "distinct" to mean recognizable as a charge on the public purse. During the minority years (2004–11), the royal recommendation rule became an important tool for the Government with respect to private member's bills as the Government did not have enough members to defeat private member's bills on a vote so it looked to the royal recommendation requirement instead. Because this introduced a contentious procedural question, a new procedural practice was required to enable the competing views to be aired: the Speaker would announce in the House that he had concerns that certain private member's bills on the Order of Precedence might require a royal recommendation and invite responses. The sponsoring member or the Government (usually the Government House leader's parliamentary secretary) would then make a case for or against requiring a royal recommendation.[43]

For example, in 2005, Bill C-280 amended the Employment Insurance Act to provide for adding thirteen new commissioners to the Canadian Employment Insurance Commission. The bill was held to require a royal recommendation because the existing legislation provided for remuneration to commissioners, which meant that the new commissioners would also need to be paid.[44] Thus, the bill proposed a "new and distinct charge" upon the public purse. According to the deputy speaker, where the legislative objective of a bill cannot be accomplished without the use of public funds "the bill must be seen as the equivalent of a bill effecting an appropriation."[45]

Another private member's bill legislated establishment of a Ukrainian Canadian museum at Banff National Park.[46] The Speaker decided that the bill required a royal recommendation: "[I]n my view, [the bill] constitutes an appropriation within the meaning of section 54 of the Constitution Act, 1867 and Standing Order 79. Alternatively, it constitutes an authorization to spend the necessary public funds and as such is the equivalent of an appropriation under section 54 or Standing Order 79." The reference in section 54 to appropriations was interpreted to include implied authorizations to spend and thus "equivalent" to an appropriation under section 54. The bill also required the Government to negotiate "a suitable payment in restitution for the confiscation of property and other assets from Ukrainian Canadians." The Government argued that this would create "a positive obligation" to spend funds and therefore should require a royal recommendation. The Speaker allowed that a royal recommendation would be required if the bill imposed a "positive obligation" on the Government to spend funds, but in this case the bill only imposed an obligation to negotiate a suitable restitution and it was possible that no restitution amount would ever be determined. For a royal recommendation to be required, the obligation to spend funds must arise immediately upon enactment of the bill, not upon fulfillment of a condition subsequent to enactment.[47]

In 2006, the Kelowna Accord Implementation Act, Bill C-292, sought implementation of the Kelowna Accord, which the previous Government had entered into with the provinces, the territories, and Canada's aboriginal people "to close and ultimately eliminate the gaps between our aboriginal Canadians and non-aboriginal Canadians." The new (minority) Government said that the bill, if passed into law, would have significant financial implications for the Government and therefore required a royal recommendation. The Speaker said that he had to decide whether the bill contained "a clear authorization for funds to be drawn from the Consolidated Revenue Fund for a distinct purpose." He reminded members of an earlier ruling that a royal recommendation is required only if the obligation to spend public funds arises upon enactment of the bill. "There should be nothing further required to make the appropriation," said the Speaker and therefore he needed to ask what specific spending was contemplated in the bill. The bill stated that the Government shall take all measures necessary to implement the terms of the accord but, said the Speaker, "it does not provide specific details on those measures. The measures simply are not described. In the absence of such a description, it is impossible for the Chair to say that the bill requires a royal recommendation."[48] Implementation of the Kelowna Accord would probably require various legislative proposals, possibly including an appropriation of public funds." When such enabling legislation appears, the Speaker will, he said, "be vigilant in assessing the need for a royal recommendation."

Financial cost or loss to the Government is not enough to require a royal recommendation. In 2004, a private member introduced a bill to remove the ten per cent luxury tax on jewellery (first introduced in 1918).[49] It was estimated by the Government that this bill, if adopted, would eliminate around $80 million of annual revenue. A Department of Finance official told the House's Finance Committee that the bill would have an impact on the Government's fiscal framework that is "similar to new spending measures" and would reduce revenues available for other spending and tax relief priorities. "It's worth noting," added the official, "that while it's not possible they could all be passed into law, there are currently roughly 20 private member tax relief bills that are either on the order paper or before the House. These could represent collective fiscal cost of as much as $2 billion per year."[50] While the possible loss of tax revenue may explain the Government's concerns, the bill did not require a royal recommendation because the House always has the power to eliminate a tax or to reduce an existing tax.[51]

The House requires a royal recommendation not only for new charges (or increases to an existing charge) on the public purse but also (and, in my view, going beyond the terms of section 54) where the "objects, purposes, conditions and qualifications" attached to a proposed charge are being amended, which would seem to rest on the language of the royal recommendation itself (rather than section 54), which typically recommends the proposed spending "under the circumstances, in the manner and for the purpose" set out in the bill.[52] Charges upon the public purse (properly called the Consolidated Revenue Fund or CRF) are made for a specific purpose. Clearly, a bill that changed the purpose of a proposed charge would require a royal recommendation: just as the Government cannot use funds for a purpose other than the purpose for which they are appropriated, so also the House cannot change a purpose proposed by the Government. More than this, however, an amendment that proposes a change to the objects, purposes, conditions, or qualifications of spending proposed in a bill to which a royal recommendation is attached would be inadmissible for "infringing upon" the royal recommendation attached to the bill.[53]

DELIBERATING

I suspect that the Court in *Vaid* found "deliberating" a convenient catch-all for those House proceedings that are neither legislating nor holding the Government to account, such as the Address in Reply to the Speech from the Throne, the debate on the Government's budget, opposition day supply motions, the estimates process, so-called "take note" debates, emergency debates, procedural and privilege debates, and debates on Government and private member motions (other than motions in the legislative process). This is not to say that these deliberative proceedings are not important.

Appropriations (Supply)

Although the appropriations or supply process results in legislation, an Appropriations Act, the process fits within deliberating for two reasons. First, the appropriations process is comprised mostly of Opposition Day motions (discussed below) that are not legislative in nature. Second, there is very little meaningful debate on the Government's spending estimates. The House's appropriations/estimates process is not done very well, although it is a function over which, as we have seen, there were once many battles between the Crown and the Commons. By parliamentary tradition, appropriations are fundamental to the relationship between the House and the Crown.[54] I suspect you won't find this proceeding of much interest, except for opposition day motions that, technically, are part of supply process, as I'll explain later.

The appropriations process runs over the twelve months of the government fiscal year, from 1 April to 31 March.[55] It starts with the Government tabling its main estimates of expenditures for the coming fiscal year.[56] Since 1997, the estimates process has included tabling a Report on Plans and Priorities in the spring and a Performance Report from each department and agency in the fall. The Treasury Board of Canada Secretariat (TBS) assembles the various departmental and agency budget estimates for presentation to the House. The information setting out the Government's proposed expenditures is both overwhelming and uninformative for parliamentary purposes. It seems informative because of its detail – if one has an eye for such matters and not many members do. In fairness, there is no way for the House to consider the estimates except in a summary manner, which is what, at best, it does.

The estimates for each department or agency are referred to the standing committee mandated with responsibility for the department or agency.[57] A committee, whether it has reported back to the House or not, will be deemed to have done so on 31 May.[58] Typically, a standing committee meets with the responsible minister, accompanied by a few departmental officials, once in the March to May period to consider the main estimates of the department. There is an exchange between committee members and the minister and the officials, which usually takes two hours. Shortly afterward the committee reports to the House that it "has considered" the main estimates, without any comment or recommended alterations. Committee reports are not allowed to comment on any of the estimates they reviewed but report only on the votes taken. In other words, it's a "yes" or "no" on each of the estimates – and it's never "no."

The estimates review by House standing committees in 2009, a minority Parliament, and in 2014, a majority Parliament, were much the same in each case.[59] One might suppose that reviews under a majority Government would be less rigorous than those under a minority Government. Not so. Of the twenty standing committees to which estimates were referred in 2014, fifteen committees met and reported to the House, while another three met but didn't report and two neither met nor reported. In 2009, eight committees met and reported to the House, nine met but didn't report and three never met. In both years, most of the committees met only once, a few twice, and only a very few more than twice. The estimates review process in the House appears to be rather superficial, whether it takes place in a majority or a minority Parliament.

As part of the estimates process, the leader of the official opposition is allowed to select two departments or agencies whose estimates will be considered in the House, sitting as a committee, rather than by a standing committee. The ministers responsible for the departments or agencies chosen, accompanied by officials, take questions from members and generally defend the estimates. As with standing committees, the House as committee of the whole may vote to eliminate or reduce an estimate but not to increase it or redirect it to another purpose. This estimates review in the Chamber enables a larger debate but leads to the same predictable result.

Once the committee reviews are completed, the Government brings in a bill for appropriation of the amounts set out in the estimates.[60] Later in the fiscal year, if the main estimates prove insufficient for the year and more funding is required, the Government may table supplementary estimates and a review process similar to the process on the main estimates takes place.

Opposition Day Motions

Running concurrently with the estimates process (rather loosely) and part of the supply process, are "opposition days," which are allotted to the opposition parties for debates on whatever issues they might choose. The debate need not relate to the estimates. These opposition days have their origins in the tradition, mentioned in chapter 2, that the Commons would not grant the king the funds he sought until the king had heard its grievances, although these days there is no tie-in between the main estimates process and opposition "grievances." Twenty-two days are allocated each year as opposition days. Only eight of these occur within the main estimates review period, which runs from 1 April to the end of June. Each of the opposition parties is assigned a number of opposition days proportionate to their numbers in the House. A motion proposed for debate on an opposition day is votable but not binding. The Government designates which sitting days will be used as opposition days.

The Budget (Ways and Means)

As prominent as the budget speech may be in the media, it is not, strictly speaking, a necessary part of House business; that is, the Government is not constitutionally obliged – nor obliged by the rules of the House - to present a budget in the House each year.[61] However the budget is perhaps THE major political event in the House for the Government in any year.

While appropriations fall under the House's supply procedure, the budget falls under the House's "ways and means" procedure, an archaic term for how the Government proposes to generate the revenues it needs. In the Budget Speech, the minister of finance sets out the Government's economic and fiscal plans for the coming year (at least) and proposes a ways and means motion by seeking House approval of the Government's budgetary policy.[62] (All taxation bills must be preceded by House approval of a ways and means motion setting out the terms of the proposed taxation bill.[63] Such ways and means motions are neither amendable nor debatable. You might ask why the House bothers with voting on a ways and means motion authorizing a taxation bill and setting out the content of the bill, when the bill will later be subject to a vote. What's the point of members voting twice on the same issues? Frankly, I don't know; one must assume that this practice serves a parliamentary purpose but it's lost on me.) The budget ways and means motion, unlike other ways and means motions seeking House approval to introduce a taxation bill, is debatable.[64]

The critical aspect of the budget motion is that it is invariably considered to be a matter of confidence. If the motion is defeated or an opposition amendment of the motion is approved, the Government, by constitutional convention, must resign. However, the opposition may not want the Government to resign as this would mean dissolution of Parliament and a general election which, if they are not ready, they might lose. However, the opposition will still oppose the Government's budgetary policy. On the 2014 budget motion, the official opposition amended the budget motion to read that the budgetary policy should not be approved and gave reasons why it should not be approved. If the amendment had been approved – which was highly unlikely as it was a majority Government – it would clearly have been a question of confidence and the Government would have had to resign.

In a minority Parliament, where the opposition parties acting together have the majority, the wording of an amendment can be critical. On the 2009 budget motion, where the Government did not have a majority but the official opposition did not want an election (or so it seemed), the official opposition amendment did not amend the budget motion to read that the budgetary policy should not be approved (a confidence motion) but rather that it be approved on condition that the Government table reports on various matters listed in the amendment (not a confidence motion). The challenge for the official opposition, if it does not want to go to an election, is to oppose the budget without being drawn into a confidence question. A conditional approval is arguably not tantamount to non-confidence. As it happened, the Government finessed the official opposition's strategy of seeming to oppose by voting in favour of the amendment. Did the Government ever meet the conditions imposed by the amendment? No doubt it met some of them in the coming months or years, but who was watching? The Budget debate ended and the House moved on to other business.

Address in Reply to the Speech from the Throne

This proceeding usually occurs soon after delivery of the Speech from the Throne by the governor general in the Senate (the other place, remember?). The prime minister moves that the House consider the Speech from the Throne. An opposition amendment to the prime minister's motion could, depending on its wording, be a confidence question. Insofar as the Speech from the Throne presents the Government's plans for the session (as happened when, back in the day, the king explained to the assembled parliamentarians why he had called the Parliament into session), the Government defends its plans in the House debate that follows – the Address in Reply debate – and the opposition parties, of course, criticize the Government's plans. The debate is a good opening to a session, enabling the respective parties to present their political positions.

Private Member Motions

The period devoted to Private Members' Business, as mentioned earlier, includes motions sponsored by private members. These motions ask the House to express an opinion on a matter of interest to the private member, propose some action pertaining to internal House affairs (perhaps amending the Standing Orders), or urge the Government to take some particular action. Because the House, following protocol and the constitution, should not and cannot tell the Government what to do, motions directed to the Government are drafted as expressions of an opinion of the House ("THAT, in the opinion of the House, the Government should ..."). Such motions do not have any legal effect but only, once passed, express the view of the House. Private member motions relating to an internal House matter, such as changing the Standing Orders or referring a matter to a committee, do take effect when passed.

Emergency Debates

Under House rules, a member may request an emergency debate on a "specific and important matter requiring urgent consideration."[65] The matter must relate to "a genuine emergency, calling for immediate and urgent consideration." The Speaker decides whether the matter warrants urgent consideration and need not give reasons for the decision. Various criteria have developed, such as that the matter proposed for debate must not be a matter of local interest, nor related to a specific group or industry, nor involve the administration of a government department.[66] Matters of chronic or continuing concern, such as economic conditions, unemployment rates, and constitutional matters are not accepted as emergency matters while work stoppages and strikes, natural disasters, and international crises and events have been accepted.[67] The motion debated is simply that the House should adjourn: the debate does not result in any decision that requires action by the Government. When the debate ends, no later than midnight or earlier if the debate collapses, the adjournment motion is deemed to have carried.

Take-note Debates

Occasionally there are matters that may not qualify as sufficiently urgent to require an emergency debate but on which members feel they should have a debate to allow them to express their views. These are called "take note" debates and must be authorized by a motion of the House.[68] Usually following negotiations between the parties, a motion is passed unanimously by consent, that is, without a formal vote. The debates take place at the end of the regular sitting day and last for no more than four hours. The House sits as a committee of the whole, which makes it possible to slightly relax the usual formalities of House debates (members may speak more than once and need not be in their assigned seats). The debate does not result in any resolution on which the Government must act.

Privilege Issues

If a member believes that the parliamentary privileges of the House, its committees, or the member have been violated and wants to bring the matter to the attention of the House, the member may rise in the House on a point of privilege, which can give rise to a lengthy debate. The basic rule is that any action, whether by another member or an outside party, that impairs the ability of the House, a committee, or a member to carry out their parliamentary functions is a breach of parliamentary privilege and only the House can decide whether there has been such a breach. Other members might rise to comment on the point of privilege. The Speaker's role is to determine whether there has been a breach of parliamentary privilege prima facie, a ruling that screens out privilege claims that are little more than public whining about a procedural issue, which happens from time to time.

If the Speaker finds that there is a prima facie breach of privilege, the member raising the point is expected to make a motion referring the matter to the Standing Committee on Procedure and House

Affairs (PROC) for further study. The motion is debatable but the debate is usually minimal as the parties will have agreed in advance to adopt the motion without a vote. If not, a debate will ensue and will take priority over other House business until concluded and put to a vote. Privilege motion debates can thus serve as filibusters. If the question goes to PROC, the committee may hold hearings with witnesses before reporting to the House either recommending dismissal of the privilege claim or upholding it with a recommendation for the House to either affirm the privilege and take further action or to take no further action. Usually, House concurrence is obtained without debate as the parties will have agreed on the outcome earlier when negotiating the content of the committee report.

There you have the legislative and deliberative functions of the House. There remains the House's third constitutional function – holding the Government to account – which is a rather tame affair in a majority parliament but more robust in a minority parliament where opposition parties have the majority. We shall look at how the House, mostly through its committees, held the Government to account in the minority years 2006–11.

Holding the Government to Account

This constitutional function gets a lot of attention and sometimes draws blood. It will interest you, especially if you're sitting on the opposition side of the chamber.

In a modern *democratic* parliamentary system of government such as we have in Canada, you might expect that holding the Government to account, the third of the House's three constitutional functions, would be a large part of its activity, second only (in theory) to its control over taxes and spending, which, as we saw in the previous chapter, is rather limited and mostly ineffectual, especially in a majority parliament. The accountability function is carried out in several House proceedings, most notably in each day's Question Period. Accountability can also be exercised through committee proceedings, unless the Government forms the majority on the committee, in which case it can control the committee's agenda and avoid accountability. The minority parliaments between 2004 and 2011 showed how accountability can work.

What is meant by holding the Government to account? According to a paper on Government or ministerial accountability issued by the Privy Council Office (the head office of the government bureaucracy): "Ministers are accountable to Parliament for the exercise of the powers, duties and functions vested in them by statute or otherwise. Ministers must be present in Parliament to respond to questions on the discharge of their responsibilities, including the manner in which public monies were spent, as well as to account for that use. Whether a minister has discharged responsibilities appropriately is a matter of political judgment by Parliament. The prime minister has the prerogative to reaffirm support for that minister or to ask for his or her resignation."[1] The statement that the Government is "accountable to Parliament" should be understood as "accountable to the House," as only the House can dismiss the Government through a non-confidence vote. Ultimately, Government accountability comes down to responding to demands from the House sufficiently to maintain the confidence of the House.

The sponsorship scandal of 2004–05 led to a great deal of public attention on accountability. Testimony before the House's Public Accounts Committee revealed that the deputy minister of the responsible department, the Public Works Department, did not know what his officials were doing under the Government's sponsorship program. In the committee's view, "the doctrine [of ministerial accountability] needs to be reaffirmed and its interpretation and practice refined and clarified to assure its continuing relevance and utility to our system of government."[2] The committee recommended adopting the British practice of designating deputy ministers as "accounting officers" who are answerable to Parliament for the activities of their departments.

In 2006, the Federal Accountability Act carried out what the committee had recommended and also put limitations on political contributions to political parties (including bans on corporate and union donations), introduced a new conflict of interest regime for ministers and public officials, established new officers of Parliament to oversee lobbyists and government purchasing practices, and protected whistleblowers from reprisals by creating a public sector integrity commissioner.[3] The act also established the position of parliamentary budget officer.

ORAL QUESTIONS (QUESTION PERIOD)

In Question Period the Government is held to account most directly and on a daily basis. Before you ask a question, be sure it complies with the procedural rules, particularly regarding length. Asking a question is not as easy as it may seem. Some members engage a coach, while others take to it naturally and need little practice. The challenge is to deliver the question, with its partisan political premise, within the time allowed (thirty-five seconds) or risk being cut off by the Speaker. Some members have the question written out in advance.[4] Some can be seen rehearsing their question as they wait for their turn, their lips moving silently as they go over the question again and again to be sure they have it right. Delivery is everything.

Questions must relate to Government business. A question may not be hypothetical, seek an opinion, seek confidential privileged information, relate to a minister's political activities, concern internal party matters or party or election expenses, or be a question from a constituent.[5] Unacceptable language can lead the Speaker to intervene.[6] Sometimes the Speaker will invite a member to rephrase a question. The Speaker may intervene before a question is answered to rule the question out of order, although the responsible minister may be allowed to answer the question.[7] There's a partisan political spin on virtually every question or answer.

In December 2013, a member asked the Speaker for guidance on permissible questions in Question Period, to which the Speaker replied, "the Speaker, as the servant of the House, can enforce only those practices and guidelines the House is willing to have enforced. Very often the particular circumstances of the moment dictate how far the Speaker can go without unduly limiting the freedom of speech of members."[8] The Speaker went on to explain the purpose of Question Period: "The main purpose of question period is undoubtedly the opportunity it provides to the legislative branch to seek information from the executive and to hold the Government to account. This opportunity is particularly important for the opposition parties. We all recognize that the opposition has the right and, indeed the duty, to question the conduct of the Government, and every effort must be made in the enforcement of our rules to safeguard that right. But the Government can only be held to account for matters that fall within its administrative responsibilities."

The Speaker acknowledged that a member might complain when a question is ruled out of order but, explained the Speaker, "I have to look at whether the matter concerns a government department, or a minister who is exercising ministerial functions, as a minister of the Crown, and not just as a political figure or as a member of a political party. The

Speaker must ask whether the question was actually touching upon those types of government responsibilities, or whether it was about elections or party finances or some other subject unrelated to the actual administrative responsibilities of the government." The Speaker expressed concern about a "growing trend" in Question Period where, "we hear preambles to questions that go on at some length to criticize the position, statements, or actions of other parties, members from other parties, and in some cases even private citizens before concluding with a brief question about the Government's policies." The Speaker called these questions "hybrid questions" in which the preamble has nothing to do with the administrative responsibility of the Government but in the final five or ten seconds manages to say something related to the Government's administrative responsibilities.

The quality of the questions and answers in Question Period, said the Speaker, is the responsibility of all members. Members should ask themselves whether Canadians can watch Question Period and conclude that it was a proper use of members' time. "The principle of responsible government is that the Government has to provide an accounting for where the money goes and to provide reasons for why decisions are made. In the [Speaker's] view, it takes a partnership between the opposition and the Government to demonstrate a willingness to elevate the tone, elevate the substance, and make sure that Question Period is being used to do the job that we were elected to do, which is to represent our constituents, advance ideas, and hold the Government to account." It is expected that the responsible minister will rise to respond to a question, although the prime minister can choose which minister will answer a question or even whether a question will be answered – there is no rule requiring that each question be answered. I recall a minister remaining seated, scowling, refusing to answer a question. A long-standing member and a senior member of cabinet, the minister had obviously taken offence at the question. There was a noticeable silence on both sides of the House as members looked on, waiting for the minister to rise. He simply sat there with his arms crossed and a look of contempt on his face. As no one else had risen to answer, the Speaker called for the next question.

An answer may not be meaningful. At times the answer is so unrelated to the question that one wonders whether the minister or parliamentary secretary actually heard it. An egregious example of a non-answer was seen in September 2014, when the leader of the official opposition asked the Government to confirm that its thirty-day commitment in Iraq would end in thirty days.[9] In the absence of the prime minister, his parliamentary secretary rose to respond to the question (though the minister of defence was present in the chamber). The parliamentary secretary said there was a great deal of confusion with respect to the official opposition's position on Israel. *What???* The question had had nothing to do with Israel. The leader of the official opposition asked the Speaker, as "the arbiter of the rules," to intervene. Receiving no response, he posed a follow-up question pertaining to Iraq to which the parliamentary secretary responded with an answer pertaining to Israel. The official opposition leader commented to the Speaker that his failure to intervene did not "speak very favourably about your neutrality in this House." Whereupon the Speaker called upon the leader of the second opposition party to ask a question, denying the leader of the official opposition a further question.[10]

The next day the Speaker responded to the leader of the official opposition's challenge to his neutrality by noting that his powers regarding Question Period were limited by the rules and practices of the House. He cited a statement by his predecessor on 8 October 2010 that a Speaker had no authority over the content of answers given by a minister or parliamentary secretary in Question Period and that it was not the Speaker's role to decide whether or not a response was an answer to the question. "Indeed," said the Speaker, "the Chair has no authority to rule an answer out of order unless the answer contains unparliamentary remarks or a personal attack on some other member."[11]

It is expected, though not required, that the prime minister will answer questions asked by the leader of the official opposition and the leaders of the other recognized parties but not questions asked by backbench members, although he could choose to do so. The leader of the official opposition is the first member to ask a question and then the rotation moves to the leaders of the other recognized parties and then to other members.

Time management is important for Question Period. Longer questions and answers in the earlier part mean less time for questions and answers by other members later. The issue of time came to a head after the 1997 election when the House found itself with five recognized parties.[12] The smaller opposition parties complained to the Speaker that the larger opposition parties and the responding ministers were using up too much time in their questions and answers at the expense of the smaller opposition parties. The time allowed for a question or an answer was reduced to thirty-five seconds.[13] Presumably it was felt that it would be better to get more questions and answers with less time for each than fewer questions and answers but with more time for each. As in other proceedings, it was optics over substance: the opposition parties want more opportunities to be seen challenging the Government and the Government was happy with less time for its answers as more time might require more substantive answers.

Each day, the Speaker is provided with a list of the members in each of the parties who will be asking a question. This practice was meant to assist the Speaker in recognizing members during QP but in the minds of some it has evolved to become a way to enable the party leadership to determine which members shall be allowed to ask a question.[14] (A similar complaint has been made with respect to members' statements, discussed earlier.[15]) In a ruling in 2013, the Speaker affirmed that he has discretion in recognizing members during QP (or any other proceeding) but that his usual practice is to recognize members according to lists provided by the parties.[16] If you are slated to ask a question, you should know from your whip before QP starts where you are on the list.

There is a set rotation for questions in QP that determines the sequence of members asking questions. The opportunities, or "slots," are assigned to each of the opposition parties in proportion to their standing in the House. There are approximately twenty-two slots for questions and answers in the forty-five minutes allowed for QP. Each slot has a lead question and some are allowed a supplemental question, which must relate to the matter raised in the lead question. Usually there are seventeen supplemental questions for a total of thirty-nine questions in each Question Period. Government members get a few questions but only a few as they have access to ministers in their caucus meetings. Questions put by members on the Government side are friendly questions designed to enable the minister to brag about something the Government has done. At the end of QP, independent members are allowed questions proportionate to their number in the House. There may be times when no independent member gets a question.

ADJOURNMENT PROCEEDINGS
("LATE SHOW")

If you are unhappy with an answer you received in QP, you may ask a follow-up question later, during the adjournment proceedings at the end of the day, a thirty-minute proceeding informally referred to as the "Late Show." To appear on the Late Show, you must notify the clerk's table immediately after QP so that a date can be assigned and the responsible minister or parliamentary secretary can attend to respond. Unlike QP, where you are allowed thirty-five seconds, you are allowed up to four minutes to ask a question and the same is allowed for the response. The thirty minutes allowed for the Late Show means that only a few questions can be asked and answered, so there is usually a time delay between the day on which you asked a question in QP and the day on which your follow-up question will be scheduled.

WRITTEN QUESTIONS

Separate and apart from QP, you may submit written questions to the clerk's table or the Journals Office and ask that the Government table a response within forty-five days.[17] If the responsible minister does not reply within this period, the question is automatically referred to a standing committee for study and the committee must convene a meeting within five sitting days to investigate why the minister has not responded to the question; this rarely happens. As the purpose of a written question is to seek and receive a precise, detailed answer, it is expected that each question will be clear enough to elicit the precise information sought.[18] In either a question or an answer, "no argument or opinion is to be offered, nor any facts stated, except as far as may be necessary to explain [the question or answer]." The objective is to "maintain the process of written questions as an exchange of information rather than an opportunity for debate."[19] Written questions have become increasingly lengthy, making a response within forty-five days increasingly difficult.

In 2012, a member complained that the answer she had received did not fully answer her question and did not contain the detailed information she sought. The Speaker pointed out that House rules do not give the Speaker power to review the adequacy of Government answers to written questions.[20] In 2015, a member complained that the answer the Government provided was comprised "almost exclusively" of opinion and debate, contrary to the House rule for written questions, and that the Government had all but ignored the member's question in its answer. The member explained that he was raising the issue "out of concern for the health of our parliamentary process ... and the 'integrity of the written question process' [quoting the Speaker in an earlier ruling], which is an essential tool for us as parliamentarians."[21]

ACCOUNTS OF CANADA (PUBLIC ACCOUNTS)

Each year, the Government tables consolidated financial statements for the previous year in the House. These statements are called the Public Accounts of Canada, and in them the Government includes its expenditures under each appropriation heading, its revenues and all other payments into and out of the Consolidated Revenue Fund (the public purse), and an audit opinion by the auditor general of Canada.[22] The Public Accounts provide "a snapshot of the Government's financial position at the end of the fiscal year – its liabilities, assets, and net debt."[23] After they are tabled in the House, the Public Accounts are referred to the Standing Committee on Public Accounts (PAC),[24] chaired by a member from the official opposition, which is mandated to review the Government's use of public funds.

For example, on 29 October 2014 the Public Accounts for 2013–14 were tabled in the House and PAC met on 6 November. The witnesses appearing before the committee were officials from the Comptroller General's Office (responsible for administering the accounts of Canada), the Auditor General's Office, and the Department of Finance,[25] who provided technical testimony about the financial information in the Public Accounts. Committee members did not ask questions in a partisan political manner (though their questions may have had political implications) because the officials, as public servants, were not expected to defend Government policies but only to explain the accounts. The auditor general (AG) provided an "unmodified and clean audit opinion" with respect to the Public Accounts. This audit opinion is not to be confused with the auditor general's annual performance report to the House (a "value for money" audit, discussed below), which may be critical of the Government's spending, but simply confirms that the Public Accounts of Canada had been managed in accordance with accepted accounting principles for Government accounts.

There is not much political hay to be made from the Government's public accounts but preparing and tabling these accounts is an important exercise as a matter of public record (and an important exercise for the Government's internal purposes). In this case the PAC committee reported to the House eighteen sitting days after the accounts had been tabled in the House. The House did not debate the committee's report or vote concurrence in the report, as the committee's report each year on the Public Accounts of Canada is little more than a parliamentary formality, although, in principle, an important one (again, more for optics than substance).

PERFORMANCE REPORTS

Under the Auditor General Act, the AG is required to report to the House at least once a year, although there may be additional reports.[26] These reports, generally referred to as performance audit reports, "shall call attention to anything that [the AG] considers to be of significance and of a nature that should be brought to the attention of the House of Commons."[27] The AG is required to report any cases where, inter alia, "money has been expended other than for purposes for which it was appropriated by Parliament" or "money has been expended without due regard to economy or efficiency." These reports are automatically referred to the Public Accounts Committee.

In February 2004, the AG tabled a performance report on the Government's sponsorship program in Quebec in the late 1990s, one of the most damaging Performance Reports ever.[28] The AG reported that the Government had "showed little regard for Parliament, the *Financial Administration Act*, contracting rules and regulations, transparency, and value for money" and had broken "just about every rule in the book."[29] PAC held extensive hearings with many witnesses – officials from the responsible government department and individuals from Quebec –and issued several reports. It was a powerful example of Government accountability although it did not result in the Government formally losing the confidence of the House (just of the people of Canada). The Government lost its majority in the 2004 election and lost power altogether in the 2006 election.

In 2006, the AG reported on the administration of the RCMP pension and insurance plans. PAC held fifteen meetings with sixty-one witnesses and reported to the House over a year later with thirty-one recommendations related to a variety of legal and administrative matters pertaining to the RCMP. The Government responded to the committee's report by supporting many of its recommendations.[30] There are numerous other examples where PAC held hearings based on an AG's performance report, sent a report with recommendations for action to the House, and received a response from the Government that committed the responsible government department or agency to taking steps to remedy the problems identified in the reports.[31] The important outcome is that the House obtained written commitments from the Government for improvements in the way it carries out its business. In most cases, there is not a lot of public attention paid to PAC reports arising from the Auditor General's reports but the work is important in setting expectations for Government action and as an exercise in holding the Government to account. At the very least, this process provides some assurance of probity and economy in public spending by departments and agencies of the Government. PAC hearings can be very embarrassing for the Government, certainly in minority parliaments.

COMMITTEE INQUIRIES

A minister is not obliged to appear before a committee and the committee cannot issue a summons against a minister who declines to appear. Most ministers will appear when invited, although there can be "scheduling problems." With the approval of the committee, ministers can send departmental officials in their place. When a departmental official is called, the minister or the deputy minister may appear instead. Government officials are not expected to explain or defend government policies but only to explain departmental administrative practices. If government policy is at issue, the committee calls on the minister (or deputy minister) to appear.

As well as the power to summon officials and individuals, a committee has the power to demand documents, whether from the Government or from a private source.[32] Demand for documents can lead to conflicts between a committee and the Government. Generally, Governments don't like to hand over documents, particularly if they contain information that may have political implications. The Government sometimes invokes cabinet confidentiality or the Privacy Act to explain why it cannot provide documents to a committee. In 2009, for example, PAC demanded that the Public Works Department produce audiotapes that had been made at a departmental conference with industry representatives and produce them "in their unaltered state." The department provided the tapes but with deletions required, they claimed, by the Privacy Act. The committee chair said that privacy concerns were not a legitimate reason to fail to provide the recordings to the committee without deletions. The departmental officials said they had an "absolute obligation" to respect the terms of the Privacy Act and had received legal advice from the Department of Justice saying this. (I noted to myself at the time that the departmental officials had not said that the Department of Justice lawyers had advised them that they need not or should not provide the committee with the information it had requested but only that the information was subject to the non-disclosure provisions of the Privacy Act, which may have been true – I might have agreed had I seen the information. What was likely untrue, however, was the inference that they were refusing to provide the information to the committee because Department of Justice lawyers had told them not to do so.) The committee insisted on receiving the information it had requested, and it was eventually provided, but the committee remained unhappy with the lack of co-operation from the government officials. The chair felt strongly that the committee needed to send a message to government departments about the right of a House committee to receive the information it requests. PAC tabled a report in the House with two recommendations: first, that the Government revise its policies "to reflect the legal right of parliamentary committees to demand the production of documents and records" and, second, that the Department of Justice provide its lawyers "with adequate training in parliamentary law."[33] The Government, in its response to the committee report, said it disagreed with the committee's assertion of unlimited powers to demand the production of documents.[34]

According to the Government, the committee's power to demand documents had to be "balanced and circumscribed by the constitutional principles of responsible government, the separation of powers, parliamentary sovereignty and the rule of law." Perhaps so but, we saw in *Vaid*, it is the House that determines how its privileges are used, not the Government. The Government said it may withhold information in those "limited categories" that have been "traditionally recognized as protected from disclosure by the Crown under the royal prerogative, the common law and statutes of Parliament." It seemed to me that the minister was confusing parliamentary tradition with legal practice and the latter was not relevant. If the minister was relying on traditional parliamentary practice, whether in Canada or in England, it is true that there are categories of information that parliamentary practice has allowed to be protected from disclosure but it was the House that decided whether the information would be protected.

In its response, the Government gave a good summary of the issue:

Based on constitutional principles, claims of parliamentary privilege should not be used to upset the balance of power and responsibilities between the branches of government, to override the will of Parliament or to subvert the established conventions or practices by which the Government is held to account. While it is the Government's view that parliamentary privilege does not include an absolute power to order the production of protected information, it is also the Government's view that these matters are best resolved within the precincts of Parliament, consistent with our parliamentary and political traditions. Despite our difference in opinion on historical parliamentary practice, the Government is confident that all parliamentarians can and should work together to ensure that the parliamentary process functions in the best way possible for the people it serves.[35]

In the meantime, another battle over documents had been heating up between the Government and the Special Committee on the Canadian Mission in Afghanistan. This committee wanted documents pertaining to the transfer of Afghan detainees to Afghan authorities by the Canadian military in Afghanistan. A Canadian diplomat stationed in Afghanistan had testified that the Canadian military had been handing over detainees despite reports that they were being tortured by Afghan authorities – which would be in violation of international law – and that he had reported this to his superiors. Opposition members requested that the Government produce the documents to which the diplomat referred. Government members said they would support the committee receiving the documents if they were "legally available."

To my mind, the Government was trying to use the law as a barrier to disclosure and therefore to accountability, notwithstanding the fact that this Government had campaigned on the issue of government accountability and its first legislative initiative had been the Federal Accountability Act.[36] In Question Period, the prime minister told the House that the Government would make "all legally available information available."[37] The minister of national defence advised the House that documents for disclosure were subject to a "vetting process" by the Department of Justice with respect to national security under the Canada Evidence Act. "This is the job of the Department of Justice," said the minister, "We act upon that advice."[38] Another senior minister referred to "mandatory legal requirements" that were "imposed on those of us in government."[39] At the bureaucratic level, yes, but such requirements did not apply to the Government, that is, the cabinet.

Section 38 of the Canada Evidence Act prohibits unauthorized disclosure in any legal proceeding of "sensitive information" or "potentially injurious" information, as defined in that act.[40] The Government had provided documents to the special committee but with deletions for purposes of section 38. Although the section did not apply to proceedings of a House committee, "the values that inform [section 38]" said the minister, "are consistent with the parliamentary convention that injurious information should not be disclosed in a parliamentary setting." This may be true as a matter of parliamentary practice, but not as a constitutional convention limiting the accountability of the Government to Parliament.

On the last sitting day before the Christmas break, the official opposition moved a motion requiring the Government to produce "forthwith" the documents that the special committee had requested and "in their original and uncensored form."[41] In response to the motion, the minister of justice said that the Government accepted that practice and procedure before parliamentary committees is governed by parliamentary convention. "However," said the minister, "parliamentary privilege does not relieve public servants of their obligation to protect sensitive information that relates to national security, national defence or international relations when appearing before a parliamentary committee."[42] Yes, but the committee was demanding documents from the Government, not its public servants (government officials).

The official opposition had doubts about the Government's bona fides: "[The] Government cannot claim, whether by convention or otherwise, total immunity for whatever it desires. The nub of the question here is that we do not believe the Government is blanking out or redacting documents in the interests of national security. It is doing so in the interest of covering its own butt. I think that is very important to remember." [43] The House approved (by a narrow margin) the motion for production of the documents and made it an order of the House before the House adjourned for the Christmas break.[44] No doubt this would not have happened had the Government had a majority in the House.

When the House met next, after the Christmas adjournment, the prime minister reiterated the Government's position about legal restrictions on what the Government could release to the special committee.[45] "The decision of redacting or not redacting documents rests with government lawyers who do that according to law," said the prime minister. "Rules for the publication of documents have been established by law ... government lawyers are the ones who make these types of decisions."[46] In the meantime, the Government was not complying with the House's order of 10 December 2009.

In my view, there was no basis in law for the "legally available" argument as a reason for not providing documents to the special committee. Information in the possession of the Government, excluding personal information that is protected by the Privacy Act, belongs to the Government and it can do with such information whatever it considers appropriate. The Canada Evidence Act prohibitions against disclosure apply to government officials or anyone in possession of information to which the act's prohibitions apply but not to the Government itself. Indeed, the act gives the attorney general the power to allow sensitive information to be disclosed in court proceedings where he thinks this is appropriate.[47]

A few weeks later, an opposition member rose in the House to say that the Government had breached the privileges of the House in failing to comply with the House's order of 10 December 2009.[48] The member relied on a statement made in Question Period by the minister of national defence and a letter from a senior Department of Justice lawyer (addressed to me as the House's lawyer) explaining the legal basis for the Government's refusal to provide the documents. The minister had said that there was a "mandatory obligation" on public officials to see that disclosures, presumably including disclosures to parliamentary committees, were made in accordance with the Canada Evidence Act. The member said the minister's words intimidated House and committee witnesses and thereby obstructed them, particularly public servants, from complying with House requests and orders, which constituted a breach of parliamentary privilege.

The letter from the Department of Justice lawyer acknowledged that a statute (such as the Canada Evidence Act) may not apply to the House or its committees, but "[this] does not mean automatically that government officials – who are agents of the executive, not the legislative branch – are absolved from respecting duties imposed by a statute enacted by Parliament, or by requirements of the common law, such as solicitor-client privilege or Crown privilege."[49] The letter went on to say that legal obligations on government officials are not set aside by any immunity that might be given to the official's testimony before the committee. "A parliamentary committee," wrote the lawyer, "cannot waive a legal duty imposed on government officials."[50] Notably, the lawyer's letter did not address the issue of parliamentary privilege, the elephant-in-the-room issue in the dispute between the Government and the special committee. The member argued that the letter "breaches the privileges of the House by, in effect, laying for witnesses a false basis for refusing to provide disclosure to the House or its committees after being ordered to do so."[51]

In his response, the minister of justice did not rely on the "legally available" argument that had been used earlier by Government members on the special committee, the prime minister, and two ministers.[52] In a lengthy presentation in the House, the minister said that questions of privilege must be considered in light of "two guiding values" – necessity and restraint – but he did not elaborate on how these values were to be applied in the case before the House.[53] The Government's right to withhold documents from the House, said the minister, was based on Crown or executive privilege (often referred to as public interest immunity) but he didn't elaborate on how this privilege applied. "The proper attitude of government officials," said the minister, "cannot be that they are instantly relieved of their legal duties when they are called to appear before a parliamentary committee."

In my reply to the Department of Justice lawyer, I had suggested that saying government officials were not "absolved" of their legal duties implied that there could be reprisals. "I state unequivocally," said the minister, "that it is not, and has never been even remotely, the intention of the Department of Justice or any of its officials to pressure or intimidate government witnesses before parliamentary committees. As I have noted, my department has great respect for the work of parliamentary committees and for the role of this House." If this is true, what had the Department of Justice lawyer meant when she wrote that government officials appearing before a House committee are not "absolved" of their legal duties?

The minister said that it was "well understood that all witnesses who testify before parliamentary committees are immune from legal and disciplinary proceedings in respect of their testimony" and that it was "the long-standing policy of the Government that officials should be as transparent and forthcoming as possible before parliamentary committees."[54] In a seeming contradiction of what he had said about officials being transparent, the minister added that relieving government officials of their legal duties (to not disclose sensitive government information) when testifying before parliamentary committees "would undermine the constitutional principles of parliamentary sovereignty and the rule of law, and would make parliamentary committees a law unto themselves." I couldn't grasp the connection between parliamentary sovereignty and testifying before parliamentary committees, although I recognized the reference to the rule of law as I had heard it used many times against committees.

The minister cited a British parliamentary committee report that said refusing, without reasonable excuse, to provide information or produce papers could be considered contempt and drew the House's attention to the expression "without reasonable excuse." Given the Government's rights under Crown privilege to protect the public interest, said the minister, the Government had a reasonable excuse in this matter:

> the Government of Canada is meeting its constitutional and legal obligations to the House and to the people of Canada in a reasonable and responsible manner. Complying with the bare terms of order would seriously put at risk our relations with other countries and our activities on the ground in Afghanistan.
>
> As a responsible Government, we cannot put these matters at risk. However, we have given parliamentarians as much of the information that they have requested as is consistent with our duties as a responsible Government.[55]

Finding a breach of privilege in this case, said the minister, would be an "an unprecedented extension of the House's privileges." The minister urged members "not to abuse the powers accorded to the House in the name of parliamentary privilege."

The Speaker was required to deliver a ruling on whether the Government's refusal to produce the documents constituted a prima facie breach of the privileges of the House. "As Speaker, one of my principal duties is to safeguard the rights and privileges of Members and of the House. In doing so, the Chair is always mindful of the established precedents, usages, traditions and practices of the House and of the role of the Chair in their ongoing evolution. It is no exaggeration to say that it is a rare event for the Speaker to be seized of a matter as complex and as heavy with consequence as the matter before us now."[56] The Speaker acknowledged that the dispute raised issues that question "the very foundations upon which our parliamentary system is built," adding that "in a system of responsible government, the fundamental right of the House of Commons to hold the Government to

account for its actions is an indisputable privilege and in fact an obligation."[57] The Speaker noted the minister's citation of a respected parliamentary text that allowed that the Government may "feel constrained to refuse certain papers on the ground that their production
would be ... injurious to the public interest."[58] However, he said, the
text went on to say that it was for the House to consider whether the
reasons given for refusing the information are sufficient: "The right of
Parliament to obtain every possible information on public questions
is undoubted, and the circumstances must be exceptional, and the reasons very cogent, when it cannot be at once laid before the houses."

With regard to the minister's contention that the House order
demanding production of the documents was an unlawful extension
of the House's privileges, the Speaker said this could only be true if
one agreed that the House's power to order the production of documents is not absolute. The question would then be whether this sub-
jugated the legislature to the executive: "accepting an unconditional
authority of the executive to censor the information provided to Parliament would in fact jeopardize the very separation of powers that
is purported to lie at the heart of our parliamentary system and the
independence of its constituent parts. Furthermore, it risks diminish-
ing the inherent privileges of the House and its members, which have
been earned and must be safeguarded."[59] The Speaker affirmed that
the procedural authorities were "categorical" in asserting the powers
of the House in ordering the production of documents by the Government. "No exceptions are made for any category of government
documents," he said, "even those related to national security."

The Speaker noted that the Government had explained to the
House that it could not produce the documents as this would cause
disclosure of sensitive information related to national security. However, in adopting the motion ordering production of the documents,
the House had decided that the Government's explanation was not
sufficient. This raised the issue of accommodation and trust. What to
do? "Is it possible," the Speaker asked, "to put in place a mechanism by
which these documents could be made available to the House without compromising the security and confidentiality of the information
they contain? In other words, is it possible for the two sides, working
together in the best interests of the Canadians they serve, to devise a

means where both their concerns are met? Surely that is not too much to hope for."[60]

With respect to trust and accommodation, the Speaker added a few observations: "There have been assertions that colleagues in the House are not sufficiently trustworthy to be given confidential information, even with appropriate security safeguards in place. I find such comments troubling. The insinuation that Members of Parliament cannot be trusted with the very information that they may well require to act on behalf of Canadians runs contrary to the inherent trust that Canadians have placed in their elected officials and which Members require to act in their various parliamentary capacities."[61] He went on to say that the House and the Government had an "unbroken record of some 140 years of collaboration and accommodation in cases of this kind." The House understood the Government's role as "defender of the realm" and the Government understood the House's role as the "grand inquest of the nation." In view of the "grave circumstances of the current impasse," the Speaker urged the House to make one further effort to arrive at "an interest-based solution to this thorny question."

The Speaker found that the Government's failure to comply with the House's order for the production of documents constituted prima facie a breach of privilege but, rather than have the question of privilege referred to a committee in the usual manner, he allowed the parties two weeks to find some way of resolving the impasse. "We would fail the institution [the House]," he said, "if no resolution can be found." Soon after, the Government and two of the three opposition parties agreed on a screening process by which documents would be provided to the special committee.[62]

What we saw in this dispute over documents was a conflict between the House's constitutional function of holding the Government to account and the Government's duty as the "defender of the realm," that is, the guardian of national security and foreign relations. We saw the constitutional separation of powers of our parliamentary system of government as it is rarely seen: prerogative powers against parliamentary powers.[63] It seemed to me that the appropriate response for the Government was simply to refuse to produce the documents, to "Just say No" (to borrow a slogan from another context) and leave the opposition parties to decide what they would do next. However, this was politically risky and if Government polls were showing weak public support for the Government, it would not want to bring on an election. The same applied to opposition party polls. I suspect, though I will never know, that neither side wanted an election at that time as neither was sure they could win. Hence, the parties came to a compromise agreement *"en arrière du rideau"* for selective disclosure through a committee of impartial jurists without a lengthy battle between the parties.[64]

A few months later, the Finance Committee made demands for information relating, inter alia, to the costs of purchasing F-35 military jets and the projected costs of some of the Government's justice bills.[65] The Government said it was "not in a position" to provide the information sought by the committee because such information was subject to cabinet confidences.[66] The Finance Committee reported to the House that the Government had refused to produce the information it sought and claimed that the refusal constituted a breach of the privileges of the House, the same approach taken earlier with the special committee's demand for Afghan detainee documents.[67] However, before the Speaker ruled on this point of privilege, the official opposition moved a motion ordering the Government to produce the documents sought by the Finance Committee by a specified date. As the opposition parties were in the majority, the motion was adopted and became an order of the House.

The Government provided some of the information requested by the Finance Committee and explained that in doing so it had preserved "the confidentiality required around documents which are classified as cabinet confidences" and had only disclosed information that was not within cabinet confidentiality. The official opposition claimed that the Government had failed to provide a "reasonable explanation" as to why some documents were not being provided or provided without redactions: cabinet confidentiality was not accepted as a reasonable explanation.

In his ruling, the Speaker reiterated what he had said on the production of Afghan detainee documents where he had affirmed the House's right to demand documents or information from the Government. Of greater concern to the Speaker was the lack of any explanation by the Government. "Only [after explanation]," he said, "can the House determine whether the reasons given are sufficient or satisfactory."[68] The Speaker noted that the Government had initially refused to produce documents and then afterwards relented and produced some but not others without explaining why cabinet confidentiality had been waived for some documents but not for others. There was no doubt that an order of the House was not being complied with and this was "a serious matter that goes to the heart of the House's undoubted role in holding the Government to account." The Speaker found a prima facie breach of privilege and the matter was referred in the usual manner to the Standing Committee on Procedure and House Affairs (PROC) for closer consideration and recommendations. I was called before the committee to advise.

The opposition members on the committee were considering recommending to the House that it find the Government in contempt of parliament. One of the members stressed that such a finding had never happened in any other country with a parliamentary system of government. I agreed but then asked why the House would hold the Government in contempt rather than voting non-confidence. It seemed to me that citing the Government for contempt rather than voting non-confidence was like firing rubber bullets: lots of noise, perhaps, but only minor injuries. I recognized that contempt was being used as a strategic alternative to a non-confidence motion but it was not my place to comment on political strategies but rather to speak to traditional parliamentary practice. "In previous Parliaments," said a Government member, "it has been traditional ... to have respect for Cabinet confidences particularly in matters of national security ... What can we do to get back that ... balance between Cabinet confidence and respecting Parliament?" I ventured that balance is obtained through trust and confidence: I had in mind the Speaker's reference to the need for "accommodation and trust" between the House and the Government in his ruling on the Afghan detainee documents.

On Monday, 21 March 2011, PROC (which had an opposition majority) reported to the House that the Government had not provided a reasonable excuse for not providing the information sought by the Finance Committee (and by the House) and was therefore in contempt.[69] It looked like the opposition parties were intent on a showdown. On Wednesday, 23 March 2011, following the morning caucus meetings, the official opposition moved concurrence in the committee's report. On Friday, 25 March 2011, before the concurrence motion had been put to a vote, the official opposition moved a motion of non-confidence in the Government. The motion carried and the next day, Saturday, 26 March 2011, Parliament was dissolved.[70] It would appear that the parties felt they were ready for an election. An election was held on 2 May 2011. The Government, after five years as a minority Government, won a majority. The days of minority Governments were over.

SENSITIVE TESTIMONY

A committee may recognize that some testimony should not be heard in a public meeting. The testimony may have national security implications, as the Government claimed in the controversy over providing documents to the Special Committee on the Canadian Mission in Afghanistan discussed above. There may also be privacy considerations under the Privacy Act. There might be concerns that the testimony will touch on a matter that is currently before the courts, or concern that testimony could be used against the witness, directly or indirectly, though it would be unlawful to do this. What are the options?

The committee could meet in camera, that is, behind closed doors, although committees generally are reluctant to do this as it is an important feature of committee proceedings that they take place in public so Canadians can see what is going on. What is said at in camera meetings is confidential and committee members must not publicly disclose what was said in the meeting. Enforcement of in camera committee confidentiality can be difficult, however, for several reasons. First, there is the relatively large number of people who will share the confidential information. Committee meetings in camera often include, in addition to the members, members' political staff as well as parliamentary support staff, perhaps as many as twenty to twenty-five people in all. Experts will tell you that the larger the number of people who share confidential information, the greater the likelihood that the confidentiality will not hold. Second, responsibility for a breach of confidentiality – a "leak" – is difficult to establish.

Finally, there is partisan rivalry: sometimes information is simply too hot to keep secret.

With respect to sensitive documents, the committee could number the documents provided to the committee and retrieve the documents at the end of the meeting to be kept in safe custody by the clerk of the committee. For some, this approach makes the offensive suggestion that committee members – who are all "honourable members" – cannot be trusted with sensitive documents. Another approach might be to form a small, all-party subcommittee to privately negotiate the terms of disclosure of a sensitive document, including an agreement on redacting parts of the document.[71] The Government's proposal for a "panel of jurists" to screen sensitive documents in respect of Afghanistan detainees was an attempt at finding such a disclosure process.

For some years, there have been attempts by some members to have the House involved in national security and intelligence matters. I found these suggestions troubling. It seemed to me that membership on such a committee would compromise parliamentary function as a member's duties in the House would conflict with duties on the committee: committee members would be obliged not to disclose information acquired through the committee but this information might have political implications. Would a member's participation in debates in the House then be constrained by membership on this committee? Or would membership on this committee give greater weight to whatever the member said in the House that touched on national security and intelligence? A member's first and only loyalty, it seemed to me, should be to the House.

Moreover, what would be the function of the committee? Oversight? If so, what could it do if it found something unacceptable? Would it have powers governing Government action? Or would it be little more than a focus group? In the United States, members of the Senate and House of Representatives Intelligence Committees receive classified intelligence information although they are not to disclose it to third parties, including members of Congress and Senators not on the intelligence committees. According to the US Senate Intelligence Committee website, the president is required to ensure that the Intelligence Committee is kept "fully and currently informed" of intelli-

gence activities, meaning that intelligence agencies are required to
notify the committee of their activities and analysis. This includes
keeping the committee informed of covert actions and any significant
intelligence failure. This idea has taken hold in Canada. In 2017, the
House approved a government bill establishing a committee of parliamentarians on national security and intelligence.[72] The committee,
which will not be a committee of either the House or the Senate or
both, will have not more than eleven members comprised of not
more than three senators and not more than eight House members of
whom not more than five may be members of the Government party.
Ministers and parliamentary secretaries cannot sit on the committee.
The committee members must have the "necessary security clearance"
from the Government, which means that members who do not have
this clearance will have to allow the Government to investigate their
lives and members joining the committee must take an oath not to
"communicate or use without due authority any information
obtained in confidence."[73] Parliamentary privilege does not apply,
and, overriding the protection given to committee testimony by parliamentary privilege, testimony before a House or Senate committee
(or statements made in the course of a committee proceeding, presumably) may be used to show that the member wrongfully disclosed
confidential information.[74] What might this mean for the parliamentary independence of the members?

The mandate of this statutory committee will be to review "the legislative, regulatory, policy, administrative and financial framework for
national security and intelligence." This looks like a mere oversight
function, that is, oversight without teeth. The committee will be
mandated to review any activity relating to national security or intelligence carried out by a government department UNLESS a minister
says such review would be "injurious to national security."[75] What
does this mean? If the Government tires of the committee or begins
to distrust its members, can it exclude the committee from some if
not all national security and intelligence matters? The committee
may seek information from government departments but the information may be denied if the responsible minister is of the view that
giving the information to the committee would be "injurious to
national security."[76]

How does the mandate of this committee comport with the House's constitutional functions? Presumably, it is seen as part of the House's oversight or accountability function, although it is not a House committee and the information obtained cannot be used outside the committee. Why are the members there – other than to offer their personal views privately – if they cannot take parliamentary action when they feel, based on the information provided to them, that the public interest is not being well served by the Government or its agencies?

MOTIONS FOR THE PRODUCTION OF PAPERS

Members can request that the Government table documents identified or described in the request[77] by putting a Motion for the Production of Papers on the Notice Paper. This piece of business occurs only on Wednesdays, immediately after Routine Proceedings and Questions on the Order Paper. It is rare that anything happens under this rubric.[78] Usually the Government agrees to the motion, it becomes an order of the House, and the documents are provided to the member. If the Government agrees with the motion but with reservations and the House accepts the reservations, the motion becomes an order of the House with the reservations included. If the Government does not accept the motion, the member is asked to withdraw the motion. If the motion is not withdrawn, a request is made that it be transferred to the Order Paper for debate under Private Members' Business. If no request for transfer is made, the motion is put to a vote immediately without debate. I don't believe any of this ever happened in my years at the House, but in theory it could, though the requesting member's motion would undoubtedly be defeated as the member, acting alone, would not get a majority of members supporting the motion.

The rules of the House do not impose a time limit by which the documents must be produced. In 1973, the Government tabled a paper setting out the general principles governing this process. Although not formally adopted by the House, these principles established the practice that has applied ever since.[79] The paper described this process as enabling members "to secure factual information about the operations of Government to carry out their parliamentary duties and to make public as much factual information as possible consistent with effective administration, the protection of the security of the state, rights to privacy and other such matters." The paper went on to list sixteen categories of documents or information that the Government will not produce, such as, inter alia, legal opinions, information adversely affecting conduct of foreign relations, information that might allow or result in direct personal financial gain or loss, or information reflecting the personal competence or character of an individual. These restrictions apply only to requests for documents by individual members and not to demands for documents made by the House.

ACCOUNTABILITY
– A CONSTITUTIONAL RELATIONSHIP

The House, like an investor who provides funding to a start-up company, funds the Government and the Government does the spending. The investor does not run the company but expects an accounting and the principals of the company want to maintain the confidence of their investor. So it is in this case: the Government must explain its policies and practices well enough that it maintains the confidence of the House. The House may withdraw its confidence at any time for any reason.

How much accountability should we expect to see between the Government and the House? This is a political question and will be answered differently according to how important the issue is that gives rise to the question. It cannot be answered in the abstract: some issues require more accountability than others. Unfortunately, in a majority parliament, the Government, through party discipline, can prevent anything other than routine accountability. The minority parliaments from 2004 to 2011 saw more robust accountability because the Government was not able to prevent it. After the elections of 2011 and 2015 produced majority parliaments, all has been quiet on the parliamentary accountability front outside of QP.

Last but not least, we must go backstage to look at House Administration, which holds the institution together at the operational level.

6

Backstage

You can't really understand the House without looking at House Administration, the backstage crew of professional staff that support you in your parliamentary functions and provide permanence to the House as an institution, ready to receive new members after each election.

Legally, the House does not exist – it is not a corporate body – but it has an administrative organization as if it were one, except that management works for the shareholders rather than the corporation. The shareholders – the members – run the business of this corporation. The board of directors is the Board of Internal Economy, which is comprised of members representing the recognized parties. The CEO is the clerk of the House, who also serves as secretary to the board.

Those who work in House Administration are public servants, much like the many thousands who work in the federal public service, but they are not employees of the federal government. They have no partisan political interests or if they do, do not allow them to affect their work. They are hired for their professional skills without reference to any political association, past or present, and work for the House in its role as a public institution, serving without regard to members' politics.

The House is a two-tiered organization, much like the English upper-class households of the Victorian and Edwardian eras that you might have seen in *Upstairs Downstairs*, the popular British TV program of the 1970s, or, more recently, *Downton Abbey*, where the servants work downstairs for the family living upstairs. The servants may have much to say downstairs about the goings-on upstairs but say little or nothing when their duties take them upstairs. They do not speak unless spoken to and go back downstairs when their tasks are done. The family upstairs is loyal to its servants because they know they depend on them and the servants are loyal to the family because that is the professional commitment they make when they sign on; it's fundamental to the workplace culture. Upstairs takes no interest in the staff working downstairs (except when it serves their political interests to do so, as I experienced). Downstairs doesn't expect to be noticed but is part of the furniture, like the people who come on stage between acts to move the props around for the next act, dressed in black to indicate that you are not supposed to see them.

In my early days at the House, a veteran procedural clerk, after recounting the many good times he had had when travelling with members on committee trips outside Ottawa or overseas, cautioned me: "Remember, they are not your friends." I found this ominous and it turned out to be both true and untrue, depending on circumstances. Generally, I found members usually very courteous and professional in their interactions with me or the lawyers in my office. The bad actors gained little by their antics, although they had to be answered in a manner that was both professional and dispassionate – and this was particularly difficult in the late 1990s when members rose in the House to criticize the work my office did in providing legislative counsel services (discussed below).

ANNUAL ESTIMATES

Each year, House Finance Services prepares an estimate of the money Parliament will need to meet the expenses of the House and members in the coming fiscal year. The clerk of the House presents the estimate to the Board of Internal Economy (discussed below) for approval and then the Speaker sends it to the Treasury Board to be tabled in the House with the estimates from the Government.[1] The important feature here is that House estimates are not subject to approval by the Treasury Board, unlike the estimates of government departments and agencies. The constitutional independence of the House means it must be self-regulating, that is, its administration and budget estimates are not subject to review or approval by the Government.

For 2016–17 House expenditures were estimated at $463.6 million (and those of the Senate at $90.1 million).[2] In 2015–16, the House had a budget of $443.4 million but spent only $424.3 million, saving $17,610,000, mostly because in 2015 the House did not return in September as it usually does after the summer break because Parliament had been dissolved in August for the election in October. The House did not meet again until 3 December 2015. (Of course, for the taxpayer, the savings for the House were more than offset by the cost of the election: $443 million, up 53% from 2011.) Approximately 63% of House funds is spent on upstairs operations – members, House officers, caucuses, committees, parliamentary associations and parliamentary exchanges.[3] The remaining 37% ($170 million in 2015–16) is spent on operations downstairs – House Administration (38% for Information Services, 17% for Procedural Services, 15% for Parliamentary Precinct Services, 10% for Finance Services and 2% for the Law Clerk's Office). Around a third of this 37%, or 12% of the House budget, is for Administration salaries and benefits.[4]

BOARD OF INTERNAL ECONOMY

The Board of Internal Economy is the House's governing body on administrative and financial matters.[5] Under the Parliament of Canada Act, the Board is given the "capacity of a natural person" with "exclusive authority" over the use of House resources[6] and the ability to adopt by-laws that regulate the internal administrative and financial business of the House.[7] There are six board members, three from the Government side (two of whom must be ministers) and three from the opposition side of the House, with the Speaker sitting as the chair.[8] A quorum of five board members, including the Speaker, is required for the board to conduct its business, which means that at least one member from the opposition side must be present even if all Government representatives are present.[9] The board sets the budgets for the offices of the Speaker, deputy speaker, and the other chair occupants, for recognized party leaders (in opposition only), House leaders (opposition parties only), whips, and caucuses (pro-rated according to their numbers in the House).[10] Members are each given a budget for their offices.[11]

The board meets behind closed doors and designates a Government board member and an official opposition board member to act as its public spokespersons.[12] It is frequently criticized for this on the grounds that, as a public body that spends public funds, it should conduct its business in open sessions. The Parliament of Canada Act requires board members to take an oath or affirmation of "fidelity and secrecy" (limited to matters of security, employment and staff relations, tenders, and investigations in relation to a member) with respect to board business but the act does not require the board to conduct its meetings in closed sessions: the oath of secrecy is not binding on the board as a whole. In 2013, the House directed the Standing Committee on Procedure and House Affairs to review the practices of the board but no changes were made before Parliament was dissolved for the 2015 election.[13] In 2017, the Parliament of Canada Act was amended to provide for open board meetings, while allowing the board to meet secretly whenever it chooses to do so provided the members are unanimous that it should do so.[14]

Many might assume that the board, as a parliamentary body, is protected by parliamentary privilege. I don't believe this is the case, though it is an open legal question. If the board were a committee of the House (like its counterpart in the Senate), it would certainly be protected by parliamentary privilege. However, it is a statutory body and as such, in my view, it is subject to the same legal rules as other statutory boards or commissions. Legally, as an administrative body, it operates separate and apart from the House. While parliamentary privilege may apply to some matters considered by the board under the House's privilege of exclusive control over its internal affairs, there would not be, in my view, a blanket application of parliamentary privilege to board meetings. We saw from *Vaid* (chapter 3) that privilege applies only where the activity for which privilege is claimed is "so closely and directly connected" with the functions of the House "that outside interference would undermine the level of autonomy required to enable [the House] and its members to do their work with dignity and efficiency."[15] In my view, the financial and administrative affairs of the House are not "so closely and directly connected" to legislating, deliberating, and holding the Government to account that they fall within the ambit of parliamentary privilege.[16]

Perhaps recognizing the board's lack of protection under the law of parliamentary privilege, in 2017 the House, at the instigation of the Government, amended the Parliament of Canada Act to make proceedings of the board "proceedings in Parliament," indirectly enabling board meetings to be protected by the law of parliamentary privilege – or so one might assume since parliamentary privilege applies to all parliamentary (House) proceedings.[17] However, I'm not sure the amendment would survive a challenge under the legal test of necessity provided in *Vaid*, that is, whether the scope of the House's recognized privilege of control of its internal affairs necessarily includes House financial and administrative matters that are under the control of the board. In *Vaid*, the House argued unsuccessfully that its privileged control of its internal affairs covered all its employees. I would expect that a claim that privilege applied to all the financial and administrative business of the House would get the same result: not all such business has the protection of parliamentary privilege.

Board By-laws

The board's rules are set out in four bylaws: Members Bylaw, Committees Bylaw, Governance and Administration Bylaw, and Rules of Practice and Procedure of the Board of Internal Economy. The Committees Bylaw provides for the funding of committees and the administration of goods and services provided to committees. Under this bylaw the Administration publishes the "Financial Management and Policy Guide for Committees." The Governance and Administration Bylaw vests responsibility for management of the House's administrative affairs in the Administration, under the direction of the clerk of the House. The Rules of Practice and Procedure of the Board of Internal Economy sets out how board meetings may be called and how members or the Administration can request direction from the board. You might want to read the Members Bylaw as it regulates the use of House resources by members, particularly the funds provided to support you in carrying out your parliamentary functions.

The fundamental principle is that House resources may be used only for a member's "parliamentary function," defined in the bylaw as: "the duties and activities that relate to the position of member, wherever performed and whether or not performed in a partisan manner, namely, participation in activities relating to the proceedings and work of the House of Commons and activities undertaken in representing his or her constituency or constituents."[18] A member's parliamentary functions are not necessarily those covered by parliamentary privilege. Some functions are covered (e.g., debates) and some are not (e.g., hiring staff). It can sometimes be difficult to determine whether a particular use falls within "parliamentary function."

Under the board's bylaws, members, House officers, and party caucuses are responsible for their use of House resources and for administration of their respective offices and staff. Each member, not the board, is understood to be the employer of his or her staff. It is the member who sets the terms of their employment and, where necessary, terminates the employment. House Administration administers but does not enforce the bylaws except when directed to do so by the board. Funds wrongly used may be recovered by withholding funds from "any budget, allowance or other payment" payable to the member.[19]

The media often says that House resources may not be used for partisan purposes. This is not true. House resources may be used for partisan purposes provided that the partisan purpose falls within a member's parliamentary functions.[20] Given that members are elected and belong to a political party, partisan activity is fundamental to their work as members. Partisan activity for the direct benefit of the member's political party, such as fund raising, soliciting memberships, or a political campaign (including party leadership contests), is considered outside a member's parliamentary functions and House resources may not be used.[21]

HOUSE ADMINISTRATION

House Administration is divided into seven operational support sectors under the direction of the clerk of the House:

• Procedural Services provides procedural support services to the House, committees, and members, and is headed by the deputy clerk.

- Parliamentary Precinct Operations provides operational support for members and the House Administration in such areas as trades, tenant operations, room allocations, catering and restaurants, postal and messenger services, transportation, printing and mailing, and maintenance and material handling. It is headed by the director-general, Parliamentary Precinct Operations.
- Law clerk and Parliamentary Counsel Office provides legislative counsel services to House committees and private members and legal counsel services to the Speaker, the board, the House Administration, and private members.
- Information Services plans, implements and maintains information technology, information management services, technology and accommodation planning related to facility renovations and is headed by the chief information officer.
- Finance Services provides advisory and operational support in the areas of policy and financial planning, financial management, and materiel and contract management to the House Administration, members and their staff and is headed by the chief financial officer.
- Human Resources Services provides support in the areas of talent management, employee relations, pay and benefits, occupational health and safety, and organizational effectiveness and is headed by the chief human resources officer.
- Corporate Security Office is responsible for security in the House of Commons Chamber, conducting investigations, coordinating visitor and event access, providing security accreditation, promoting security awareness and administering parking services and is headed by the deputy sergeant-at-arms and corporate security officer.

Clerk of the House

The clerk of the House is the chief administrative officer of the House, the equivalent of a deputy minister if the House were a government department, as well as the Speaker's chief procedural adviser. The clerk's official title is "Clerk of the House of Commons," which means that the clerk is not, strictly speaking, the Speaker's clerk.

Under the Standing Orders, the clerk is responsible "for the safekeeping of all the papers and records of the House" and "has the direction and control over all the officers and clerks" employed by the House.[22] The clerk serves the board not as the clerk of the House but as secretary to the board.[23] In this capacity, the clerk oversees the financial and administrative business of the House on behalf of the board.[24] The Clerk's Office includes three operational units: Corporate Communications, Preparedness and Planning, and Internal Audit.

Procedural Services

Procedural Services, headed by the deputy clerk, provides procedural and operational support to the House and its committees and to parliamentary associations. Procedural clerks are experts in parliamentary procedure and practice: they develop their expertise on the job because it cannot be learned anywhere else. Clerks are assigned to any of four operational divisions within the sector: Table Research, which supports the table officers in the House on emerging procedural issues and keeps track of procedural precedents; the Committees Branch, which provides procedural clerks and administrative support for each of the House standing committees; the Journals Branch, whose clerks provide support for House proceedings in the chamber and keep records of those proceedings; and Inter-parliamentary Associations and Protocol, whose clerks support the activities of members participating in inter-parliamentary activities in Canada and abroad.

Before the start of each sitting day, the table officers, including the clerk and me in my role as law clerk, met in the basement of the Centre Block to go over what was planned for the day in the House and in committees – an intelligence briefing, as it were.[25] The meeting began with a Journals Branch clerk reporting on the items expected to be called that day in the House and whether the Speaker would be delivering any rulings. Next, a clerk from the Committees Branch reported on the agendas of the committees meeting that day. Then the clerks at the table on the previous day reported on procedural issues that had arisen in the House and whether these might have ongoing implications. Finally, the meeting looked at jokes and rumours about House business, committees, and members – mostly rumours – which could be quite funny and often provided some comic relief. Sometimes a "heads up" is given the clerks scheduled to be at the table that day that a member might be seeking advice on a procedural issue (table officers should be "on the same page" on procedural issues so it was important to have these questions settled in advance) or that a member or group of members was unhappy about something in the House or in committee and might rise on a point of order or a point of privilege and make a fuss. The objective was to be prepared for, and not be surprised by, anything that came up in the course of the day. The information exchanged was treated as confidential and did not leave the room. Immediately after this meeting, the clerk, the deputy clerk, and the table officer overseeing the table for the day briefed the Speaker on the business expected to be called in the House that day. In my earlier years at the House, when I was trying to learn as much as I could about House proceedings and the procedural rules, I found these morning meetings very helpful – at times there were some great procedural debates between the clerks.

Parliamentary Precinct Operations

Parliamentary Precinct Operations is responsible for seeing that members are installed in their offices and for supplying the requisite office furnishings and equipment, which can be quite challenging after an election, depending on how much time there is between the election date and the opening of the new Parliament. If there is a change of Government, more offices see a change in occupant than if the governing party stays in power. In 2011, for example, there was only a month between the 2 May election, in which there had been significant changes in party standings, and the opening of the next Parliament on 2 June. The governing party went from a minority to a majority in the House, the official opposition became the second opposition party, the second opposition party lost so many members that it lost its status as a recognized political party, and the third opposition party became the official opposition, all of which led to many changes in who occupied which office. By tradition, perhaps to be consistent with the election outcome, choice of office is based on how well the party did in the election. The governing party has first choice of offices, followed by the official opposition, then by the other opposition parties, and finally the independent members, if any, which means changes in party rankings can significantly affect office distribution. Some members will be quite pleased to find themselves moved to a larger office, possibly in a better location such as Centre Block, while others will not be pleased with a smaller office and likely not in Centre Block. As a new member, your office is probably in either the Confederation or Justice Building, if not across Wellington Street in the Wellington Building.

Precinct Operations is also responsible for the little green buses seen around Parliament Hill, a shuttle bus service that transports members between the Centre Block and the other parliamentary buildings. You'll probably want to use these buses for the back and forth between your office and the chamber in Centre Block or for committee meetings wherever they are held.

Law Clerk and Parliamentary Counsel

The Law Clerk's Office has two parts – legislative and legal – with four or five lawyers in each part. On the legislative side (the "law clerk" side of the office), the lawyers draft private member's bills and amendments to government bills. In addition, staff editors review draft legislative text, translators put the text into the second official language, and high-tech text treatment operators put the text into the required format (bilingual, dual column), ready for printing and posting on the parliamentary website.

Each legislative year, from September to June, the work was steady until the "crazy times" in the last three weeks before the six-week Christmas break and the last six weeks before the eleven-week summer break. In these weeks, private members would press us for their bills in order to get them into the House and then published and posted ahead of the long summer break, presumably so they could show their constituents how productive they had been in Ottawa.

Also in the weeks leading up to the summer break, there would also be increased demand for amendments to government bills as the Government was pushing its bills through before the summer break. The Standing Orders provide for late sitting hours on Government Business during the last two weeks before the scheduled summer break in late June.

On the legal side (the "parliamentary counsel" side of the office), legal counsel advise administration officials on issues within their respective domains. A significant part of our legal counsel work related to members' problems as employers. Too often, the member would terminate an employee before seeking legal advice, which created legal problems. In some cases, there was concern that the employee might take the member to court and make the political business of the member public. Invariably, the parties came to an agreed settlement without going to court, although the employee usually needed to hire a lawyer from off the Hill.

There have been fourteen law clerks since Confederation and some of them made a mark in ways they might not have chosen. Difficulties with my two predecessors had resulted in the position being vacant for nine years until my appointment. The first law clerk, G.W. Wicksteed, had been the assistant law clerk for the Parliament of the Province of Canada (1840–67) before becoming, in 1867, law clerk for the House in the Parliament of the new Canada. He reported to the Speaker, not the clerk. This reporting relationship continued until around 1980 when, for administrative purposes, the law clerk began reporting to the clerk. Wicksteed was a man of letters, his chief literary production being a book of *vers de société*, *Waifs in Verse* (1878). In an "apology" added to *Waifs in Verse*, he wrote about his parliamentary career: "Before this year is out, I shall have been fifty years in my office of law clerk and translator, and forty of these as chief; nor has anyone ever said that I gave undue preference to any party or person, though it has depended on me that many thousands of bills should be examined, printed, corrected, noted, translated and put through all their stages into lawful order and turn; and a very considerable portion of them had to be drafted or amended."[26] In a letter dated soon after Wicksteed's retirement, Prime Minister John

A. Macdonald offered his old friend these consoling thoughts: "I hold in pleasant remembrance the many measures in the way of law reform in which we were co-labourers, and although the reforms which were effected as the result of our labours will be forgotten by a grateful public, yet I think we can justly congratulate ourselves on the benefits that we have by these measures conferred on our adopted country."

Mr Wicksteed's successor as law clerk was both a lawyer and a medical doctor and died in office. The next law clerk served for nineteen years and died suddenly at the end of the session in 1908. The fourth law clerk, A.H. O'Brien (1908–13), had internal office problems (as I would almost ninety years later) that were so severe the Government appointed a Royal Commission "to investigate the workings of the Law Branch" and to make suggestions on how to make the service "efficient and satisfactory." The commission reported that there had been "no proper management of the office" nor "harmony either in the methods of workings or in the relations of the lawyers among themselves."[27] The clerk of the House testified that O'Brien, "by an exaggerated view of the responsibilities of his office," had on occasion amended bills without getting parliamentary approval. O'Brien maintained that the Law Branch had always made such changes "as would express the intention sought to be conveyed by a bill in proper parliamentary language." He felt it was one of the duties of the law clerk to make changes in bills *after* they had passed the House, provided the changes did not affect or alter the clear meaning and intention of the bill. In my time as law clerk, we *never* made changes to bills, whether before they were adopted by the House, after adoption and before they went to the Senate, or after they came back from the Senate, except for obvious typographical corrections or numbering changes consequential to amendments.[28] The 1912 commission recommended that Law Clerk O'Brien be demoted to deputy law clerk and a new law clerk appointed who could manage the Office of the Law Clerk and respect the rule that only the House can amend a bill once it has begun the legislative process.[29]

O'Brien's successor had been an assistant deputy minister at the Department of Justice before his appointment. The Treasury Board recommended that he be formally designated "draughtsman of government bills" with the rank of deputy minister. (In my time, the position of law clerk was considered equivalent to that of an assistant deputy minister). In 1923, a law branch re-organization provided for the appointment of two joint law clerks, one for common law and the other for Quebec civil law.[30]

In 1924, the legendary Paul Maurice Ollivier became one of the joint law clerks and in 1951 sole law clerk. In 1956, his title was changed to "Law Clerk and Parliamentary Counsel," the title used today. Ollivier is credited with breaking the taboo against alcoholic beverages on the Hill when he brought a bottle of wine with him to the parliamentary restaurant in the Centre Block and asked for a glass. He is also credited with contributing to broadening the grounds for divorce in the late 1960s when, during hearings on the divorce reform bill, he commented that adultery was not a crime but a pastime. He is the longest serving law clerk, having retired on 31 December 1970.

Drafting government bills had always been the responsibility of the sponsoring government department or agency, though the Office of the Law Clerk was closely involved in the preparation process. By 1948, however, responsibility for drafting government bills had moved entirely to the Department of Justice. The Law Clerk's Office retained its traditional watchdog role and "scrutinized, revised and often redrafted" government bills as well as having responsibility for determining whether a government bill required a royal recommendation in accordance with section 54 of the Constitution Act, 1867 (discussed in chapter 4).[31]

Law Clerk J.P. Joseph Maingot (1971–82), who would later write a leading text on the law of parliamentary privilege, got himself into trouble in the so-called "bells incident" in early 1982. The opposition thought an omnibus government bill should be broken into several bills. The Speaker felt that she did not have the power to divide a government bill. Trouble began when a recorded vote was demanded on an adjournment motion and this required that the bells be rung to call the members to the chamber for the vote. The procedure then and now is that the bells must ring until both the government whip and the official opposition whip enter the chamber together for the start of the vote.[32] The bells in those days were like fire alarm bells, very loud.[33] To protest the Government's use of an omnibus bill, the official opposition whip refused to enter the chamber, which meant that the bells continued ringing, echoing down the corridors of Centre Block and the other parts of the precincts. The House was effectively shut down for two weeks and the constant ringing of the bells drove everyone crazy.[34] The Government and the opposition parties eventually came to an agreement and the Government divided its bill into several parts.

During the two-week shutdown, the clerk and the law clerk offered the Speaker conflicting advice on what she may or may not do. Not unexpectedly, the Speaker was not happy with this. It was later settled that the clerk alone would be the Speaker's advisor on procedural matters and the law clerk would be consulted only when there was a legal issue. This limited role for the law clerk has applied ever since, much to the relief of the clerks, I'm sure. Maingot resigned as law clerk soon after.

Joe Maingot's successor, M.R. Pelletier (1983–90), had problems as a law clerk that lead to his (unhappy) resignation a few months before I arrived as general legislative counsel in 1991. The law clerk position remained vacant for nine years, until I was appointed to the position in December 1999.

After I had agreed to go to the House as its general legislative counsel but before I arrived, I read in the Toronto *Globe and Mail* that the law clerk had launched a lawsuit against the prime minister and the clerk of the House. *What???* It was too late to change my mind about going to the House but I was intrigued by this, to say the least. I resolved to get to the bottom of what happened once I got there lest I get into the same or similar difficulties.

I began my discreet enquiries soon after I arrived. Apparently, there had been problems between the previous law clerk and the clerk for several years. Some believed their difficulties began when the clerk was appointed to the clerk position over the law clerk, who had thought he would get the appointment. Who knows why he felt this way; it didn't matter for my purposes. My problem – and an immediate problem when I arrived – was that the conflicts between the clerk and the law clerk had trickled down to the procedural clerks and lawyers. The clerk had "won" his battle with the law clerk – who had left the House a few months before I arrived – but the blood was still on the floor. The clerks thought the lawyers were arrogant jerks and the lawyers thought the clerks were know-nothings. Oh boy.

The lawyers were an unhappy lot regardless. Lawyers do not take easily to being managed by persons who are not lawyers. The clerk was then and has been ever since a career procedural clerk, not a lawyer. As manager of the legislative lawyers, in my early years at the House I reported to the deputy clerk, also a career procedural clerk. By contrast, government lawyers in the Department of Justice had managers who were also lawyers. The House lawyers, for the most part, felt that Administration management, because they were not lawyers, did not understand their needs. They also believed that, given the confidential nature of their work as legal advisors, they should function separate and apart from House Administration and that the law clerk should not report to the clerk but only to the Speaker and the board. This was the nub of the discontentment in the law branch when I arrived and it proved intractable for many years to come.

In the mid-1990s, my problems in the office reached the floor of the Chamber. I was in trouble and conditions were right for a perfect storm. The House, as its contribution to the Government's commitment to reduce the federal deficit, had introduced a program to cut back on staff by offering financial inducements for early departures or early retirements. Some members feared that staff reductions in our office would mean they would have to wait even longer to get their private member's bills drafted for introduction in the House. At the same time, the opposition parties were demanding the drafting of large numbers of amendments in an attempt to slow down the legislative process on government bills. We were working as hard as we could to meet private members' demands but had only three lawyers and could not hire more.

It became evident that the members who were complaining were receiving insider information from a person or persons in the Office of the Law Clerk. I was advised that the members had their own agendas vis-à-vis the Speaker and the Government and that the problems in my office were useful fodder for their purposes. At the personal level, however, I couldn't help but feel that members publicly complaining in the chamber about my office put my position in jeopardy: another problem law clerk. Some administrative changes were made to relieve the pressure on the office but made little difference. The lawyers continued to be discontented over the amount of work they were being asked to do and nothing I did as their manager offered any relief.

This unhappy situation continued for several years until events came to a head in 2000 and almost cost me my job. On or about St Patrick's Day (of all days), a Bloc Québécois member rose in the House to complain about a breach in the confidentiality of the amendments that the Bloc had requested from my office relating to the Government's so-called Clarity Bill affecting future referenda on separatism in Quebec.[35] By accident, an amendment that the Bloc had not intended to use had gotten into the hands of the procedural clerks reviewing amendments. The Bloc felt this was a breach of the confidentiality that they expected with my office, where their amendments were drafted. The Bloc moved a motion of non-confidence in the Speaker (as the Speaker is responsible for the services provided to members by House Administration).[36] The non-confidence motion was debated for a full day before it was withdrawn by agreement of the parties (which saved the Speaker from the unprecedented humiliation of a non-confidence vote) and a new motion was substituted that referred the issue of confidentiality in the work of my office to a House committee. This was highly unusual. Difficulties with any of the Administration services were usually referred to the clerk to resolve as administrative matters, but not this time. I would be required to defend the operations of my office before a House committee!

My office was being used as a political football in the Bloc's fight with the Government over the Clarity Bill but there was little I could do except prepare to appear before the committee. Lawyers in my office were called before the committee, which was highly unusual (and confirmed in my mind that they had had a role in these events) as committees would not normally ask Administration staff other than senior management to testify about operations downstairs. In the end, the committee found that there had been no breaches of confidentiality in the work of my office.[37] I took this to mean that controversy about confidentiality was over. The House would soon be adjourning for the summer break and members would be gone.

A few days later, however, the clerk to the committee called to tell me I had to appear before the committee again. "What for?" I asked. I was stunned. The clerk explained that the committee wanted me to explain a breach of confidentiality in the statistics I had provided to the committee. *What????* It had been shown that there had not been any breach of confidentiality but I was now being accused of breaching confidentiality. I immediately reviewed the statistics and found, to my horror, that the statistical information included data showing amendment requests on three bills that had not yet been put on notice, meaning the data was still confidential. I had not checked the status of these bills when I authorized the statistics to be given to the committee. The data was only numbers but experienced political staffers could read between the lines and deduce from the content of the bills and the respective positions of the parties on those bills that it was probably the Bloc that had requested most of the amendments, and knowing this disclosed the Bloc's parliamentary strategy. I had to go back to the committee and explain – the committee had me dead to rights on this.

The Bloc member on the committee seemed out to get me personally, for some reason. I had never had a problem with this member before so I had a hard time understanding the attacks. I read the transcript of the committee meeting where it was decided that I should be called back, to get an idea of what I might be facing. "The law clerk and parliamentary counsel," said the member, "is held to the strictest confidentiality because of the highly confidential information circulating in his office." Having set the premise, the member went on, "Either he does not care about confidentiality, either he does not understand the full importance of the discretion his administrative service must observe, or he has shown a carelessness that should worry us to the highest degree, Mr. Chair, taking into account the high functions he has within the administrative machine of this House of Commons. In any case, Mr. Chair, allow me to doubt the seriousness Mr. Walsh has shown for the matter the House referred to this committee."[38] Wow. He wasn't pulling any punches. I developed a sinking feeling; was this the beginning of the end?

A colleague suggested that with all the controversy about my office over the past several months perhaps I should offer the Speaker my resignation. I did not feel that my oversight warranted resignation. I was assured that the Speaker would probably not accept my resignation but this was small comfort. On the other hand, the Speaker might accept it as part of a larger agreement between the parties to bring the matter to a close. There comes a point with any political dispute – and this was a dispute between the Bloc and the Government – when the Government decides that the dispute is taking precious time away from more important parliamentary business and should be settled, if possible. I feared that my resignation would be seen as a convenient price to pay if it brought the dispute to an end; unfortunate road kill, as it were. Nonetheless, I decided I should offer my resignation and hope for the best. It wasn't an easy letter to write.

I knew I would not win any argument with the Bloc, whatever I might say in my defence. I had to disarm the Bloc member. Accepting responsibility for the breach unreservedly, with apologies, would be a good start. The offer of resignation should remove any doubt about whether I accepted the gravity of my offence.[39] The committee accepted my apology and the Speaker did not accept my offer of resignation. A week later, the House adjourned for the summer break and returned in mid-September; soon after Parliament was dissolved for an election on 27 November 2000. The new Parliament did not open until the end of January 2001. I had the summer and fall period to rebuild the Law Clerk's Office. The dissident lawyers departed, new blood was brought in, and everything worked well for the rest of my years at the House as law clerk and parliamentary counsel. So well, in fact, that at times I have felt like the boy in the proverbial bubble, waiting for it to burst and for the troubles of the past to return but, *grâce à Dieu*, they never did.

When I was first appointed law clerk, the clerk said to me that the House should have "the best parliamentary law firm in the country." I was pleased to hear this as it told me that the clerk would support my efforts to rebuild the law branch after so many years of internal difficulties and nine years without a law clerk who could take responsibility for lawyer services at the House. My formative years as a lawyer had been in a law firm and, while I recognized that the House as a working environment had features that were unlike anything in the outside world, this provided a business model. It would be a *parliamentary* law firm, serving a variety of "clients" in an institution driven and dominated by partisan political interests. The Law Clerk's Office had to function credibly as a law office adapted to the parliamentary environment.

Information Services

Coming to the House in 2015, you won't appreciate the transformations made to the operations of the House and for members by digital technology. Changes in technology kept us all – including members – dancing as fast as we could to stay ahead of the rapidly appearing changes. I remember when voicemail came in and I had to learn how to use it – I had no idea how many changes were still to come. It's quite a story, really, that I can only skim over here.

It's important to remember that words, whether oral or written, are the currency of a place like the House. The business of the House and its committees – politics – is driven by talk, more talk, and even more talk; the need to know what is going on as soon as possible. If you aren't already, you'll soon find yourself constantly checking your cell phone for the latest messages or calls. I doubt that there is any professional group, except perhaps journalists, that has been as well served as politicians by the arrival of digital word processing and communications technology.

Fortunately, the House was blessed with a "tech-smart" clerk of the House who recognized early on what technology could do for the House and for members. At the same time, members saw that each new technological development would be more useful than what they already had and pressed the clerk and the board for the latest version. The clerk recruited a chief information officer (CIO) who had both short-term know-how and long-term vision. Between them, they understood that incorporating this new technology into the House's workplace infrastructure was a priority. The CIO was "the boy with the toys" who could play Santa Claus to members when a new device or software came along.

In the mid-1980s, members were provided with desktop computers with an average memory capacity of sixteen megabytes. (Today's computers typically have two gigabytes of memory or 128 times more.) In 1991, the board approved giving members a second personal computer in their offices. The clerk and the CIO recognized that technology infrastructure in the House had to be centralized if it was to be supported by Administration staff. A House-wide operating platform was needed to prevent operational incompatibility with devices having trouble exchanging information. The House had to think strategically in the face of the new technologies coming along; members could not be allowed to choose their own computer operating systems.

In 1994, the House moved to a networked "precinct campus" with a stable infrastructure on which to base future technologies. In 1995, a parliamentary internet site was launched and in 1997 an internal parliamentary *intra*net site that was accessible only on the Hill to provide members and their staff with information and services supporting them in their work.[40] With 200 newly elected members arriving in 1993 and 100 in 1997, members were increasingly computer literate and knowledgeable about the potential of digital technology. Their expectations brought increased demands.

By 1998, Information Services recognized that communications between a member's constituency office and the Hill or from remote locations while a member was travelling the country required a Canada-wide high-speed access service. Local solutions existed in the larger metropolitan areas but most of the rural areas, where forty per cent of members' constituency offices were located, were not served by any of these. The House had to create and manage its own private, high-speed, Canada-wide network. In 2001, the House began using government satellite services to implement a high-speed access communications network system from coast to coast to coast.

It became evident around 2003 that the audio, televising, and recording technology that had been installed in the Chamber and the adjacent lobbies in 1978 had to be replaced. An electronic infrastructure was installed that allows electronic voting (if the House should ever choose to adopt this practice) and internet access within the Chamber. Three computers with a small network hub were installed at the table. This configuration supports several applications designed to facilitate management of the Chamber's activities from the table. A seventeen-inch flat-screen monitor was installed at the Speaker's feet, hidden from public view behind a small wooden wall.

Television soon moved from analogue to digital to accommodate high definition as the consumer market migrated to this technology – the House had to be mindful of its television viewing audiences across Canada. Cell phones, blackberries, and personal laptop computers provided operational portability or mobility: office work could be done anywhere, anytime. As electronic text, ideas and messages could now travel over great distances at the speed of light.[41] Messages could be answered almost instantly. Information Services established a 24/7 help desk that members could access from anywhere in Canada by phone, fax, e-mail, or the website. By 2010, the Information Services help desk supported approximately 6,000 clients and received from 280 to 450 calls per day. Technical support from Information Services is constantly in demand by members and by Administration staff.

Last year the House began providing wi-fi and mobile access across parliamentary precincts by implementing a private cloud computing infrastructure that brings much of the efficiency and agility of public cloud computing to the House.[42]

Information Services has also developed a website, *Our Commons*, designed to ensure that members and their staff, as well as the general public, remain connected to daily House business "while on the go."[43] This website (www.ourcommons.ca) provides an opportunity to view the democratic process in action, demonstrating the House's commitment to providing access to the work of members both in the

Chamber and in committees, and has search capabilities for both members and legislation.

PUBLICATION OF DEBATES (HANSARD)

Prior to Confederation in 1867, debates in the Canadian parliaments were reported only in newspapers and it was widely believed that political considerations influenced many of these reports. The idea of a "scrapbook Hansard," that is, a collection of newspaper reports of speeches in the House, eventually developed. Newspaper publishers liked this idea but the prime minister, Sir John A. Macdonald, thought the story the "scrapbook" would tell would be incomplete at best. Legislators agreed that the parliamentary debates were too important not to be recorded. (Many might not agree with this today.) However, resistance to published *verbatim* debates continued. In 1874, the *Daily Globe* in Toronto ran an editorial against the publication of a full-length Hansard, arguing that if members knew they were being recorded in full, the parliamentary report would become a platform for members' egos. (What would they have said when television coverage of debates was first proposed?) Besides, said the *Daily Globe*, the Hansard reports would never be produced as quickly as those in the newspaper.

In 1880, the Parliament of Canada began producing an "official report" of the debates in the House and the Senate. The emphasis was not on verbatim reporting but rather on the meaning and effect of the words spoken: Hansard reporters took notes on the debates and then dictated their accounts to assistants who wrote them up. By the 1960s, the Hansard staff was comprised of eight two-person teams, which rotated every ten minutes. By the late 1960s analogue recorders were being used to verify the accuracy of reporters' shorthand notes.

Today, Information Services produces written and electronic text, in both English and French, of House and committee debates for each sitting day, usually by 9 a.m. of the next morning. These are publicly available on the internet by the early hours of the next day. Committee debates sometimes take a back seat to production of House debates. Members are given a proof copy of the text of what they said in debates, which provides them with the opportunity to correct any error in the transcription or to clarify what they meant where their language is unclear, but they are not allowed to change the meaning of what is recorded or to delete anything.

Finance Services

You will want to make these people your friends – they will explain how you should manage your finances as a member and probably keep you out of trouble if you make a mistake that could seriously embarrass you were it made public.

Finance Services prepares the House's estimates of spending for the coming year after receiving input from the managers responsible for each sector of House Administration. At the end of the year, Finance Services prepares financial statements covering the spending by the House in the past year. Finance Services also provides policy advice to the board, reimburses members for expenses permitted under board by-laws and policies, provides access to financial tools, and tracks all member expenses involving public funds and regularly discloses these in the format approved by the board.[44] Finance Services also provides budgetary administrative support to members with respect to their office budgets. In 2013, the House chief financial officer (CFO) advised a House committee that Finance Services makes an average of over 70,000 member expenses payments each fiscal year and has an average of 20,000 calls or e-mail exchanges with members each year. In the most recent fiscal year, the CFO reported that Finance Services sent members 4,365 "regret letters" advising them of a problem with an amount claimed. Of these "regrets," only seven went to the board for resolution.[45]

When there is a finance problem with a member, the whip for the member's party may become involved and the problem is resolved quickly. If not, either the member's whip, on behalf of the member, or the CFO could take the issue to the board for a decision. The vast majority of members respect the administrative rules but there will always be a few who are innovative in their interpretations of the rules and need to be advised. It's important to remember that infractions of the rules are usually honest mistakes, either by the member or staff. Finance Services, on behalf of the board, keeps members as fully informed as possible about the meaning to be given to the board's by-laws and administrative policies.

Sometimes members, when faced with accusations that they had misused House resources, would plead that their expense had been approved by Finance Services, as if this meant the expense was permissible. While Finance Services may identify some expenses as irregular and bring them to the attention of the member or, if necessary, the member's whip, they must rely on the information provided by the member (or the member's office). As all members are "honourable members," Finance Services must accept at face value whatever they are told. They do not examine each expense claim to determine whether the member's representations of the expense are true. Finance Services does not have a policing or enforcement function; it does not have resources for this. Compliance with board by-laws on the use of House resources remains the responsibility of each member for which the member alone is accountable.

Human Resources Services

Human Resources Services administers the terms and conditions of employment and the collective agreements that apply to House employees. This directorate also administers internal training programs, performance evaluations, promotions, and grievances. There are seven bargaining units on the Hill, represented by four unions: the Public Service Alliance of Canada (PSAC), the Professional Institute of the Public Service of Canada (PIPS), the Communications, Energy and Paperworkers Union (CEP), and the Security Services Employees Association (SSEA). Employees of members of Parliament are not able to join a union, but the employees of NDP members have organized for bargaining purposes and are represented by a recognized union (CEP), although this collective bargaining relationship is not legally sanctioned by legislation and is not recognized by the board.

About half of the approximately 1,700 House Administration employees are not represented by a union. The terms and conditions of their employment are set by the board and are usually the same as those of unionized employees.[46] Pay increases for unrepresented employees are generally set to match the pay increases negotiated with the unions for represented employees. Administration employees are included in the federal public service pension plan, the Public Service Superannuation Plan. Administration employee grievances, including terminations, are governed by the Parliamentary Employment and Staff Relations Act (PESRA) and adjudicated by the Public Service Staff Relations Board.

These are the administrative ligaments that hold the House together day in and day out, from one Parliament to the next, giving the House continuity and permanence as an institution despite the turnover of members with each election or two.

Epilogue

I've shown you the House as I came to know it, from downstairs. You will be working upstairs, of course. Are you ready for what awaits you? Not to worry; you're as ready as any new member ever is, which is not very but you'll manage somehow; there will be ups and downs, good days and bad days. Before leaving you, I offer some thoughts on how the House might improve its proceedings, in furtherance of greater democratic representation in the business of the House and for the benefit of Canadians generally.

One has to keep in mind that the business of the House is the debate and resolution of issues of public policy, driven by political parties that are competing for public approval and hoping for more seats in the House after the next election, possibly the most seats so they can form the next Government. The political goals of the parties, enforced through party discipline, govern the members and their debates. Given the House's partisan political environment, at times questions from opposition members in Question Period will be more bombast than substance and responses from ministers will be dismissive and less than fully honest. However, Question Period, despite its faults, serves the broad political purpose of challenging the Government, which at the very least makes the Government conscious of its accountability to the House and indirectly to Canadians generally. Nonetheless, partisan politics is unavoidably the driving force of the House, though this could be moderated through changes to the rules of the House.

You might want to see less hostile partisanship in the Chamber but there's little you can do as an individual private member except avoid being part of it and in caucus urge your colleagues to remember where they are. In 2010, a private member tried to get the House to do something about Question Period.[1] "If the heart of our democracy is Parliament," said the member, "then the heart of Parliament is Question Period," which, he said, had become "more about scoring cheap political points than dealing with the issues that really matter to Canadians." The House gave the member its support, or so it seemed, when it instructed a committee to consider the member's motion and report back within six months. The committee held one meeting and had not reported back to the House before Parliament was dissolved for an election, almost a year later.[2] With dissolution, of course, this piece of business died. And so it goes.

If holding the Government to account is an important function of the House, as I would argue it is, the House's rules should be changed to minimize a majority Government's ability to control House and committee proceedings. The parties should allow their members free votes more often. A majority Government should not be allowed to introduce omnibus bills of the kind seen in 2012 and 2015 and most recently in 2017.[3] The Standing Orders should be amended to enable the Speaker to rule such bills out of order and to direct that they be broken down into several separate bills to enable separate debates and separate votes on each of the different subject matters.

The business of the House could be improved through some changes in committee practices. A majority Government should not be allowed to use its majority to put a committee meeting behind closed doors (usually done for self-serving political purposes). Committee meetings should take place in camera only if members from at least two recognized parties support this idea. With respect to committee reports, minority views should automatically be affixed to the report (and not only by approval of the majority).[4]

I would also suggest introducing Opposition Days in committees, much as already happens in the House (discussed in chapter 4). Also, members should be allowed to raise objections in the House about actions by a committee chair or a committee majority, which they cannot do now: "Committees are the masters of their own proceedings" (discussed in chapter 6). The Standing Orders pertaining to committees should not be revised or suspended by the House except on a motion supported by members from at least two recognized parties.

These changes – and some might suggest others – would, I feel, enhance the work of committees. They would make their work, including their reports to the House, more representative of the contending viewpoints of the political parties. They would enable us to see more of what committees are doing or, as the case may be, more of why they are not doing more. It's all about political transparency in the business of committees.

Looking elsewhere, the House should allow persons outside the House – including public officials – who feel they have been misrepresented or defamed by something said in the House or in a committee to submit a response that would be tabled in the House. Where the response relates to statements made in a committee, the House should automatically refer the response to the committee.

There is much public confusion or uncertainty about the powers and privileges of the House and its committees, notwithstanding the Supreme Court of Canada's lengthy disquisition on parliamentary privilege in *Vaid*. It's time that the House review its privileges as traditionally understood and update them to suit the times, especially its privilege of exclusive control of its internal affairs, codifying its privileges in an appendix to its Standing Orders. There can be no doubt that parliamentary privilege is important for the House but its purpose is too frequently challenged because the privilege claimed seems outdated or is not properly understood.

Finally, the House should do a major revision of the Standing Orders to modernize some of its practices and make them comprehensible to members, government officials, and the general public. Have a look and see if you can understand them; you should at least try. Fortunately, you will find the Standing Orders explained in plain language in the House publication, *House of Commons Procedure and Practice*, on which I have at times relied here. Nonetheless, the rules themselves – the primary authority on House procedure – should not be virtually unreadable by members or their staff. Finally, the layout and content of the House's Order Paper, Notice Paper and Journals should be reviewed to make them more user-friendly and informative for members and the general public. After more than twenty years at the House, I still had difficulty using these papers.

In my view, a session of Parliament ought not to be prorogued by the governor general (on the advice of the prime minister) without first having the House's consent. However even if the Government were required to move a motion for prorogation and allow a vote on it, this would not be a meaningful exercise in a majority Parliament where the Government could use its majority to pass the motion. It seems to me a rule of the House should provide that any such motion must be supported by a majority comprised of members from at least two recognized parties. Also, the motion should specify the date for commencement of the next session.

The composition of the Board of Internal Economy should not be tied to party standings in the House. The recognized parties in the House should be represented equally to avoid or minimize partisan influence. Ministers and other House officers, other than whips, should not sit on the board and appointments to the board should be made by each caucus. The Government has amended the Parliament of Canada Act to open board meetings and I agree with this.[5] The board should table its minutes in the House no later than the first sitting day immediately following the next board meeting. At the end of each Parliament, other than those that last less than a year, the auditor general should audit, or in some manner review, the financial decisions of the board through random annual audits of members, with enforcement measures put in place to recover funds found to have been wrongly spent.

I was asked once by a committee what I thought of establishing an outside independent body to avoid members "policing themselves." I disagreed with the premise of such action: members of Parliament need not and should not be "policed" by an outside agency. I acknowledged that public confidence in parliamentarians with respect to internal financial matters (troubles in the Senate were very much in the news at the time) was suffering and that credibility meant that the public needed to be confident that members were not simply serving their collective self-interest when they met as the Board of Internal Economy. If the boards' meetings are opened, members on the board will be publicly accountable for their decisions.

Prospects for House reforms are not good, in any Parliament. A majority Government can use its majority to push through reforms of its choosing, although this would be contrary to House tradition,

where procedural changes are first discussed among the House leaders. In March 2017, the Government proposed changes that seemed to
serve the Government's interests but not those of the opposition parties, except where they empowered the Speaker to split up omnibus
bills.[6] As there had been no prior discussion with the opposition parties, the Government's proposals were met with loud protests from
the opposition parties, including a filibuster debate when the reforms
came before the Standing Committee on Procedure and House
Affairs, where at the time of writing they remained.

Reforms don't relate to House procedural practices only. A private
member in the previous Parliament – a widely respected member on
the Government side of the House at that time and a former minister
– proposed amendments to the Parliament of Canada Act and Canada Elections Act to restore the balance between members and their
leaders.[7] "It is clear that over the last number of decades," said the
member, "power has flowed out of the people's elected Chamber [the
House] into the party leaders' offices and this has weakened Canadians' connection to Parliament."[8] The bill set out the parliamentary
principles that it was designed to serve:

> Whereas members of Parliament are elected by their constituents
> to represent them in the Parliament of Canada;

> Whereas the leadership of political parties must maintain the con-
> fidence of their caucuses;

> And whereas, in Canada, the executive branch of government is
> accountable to the legislative branch in accordance with the con-
> cept of responsible government, which is the foundation of the
> Westminster system of parliamentary democracy.

Specifically, the member's bill proposed enhancing the powers of
the local riding associations (giving control of candidate selection to
the local riding association by removing the requirement that every
candidate has to be approved by the party leader, removing the power
of the party leader to "deregister" a local riding association, and giving
riding associations the power to determine the time, date, and rules

for candidate nomination elections) and giving House caucuses the power to expel or re-admit members through secret ballot and to elect the caucus chair. The bill proposed giving more power to the local riding associations and to members sitting in caucus at the expense of the party leader. At the time, and not coincidentally, the private member's party leader was the prime minister.

A few months later, after receiving comments from members and others, the private member introduced a revised version of his bill. The local riding association's control over selecting the party candidate was reduced (the party leader's exclusive power to authorize a candidate to represent the party was replaced by authorization by "the person or persons authorized by the political party to endorse prospective candidates," that is, the party leader OR some other official named by the party) and a new provision added to enable a caucus to impose a party leadership review.

In committee, the bill was amended (by the Government majority) to require each caucus, at its first meeting following each general election, to decide (not necessarily by secret ballot) whether the bill's provisions relating to expelling and re-admitting members and to leadership reviews would apply to the caucus in that Parliament.[9] The reforms were thus made optional for each caucus and, it should be noted, the caucus vote of its members on whether the reforms would apply was to be open and recorded (within the caucus). Imagine: an open and recorded vote on the party leader. God help you if the leader survived the vote and you voted on the other side.

One has to ask: what are the chances that a caucus, immediately after a general election and in an open vote, would vote to adopt these rules, particularly if their party had done well in the election? If their party had done badly in the election, they might do so, but the leader would probably have resigned before the caucus met. In short, adopting these rules will only happen, perhaps, where a leader refuses to resign after failing the party in an election (as with Prime Minister John Diefenbaker after the 1963 election that he lost).

When the bill, as amended in committee, came back to the House for its final reading, the sponsoring member admitted that the bill, as amended, was not perfect but he thought it was still very good.[10] "If not amended," said the member, "the bill would not pass the House.

The important point for people to know is that in this case perfection would have been the enemy of the good."[11] The member was putting a good face on what, in my view, had become a largely empty bill. It was approved by an overwhelming majority of members (260) with only a few dissenters (17), which could have been expected, given the very limited content of the bill: voting against a reform bill would have looked bad, while voting in favour, after the amendments, was harmless.[12] As to whether any of the bill's reforms would be adopted by the parties, we were left to await the opening of the next Parliament following the election on 19 October 2015. As of the time of writing, there have been no reports of any of the parties adopting the proposed reforms in caucus.[13]

As you can see from the legislative saga of this private member's bill, reforms that threaten the power of the incumbent party leaders, especially the leader of the governing party, the prime minister, will probably go nowhere although appearances of reforms may be allowed (optics over substance).

As I have said earlier, politics is about power and in a democracy power is about winning and losing – and for the parties in the House, it's definitely – above all – about winning, whether in the near term in the polls or in the longer term in the next election. Facts can be spun until the truth is unrecognizable and fair comment is, at best, an after-thought. This might bother you at times, as it does me and most Canadians. However, there must be full, free, and public debate on matters of public interest, which means we must, in the end, depend on members – and their parties – to discipline themselves and draw our own conclusions about which members are honourable and which are not. Moreover, we must have a Government that is publicly accountable to the elected House, which means opposition parties must have unlimited latitude to challenge the Government. The relationship between the Government and the opposition is adversarial by nature and understandably the heat of battle may at times give rise to some untoward behaviour.

The changes I have suggested would, in my view, improve the House's performance and do so in the public interest. But they would require that the governing party give up some of the powers it has through its majority. The chances of this, like those of original Reform

Act, 2014, are slim indeed. As Winston Churchill once said, democracy is the worst form of government, except for all the others. It's messy and it disappoints but it must have a place to play itself out between elections and that place is the House. We cannot do without it and we ought to value it, warts and all.

As a member, you have a chance, upstairs, to make a positive contribution that those off the Hill and I, downstairs, cannot. You will find your job very demanding – and the struggle to balance your personal life with your political life difficult – but, at the end of the day, be sure that you give no one reasonable cause to doubt that you are, as they say, an Honourable Member. If you manage this, you'll come out ahead in the end. Good luck.

Notes

PROLOGUE

1 Constitution Act, 1867, RSC 1985, s. 128, Appendix II.

2 According to the governing legislation "proportionate representation of the provinces must balance the fair and equitable representation of faster-growing provinces and the effective representation of smaller and slower-growing provinces." See preambles to the Fair Representation Act, SC 2011, c 26., for a more complete explanation of why and how the reconfiguration provided fifteen new members for Ontario, six each for Alberta and BC, and three for Quebec for an estimated additional annual cost, according to government estimates, of $34 million: $19 million in operational support for the new members and $15 million for the increased number of riding elections. As the size of the Chamber could not be increased, the last two rows had to have five seats between each aisle, rather than two as in other rows, which gives each member direct access to an aisle. Drop-down seats were required in the second-last back row to enable members with an inside seat to get by other members when taking or leaving their seats. The reconfiguration was done pursuant to section 51, Constitution Act, 1867. Boundaries of ridings were adjusted to reflect the increase in member representation: see Electoral Boundaries Readjustment Act, RSC 1985, c E-3., as amended by the Fair Representation Act, supra.

CHAPTER ONE

1 Seats are assigned by the Speaker on the advice of the whip of each of the political parties. Independent members are seated at the far end of the Chamber, on the left side.

2 The British House of Commons provides only benches without desks for its members. According to John George Bourinot, clerk of the House from 1880–1902, the idea of installing desks for members came from the Legislative Assembly of Lower Canada (Quebec) and has never been adopted by the British House: see Banks, infra, at p. 82. As well, the British House is too small to seat all its members. When all members attend, a large number of them can be seen standing at the bar of the House for lack of a place to sit.

3 The dress code for the Chamber is business dress, which means a jacket, shirt, and tie for men and whatever current standards permit as business dress for women. No jeans, hats, or sandals. Failure to respect the business code may mean that the Speaker will not recognize the member.

4 In a few years, the House will be moving again, this time to the West Block building where it will sit for as long as ten years while the Centre Block, including the Chamber, is renovated. For details see Public Services and Procurement Canada, last modified 9 November 2016: http://www.tpsgc-pwgsc.gc.ca/citeparlementaire-parliamentary-precinct/rehabilitation/ouest-west-eng.html.

5 For a more detailed account see the House of Commons Chamber, last modified February, 2016: http://www.parl.gc.ca/About/House/Collections/heritage_spaces/chamber-e.htm.

6 The Speaker's chair seat can be electronically raised or lowered to a level that suits the occupant.

7 The pages are university students recruited from across Canada who work part-time as pages during the academic year. Whenever the Speaker or other chair occupant stands up, the pages, seated at the foot of the Speaker's chair, must stand up. There can be a lot of bobbing up and down.

8 The Government majority after the 2015 election was greater than the number of seats available on the Speaker's right side, which meant that some Government members were seated on the "opposition" side.

9 O'Brien and Bosc, *Procedure and Practice*, 280–2, especially fn. 58 on 282.

In medieval times, a mace was a large club that was used to defend one-self when attacked. The monarch's sergeants-at-arms carried one to be ready to defend the king (or queen). In the early days of parliamentary history, the Crown assigned one of its sergeants-at-arms to the Speaker of the House to protect the Speaker against assaults or other disrespect-ful affronts. The mace also gave the sergeant the power to arrest without a warrant, which meant that the Commons had the power to arrest per-sons without going through the legal process that would otherwise apply and supported the House's right to act in the defence of its privi-leges, as it can today.

10 The four chair occupants are the Speaker, the deputy speaker and chair of committees of the whole, the assistant deputy speaker and deputy chair of committees of the whole and the assistant deputy speaker and assistant deputy chair of committees of the whole.

11 Standing Orders of the House of Commons, s 1 provides: "In all cases not provided for [in the Standing Orders of the House of Commons], or by other Order of the House, procedural questions shall be decided by the speaker…whose decisions shall be based on the usages, forms, customs and precedents of the House…and on parliamentary tradition."

12 O'Brien and Bosc, *Procedure and Practice*, 307.

13 Ibid., 308; Standing Orders of the House of Commons, s 10; see Speak-er's ruling, House of Commons Debates, 41st Parl, 1st Sess, No 238 (23 April 2013), at 1505.

14 Appeals of Speaker's rulings to the whole House were abolished in 1965 but remain available in the Senate.

15 Standing Orders of the House of Commons, s 9; see also Constitution Act, 1867, s 49.

16 See House of Commons Debates, 37th Parl, 2nd Sess, No 120 (16 Sep-tember 2003); House of Commons Debates, 38th Parl, 1st Sess, No 91 (4 May 2005); House of Commons Debates, 38th Parl, 1st Sess, No 102 (19 May 2005); House of Commons Debates, 40th Parl, 2nd Sess, No 48 (29 April 2009); House of Commons Debates, 40th Parl, 2nd Sess, No 93 (8 October 2009) and House of Commons Debates, 40th Parl, 2nd Sess, No 128 (10 December 2009). A tie-breaking vote on 22 June 2005 by the deputy speaker was later set aside when it was shown that the vote had not actually resulted in a tie.

17 Excluding four tie-breaking votes cast in the Committee of the Whole,

the previous tie-breaking votes in a House proceeding were cast on 6
May 1870, 28 February 1889, 31 March 1925, and 11 March 1930; the
last was later set aside when it was found that the House vote had been
incorrectly recorded as a tie vote.

18 House of Commons Debates, 37th Parl, 2nd Sess, No 120 (16 September
2003) at 1800.

19 House of Commons Debates, 38th Parl, 1st Sess, No 102 (19 May 2005)
at 1810.

20 House of Commons Debates, 40th Parl, 2nd Sess, No 93 (8 October
2009) at 1120.

21 House of Commons Debates, 40th Parl, 2nd Sess, No. 128 (10 December 2009) at 1825.

22 Standing Orders of the House of Commons, s 11(1); see O'Brien and
Bosc, *Procedure and Practice*, 308–11.

23 Speaker Gilbert Parent (1993–2000), a former teacher, would rise from
the Speaker's chair and stand, with his hands clasped to his speaker's
gown, waiting for members to stop misbehaving. It brought the noise to
an end but was not a lasting cure.

24 For a House debate on QP reform see House of Commons Debates,
40th Parl, 3rd Sess, No 50 (27 May 2010), House of Commons Debates,
40th Parl, 3rd Sess, No 73 (29 September 2010), House of Commons
Debates, 40th Parl, 3rd Sess, No 78 (6 October 2010). See also Evidence,
Meeting No. 28, Standing Committee on Procedure and House Affairs,
House of Commons, 40th Parl, 3rd Sess (28 October 2010). No committee report was tabled in the House.

25 In addition to a member's annual pay ("basic sessional indemnity"), the
Speaker is paid a supplement ("indemnity") that in 2016 was $81,500
(the same as for ministers). The deputy speaker is paid a supplement
that in 2016 was $42,200 and the other chair occupants were paid sup-
plements that in 2016 were $16,800.

26 In addition to a member's annual pay ("basic sessional indemnity"), the
leader of the official opposition is paid a supplement ("indemnity"),
which in 2016 was $81,500 (the same as a minister and the Speaker)
while the leaders of the other recognized parties are paid a supplement
that in 2016 was $57,800. The official opposition House leader's supple-
ment in 2016 was $42,200 (the same as the deputy speaker) and that for
the House leaders of the other recognized parties was $16,800 (the same

as a parliamentary secretary). The Government and official opposition whips supplement in 2016 was $30,500, while the whips for the other recognized parties received $11,900 (the same as committee chairs).

27 A private member's annual pay ("basic sessional indemnity") for 2016 was $170,400. If also a committee chair, the private member receives a supplement ("indemnity") that in 2016 was $11,900.

28 The 2015 general election resulted in eleven independent members, ten of whom belonged to the Bloc Québécois and one to the Green Party.

29 A member who leaves or is expelled from his or her caucus will sit as an independent member unless the member joins the caucus of another recognized party. Independent members rarely get re-elected.

30 Proceedings on private member motions and bills are discussed in a later chapter on the House's legislative and deliberative functions.

31 In addition to a member's annual pay ("basic sessional indemnity"), the prime minister is paid a supplement ("indemnity") that in 2016 was $170,400 and ministers, including the Government House leader, were paid $81,500. Some say the ambition to become a minister leads private members on the Government side to be too subservient to directions from the Government.

32 Parliamentary secretaries receive a supplement that in 2016 was $16,800 (same as House leaders other than the official opposition House leader).

33 Standing Orders of the House of Commons, s 30-36.

34 The published debates are traditionally referred to as Hansard in tribute to Thomas Curson Hansard who in the early nineteenth century became the first authorized printer of the debates of the British House of Commons.

35 On 7 November 1867, following Confederation on 1 July 1867, the House adopted the procedural rules of its predecessor institution, the Legislative Assembly of the Province of Canada (1840–1867).

36 O'Brien and Bosc, *Procedure and Practice.*

37 Those who sit at the clerk's table are known as table officers and provide procedural advice to the Speaker and to members of the House. They also take the votes and keep the minutes of proceedings.

38 This is not unlike an experience I once had in Manitoba when I was drafting a revised statute for the Manitoba government. Too often, when I asked the departmental officials what they thought a section meant, I found their interpretations unsupported by the wording of the section.

I indicated that the section would need to be redrafted to reflect their interpretation. "No," they said, "don't redraft it. It's been worded like that for years. We know what it means and that's good enough." So much for the clarity of laws!

39 Standing Orders of the House of Commons, s 51.

40 House of Commons Debates, 42nd Parl, 1st Sess, No 89 (6 October 2016) at 1010.

41 "Modernization of the Standing Orders of the House," released 10 March 2017 by the Government House leader, proposed changes that served the Government's interests but not those of the opposition parties, except for empowering the Speaker to split up omnibus bills.

42 House of Commons, Standing Orders of the House of Commons, s 29 (November 2016).

43 House of Commons, Standing Orders of the House of Commons, s 30(1) (November 2016). The non-denominational prayer reads as follows: "Almighty God, we give thanks for the great blessings which have been bestowed on Canada and its citizens, including the gifts of freedom, opportunity and peace that we enjoy. We pray for our Sovereign, Queen Elizabeth, and the Governor General. Guide us in our deliberations as Members of Parliament, and strengthen us in our awareness of our duties and responsibilities as members. Grant us wisdom, knowledge, and understanding to preserve the blessings of this country for the benefit of all and to make good laws and wise decisions. Amen."

44 On one occasion in 2011, while a minister was answering a question in Question Period, a backbench member, seated behind the minister, could be seen struggling to stay awake and at times seeming to fall asleep. Media outlets showed this to their viewing audiences and the video was posted on YouTube.

45 O'Brien and Bosc, *Procedure and Practice*, 1223–1224.

46 Constitution Act, 1867, s 44.

47 The election of a Speaker on 3 December 2015 was by preferential balloting for the first time, pursuant to a private member's motion (M-489, Scott Reid) adopted by the House on 17 June 2015 by concurrence in the recommendation of the Standing Committee on Procedure and House Affairs, Report No. 21, tabled 3 October 2014: House of Commons, 41st Parl, 2nd Sess, Nos. 231, 232 & 233 (15, 16 & 17 June 2015) at 1510, 1915 and 1620 respectively; see Standing Orders, chapter 1, s. 4(8).

48 In the last three ballots, all the remaining candidates were Progressive Conservative members. In the 1984 general election, the Progressive Conservatives under Brian Mulroney had won the largest House majority in Canadian electoral history. It seems fair to say that, with their majority, PC members were able to ensure that the successful candidate would come from their caucus and on the final ballot, perhaps under direction from the PC Government, which PC member would be elected. See House of Commons Debates, 38th Parl, 2nd Sess, Vol 1, (30 September 1986), at 6–8.

49 The new speaker was elected on the first ballot: House of Commons Debates, 42nd Parl, 1st Sess, No 1 (3 December 2015).

50 House of Commons Debates, 35th Parl, 1st Sess, No 1 (17 January 1994).

51 Following the election of 22 May 1979, where the Progressive Conservative Party formed a minority government, the incumbent Speaker (Liberal member James Jerome) was "elected" Speaker (on a motion by the prime minister) and became the first Speaker from an opposition party: see House of Commons Debates, 31st Parl, 1st Sess, Vol 1 (9 October 1979).

52 For example, see Debates of the Senate, 39th Parl, 1st Sess, Vol 143, Issue 2 (4 April 2006). The same ceremony opens a new session of a parliament.

53 O'Brien and Bosc, *Procedure and Practice*, 425–72.

54 Bill numbers from C-1 to C-200 are reserved for Government bills while private member bills are numbered from C-201. A bill that originates in the Senate is given an S- number and retains this number when it comes before the House.

55 House of Commons, Standing Orders of the House of Commons, s 34 and 35 (November 2016).

56 House of Commons, Standing Orders of the House of Commons, s 66(2) (November 2016).

57 House of Commons, Standing Orders of the House of Commons, s 33(1) (November 2016). If a statement is made by the prime minister, it is expected that the leaders of the opposition parties will make responses. Independent members require the unanimous approval of the House before they can make a response.

58 A former Conservative member recently recounted that in response to a question he had put on the Order Paper asking for the amount of the salaries of certain high-profile persons who worked for a crown corpora-

tion, he was told that disclosure of such information was prohibited under the Privacy Act.

59 O'Brien and Bosc, *Procedure and Practice*, 465–8.

60 House of Commons, Standing Orders of the House of Commons, s 36 (November 2016).

61 O'Brien and Bosc, *Procedure and Practice*, 1157.

62 House of Commons, Standing Orders of the House of Commons, s 36(8) (November 2016).

63 House of Commons, Standing Orders of the House of Commons, s 36(2) (November 2016). Electronic petitions are posted on the parliamentary website and are open for signatures for 120 days; they are presented to the House once 500 e-signatures are obtained.

64 House of Commons, Standing Orders of the House of Commons, s 31 (November 2016), introduced in 1982.

65 See O'Brien and Bosc, *Practice and Procedure*, 422–4.

66 House of Commons Debates, 41st Parl, 1st Sess, No 226 (26 March 2013) at 1013 (Mark Warawa); see also House of Commons Debates, 41st Parl, 1st Sess, No 232 (15 April 2013) at 1520 (Michael Chong).

67 House of Commons Debates, 41st Parl, 1st Sess, No 226 (26 March 2013) at 1020 (Gordon O'Connor); see Speaker's ruling, House of Commons Debates, 41st Parl, 1st Sess, No. 238 (23 April 2013) at 1505 (Speaker Scheer).

68 See House of Commons, Standing Orders of the House of Commons, s 37(1) (November 2016).; O'Brien and Bosc, *Practice and Procedure*, 492–510.

69 See O'Brien and Bosc, *Practice and Procedure*, 579–80.

70 The New Zealand House of Representatives allows for three kinds of votes: voice votes, party votes, and individual member votes. The latter are done in the same way the House in Canada does its recorded votes, with each member voting in the Chamber. The party votes are done in a block, with the representatives of each party, typically the whips, advising the House which way their members are voting and submitting the number of their members so voting (there may be some who dissent); the members do not need to be present in the House for the vote. One might suppose that in, say, a three-party House, only the three whips would need to be in attendance on a party vote. Certainly must save time.

71 House of Commons Debates, 41st Parl, 1st Sess, No 135 (6 June 2012) at 2200.

72 House of Commons, Standing Orders of the House of Commons, s 74 (November 2016).

73 House of Commons, Standing Orders of the House of Commons, s 78 (November 2016).; see also Plante, "The Curtailment of Debate in the House of Commons."

74 House of Commons Debates, 20th Parl, 3rd Sess (29 May 1947), cited in O'Brien and Bosc, *Practice and Procedure*, 607, fn. 101.

75 House of Commons, Standing Orders of the House of Commons, s 104 (November 2016). Joint standing committees are comprised of members of Parliament and senators, with joint chairs.

76 House of Commons, Standing Orders of the House of Commons, s 108 (November 2016).

77 House of Commons, Standing Orders of the House of Commons, s 106(2) (November 2016).

78 The Special Committee on the Canadian Mission in Afghanistan was first created in the 40th Parliament, 2nd Session by resolution of the House on 10 February 2009 and after prorogation in December 2009 was continued by resolution of the House on 3 March 2010 but after the election of 2 May 2011 was not continued in the 41st Parliament. The Special Committee on Co-operatives was established by resolution of the House on 30 May 2012. The Special Committee on Violence Against Indigenous Women was created by resolution of the House adopted unanimously on 26 February 2013.

79 House of Commons, Standing Orders of the House of Commons, s 112 and 113 (November 2016).

80 House of Commons, Standing Orders of the House of Commons, s 108 (November 2016).

81 Evidence, Meeting No. 49, Standing Committee on Procedure and House Affairs, House of Commons, 40th Parl, 3rd Sess (16 March 2011) at 1110 (Scott Armstrong).

82 For an example of a witness being difficult in responding to a committee's request to appear, see Evidence, Standing Committee on Public Accounts, House of Commons, 40th Parl, 3rd Sess (15 February 2011).

83 Parliament of Canada Act, RSC 1985, c P-1, s 12 provides: "Any person

examined under this Part who willfully gives false evidence is liable to such punishment as may be imposed for perjury."

84 Fourth Report, Standing Committee on Government Operations and Estimates, House of Commons Debates, 37th Parl, 2nd Sess, No 118 (13 June 2003).

85 House of Commons Debates 37th Parl, 2nd Sess, No 151 (5 November 2003) at 1510 (Paul Forseth).

86 Ibid.

87 House of Commons Debates, 37th Parl, 2nd Sess, No 152 (6 November 2003) at 1015 (Ken Epp).

88 House of Commons Debates, 37th Parl, 2nd Sess, No 152 (6 November 2003) at 1015 (Pat Martin).

89 Second Report, "Restoring the Honour of the RCMP: Addressing Problems in the Administration of the RCMP's Pension and Insurance Plans," Standing Committee on Public Accounts. House of Commons Debates, 39th Parl, 2nd Sess, No 34 (10 December 2007).

90 See Evidence, Meeting No. 9, Standing Committee on Public Accounts, House of Commons, 39th Parl, 2nd Sess (11 December 2007) at 0920 (Barbara George).

91 Third Report, Standing Committee on Public Accounts, *House of Commons*, 39th Parl, 2nd Sess (12 February 2008). This report can be found on the Parliament of Canada website.

92 House of Commons Debates, 39th Parl, 2nd Sess, No 76 (10 April 2008) at 1005 (Shawn Murphy).

93 Apparently, the Speaker's ruling had a "chilling" effect on Department of Justice lawyers, who felt that they could no longer give legal advice to government officials about their duties or obligations to the government when faced with appearing before a House committee.

94 For more information, see House of Commons, "Guide for Witnesses Appearing Before House Committees," (2013): http://www.parl.gc.ca /About/House/WitnessesGuides/guide-witness-e.pdf.

CHAPTER TWO

1 Not being a historian, I am indebted to the work of professional historians, such as Ronald Butt, John Field, and Christopher Hill, who are cited in the bibliography.

2 Royal charters, such as the Magna Carta (as it would later be called), usually lasted only the length of the monarch's reign. They were not statutes that made permanent laws but were more like personal pledges by the king. In 1225, Henry III renounced the Magna Carta, saying it had been attained through force. However, in a "cash for charter" deal he was brought to affirm a modified version, which would later be treated as the authoritative version: see Hindley, *The Magna Carta*, 263–6.

3 Field, *The Story of Parliament*, 44.

4 Ibid., 97ff.

5 Ibid., 97ff.

6 Butt, *A History of Parliament*, 120.

7 Ibid., 131.

8 Ibid., 122; see also Butt, *A History of Parliament*, 34–6.

9 Field, *The Story of Parliament*, 52.

10 Butt, *A History of Parliament*, 187–91.

11 Ibid., 268–71.

12 These "grievances" are heard today through Opposition Day debates and members' petitions tabled in the House.

13 Today, we do this by the Speech from the Throne, which is delivered by the governor-general in the Senate Chamber to members of Parliament and Supreme Court justices.

14 Butt, *A History of Parliament*, 265; see also Field, *The Story of Parliament*, 55.

15 Field, *The Story of Parliament*, 55.

16 Butt, *A History of Parliament*, 341–7.

17 Parliament of Canada Act, RSC 1985, c P-1, s. 32., at the time of writing being amended to allow members of Parliament and senators to be paid by the government for sitting on the National Security and Intelligence Committee of Parliamentarians: see footnote 74, chapter 5. It was once required, in the UK and in Canada, that a member appointed to cabinet had to resign from the House and run in a by-election to be both a member and a minister. This requirement was abolished in the UK in 1926 and in Canada in 1931: An Act to remove the necessity of the re-election of members of the House of Commons of Canada on acceptance of office, SC 1931, c 52.

18 Auditor General Act, RSC 1985, c A-17, s 6-7.

19 Butt, *A History of Parliament*, 457.

20 Ibid., 478.

21 See Constitution Act, 1867, s 53.

22 Butt, *A History of Parliament*, 488–9.

23 Ibid., 631.

24 Ibid., 585–6.

25 Field, *The Story of Parliament*, 75.

26 The House debate on the Speech from the Throne is held under the rubric of an Address in Reply to the Speech from the Throne.

27 Field, *The Story of Parliament*, 86.

28 *Blackstone's Commentaries* – an influential and now classic – eighteenth-century treatise on the common law of England by Sir William Blackstone, published in four volumes between 1765 and 1769, said famously, "[that] The King can do no wrong is a necessary and fundamental principle of the English constitution." This principle applies today inasmuch as Queen Elizabeth II, as the queen of Canada (or the governor general as her representative in Canada) cannot be held liable for the consequences of his or her official actions.

29 Field, *The Story of Parliament*, 92–4.

30 Butt, *The Power of Parliament*, 43–4.

31 Field, *The Story of Parliament*, 99.

32 Adjournments are the end of a sitting of the House (usually at the end of the day) and are not to be confused with prorogations, which end a parliamentary session (and may include periods when the House is not sitting) or a dissolution, which ends both a parliamentary session and a parliament by dissolving the parliament (this is usually done for an election).

33 Field, *The Story of Parliament*, 101.

34 Ibid.

35 Zagorin, *A History of Political Thought*, 191.

36 Field, *The Story of Parliament*, 105–6.

37 Royle, *The British Civil War*, 150.

38 Ibid., 153

39 Ibid., 157.

40 Ibid., 159.

41 Zagorin, *A History of Political Thought*, 191–2.

42 Field, *The Story of Parliament*, 108.

43 Royle, *The British Civil War*, 165.

44 Field, *The Story of Parliament*, 109.

45 Royle, *The British Civil War*, 476.

46 Wedgwood, *The Trial of Charles I*, 29.

47 Ibid., 32.

48 The fact that authority to proceed had been secured from a Commons that was not representative of the people was not acknowledged.

49 Field, *The Story of Parliament*, 116–17.

50 Ibid., 122.

51 Other rights granted included freedom from taxation by royal prerogative, freedom to petition the monarch, freedom to elect members of Parliament without interference from the sovereign, freedom from cruel and unusual punishment, and freedom from fine and forfeiture without trial.

52 Some would argue that the UK lost its parliamentary sovereignty when it joined the European Union in 1973, as that enabled European laws to apply in the UK. It is widely believed that the so-called "Brexit" referendum vote of 23 June 2016 in favour of UK withdrawal from the EU was driven in part by a desire to reclaim England's sovereignty (particularly to deal with the level of immigration from EU states). Some would argue that the referendum vote was an extra-constitutional exercise in "people's sovereignty" as in a republic ("We, the people …") at the expense of constitutional parliamentary sovereignty. The UK prime minister announced that she would use Crown prerogative powers to give notice of UK withdrawal under Article 50 of the EU Treaty, but this approach was challenged in court. The applicant, Miller, argued that the Government was constitutionally required to consult Parliament; that is, it could not act alone under its prerogative powers. In late 2016, the UK High Court held that parliamentary approval was required: see *R (Miller) v Secretary of State for Exiting the European Union*, [2016] EWHC 2768 (3 November 2016). This decision was upheld on appeal to the UK Supreme Court: [2017] UKSC 5 (24 January 2017). On 1 February 2017, the UK House of Commons approved the Government giving notice under Article 50. These two decisions are a useful read on the constitutional limits of Crown prerogative powers against parliamentary sovereignty. In March 2017 the UK Parliament gave the British Government

permission to issue a Notice of Withdrawal from the EU and this was done on 29 March 2017, triggering the start of a two-year period for withdrawal negotiations.

53 For Canada, Article 8 would become s 37 of the Constitution Act 1867. The electoral system at that time (such as it was) was not changed by the 1689 Bill of Rights. Electoral reform in England would not come for another 143 years, with the Reform Acts of 1832 and 1864.

54 1689 Bill of Rights, article 9, applies to the House in Canada today.

55 Birch, *Representative and Responsible Government*, 133.

56 Ibid., 135.

57 The use of the descriptives Lower and Upper here are not to be confused with the use of these terms in reference to the House of Commons as the lower house and the Senate as the upper house, which is modeled on the British practice of referring to the House of Commons there as the lower house and the House of Lords as the upper house. Lower Canada was lower than Upper Canada only in the sense that it was further down the St Lawrence River.

58 For a detailed account of the struggle for responsible government in the Province of Canada, I recommend Stephen Leacock's *Baldwin Lafontaine Hinks*; see also Careless, *The Union of the Canadas, infra*.

59 Birch, *Representative and Responsible Government*, 131-2.

60 Ibid., 132.

61 Careless, *The Union of the Canadas*, 115.

62 Ibid., 119.

63 Ibid., 120.

64 Ibid., 115. According to Canadian historian J.M.S. Careless, Lord Elgin's "firm convictions were tempered by cool common sense and a keen awareness of the current of popular opinion."

65 Under the Constitution Act 1867, the maritime colonies of New Brunswick and Nova Scotia were joined with the two parts of the Province of Canada (Lower and Upper Canada) to form four provinces of the Dominion of Canada. The other provinces of Canada joined later.

66 The Supreme Court of Canada has interpreted the descriptive "similar in principle" to mean that Canada's parliamentary system operates on the same principles as apply to the British model of parliamentary government: *New Brunswick Broadcasting Co v Nova Scotia*, [1993] 1 SRC 319.

67 Most modern-day democratic systems of government have the same
    three branches but may differ on the degree to which these functions
    operate separately. For example, the congressional system based on the
    American model, unlike the parliamentary system based on the British
    model, separates the three branches completely, while the parliamentary
    system has the executive branch sitting in the legislative branch.

68 The Marketing Freedom for Grain Farmers Act, SC 2011, c 25.

69 Canadian Wheat Board Act, RSC 1985, c C-24, s 47.

70 See Federal Court of Canada decision, *Friends of the Canadian Wheat
    Board et al v Attorney-General for Canada et al*, 2011 FC 1432.

71 See Russell, "Does It Matter If Our Laws Are Passed Illegally?"

72 In the notorious King-Byng affair of 1926, Governor General Lord Byng
    disregarded the advice of the prime minister to dissolve Parliament and
    call an election and instead appointed a new prime minister. Up to this
    time, the governor general had been seen as representing the king or
    queen in both the imperial Privy Council in London and the Canadian
    Privy Council and therefore had divided loyalties. The governor general
    as representing the king or queen in the Canadian Privy Council only
    was accepted at the Imperial Conference of 1926 and enacted by the
    Statute of Westminster in 1931.

73 On an Opposition Day motion by a vote of 139–135: House of Com-
    mons Debates, 40th Parl, 3rd Sess, No 11 (17 March 2010) at 1510.

74 See Evidence, meetings Nos. 10 to 15, 17, 20, and 26, Standing Commit-
    tee on Procedure and House Affairs; House of Commons Debates, 40th
    Parl, 3rd Sess (27 April 2010) to House of Commons Debates, 40th Parl,
    3rd Sess (21 October 2010).

75 Bill C-16, An Act to amend the Canada Elections Act, 1st Sess, 39th Parl,
    2006–2007 (assented to 3 May 2007), SC 2007, c 10.

76 Section 1, An Act to amend the Canada Elections Act, supra, adding sec-
    tion 56.1(1) to Canada Elections Act, S. 2000, c 9. "[A]t the governor
    general's discretion" is misleading as the governor general has little or
    no discretion on whether to dissolve Parliament and call an election.
    The election date formula prescribes an election date that could be less
    than four years or almost five years after the previous election, depend-
    ing on the month in which the previous election was held. Constitution
    Act 1867, section 50, limits the term of a House of Commons (effective-
    ly, parliament) to five years.

77 *Conacher v Canada (prime minister)*, 2009 FC 920.; appeal dismissed 25 May 2010, *Conacher v Canada (prime minister)*, 2010 FCA 131.; Supreme Court of Canada denied leave to appeal on 20 January 2011, *Conacher v Canada (prime minister)* (2011), 225 CRR (2d) 375.

78 For a good discussion of the governor general's power of prorogation and residual powers generally, see Blowden, "Dawson and Forsey Clash on the Prorogation of 2008 and Over Responsible Government."

79 Notable Canadian constitutional expert Eugene Forsey (1904–1991), maintained that the Crown (the governor general) had a constitutional function independent of the Government.

80 In Manitoba in 1988 the Government lost a confidence vote and the next day the premier announced the date for the next election and that he had resigned as the leader of his party. The word in my office (I was working for the government of Manitoba at the time) was that the premier's resignation included resigning as premier without giving any advice to the lieutenant governor on a successor appointment pending the election. We had to consider the constitutional implications for appointing an interim premier. As it happened, I believe, constitutional difficulties were managed ex post facto until the new party leader was elected three weeks later, less than a month before the election, though, if memory serves, the new leader did not become premier for the few weeks remaining before the election (which the Government lost).

81 A senator can be appointed a minister and would still sit in the Senate. A prime minister might appoint a private citizen to cabinet but would also recommend the individual for appointment to the Senate (unless there was a by-election available to give the individual a seat in the House).

82 Winetrobe, "The Autonomy of Parliament," in Oliver and Drewry, eds., *The Law and Parliament*, 14.

83 Ibid., 15. A senior government official once privately described the House as a "minor process obstacle."

84 Mill, *Considerations on Representative Government*, 58.

85 Constitution Act, 1867, s 53-54.

86 Constitution Act, 1867, s 96.; Federal Courts Act, RSC 1985, c F-7, s 5.2-5.4; Supreme Court Act, RSC 1985, c S-26, s 4.

87 Constitution Act, 1867, s 99(1). The only instance of removal by the House of Commons and the Senate was the 1967 case of Justice Leo Landreville of the Ontario Supreme Court.

88 Supreme Court of Canada Act, RSC 1985, c S-26, s 53.

89 Order-in-Council P.C. 1996-1497, 20 September 1996; Reference re Secession of Québec, [1998] 2 SCR 217 [Secession].

90 Secession, supra para 49.

91 This issue was prominent in *R v Nur*, 2015 SCC 15., where the Supreme Court of Canada, in a 6–3 split decision, struck down legislation that established minimum mandatory sentences, which the Court said imposed a cruel and unusual punishment. The dissenting decision criticized the majority for interfering with the will of parliament.

92 McLachlan, "Unwritten Constitutional Principles."

93 Complaints about a judge may be put through a formal committee inquiry and result in a report that is made public (available online), possibly including a recommendation to the minister of Justice for removal of the judge, or may be resolved by an agreed outcome, including a "voluntary" resignation. Since its formation in 1971, the Council has conducted eleven formal committee inquiries: see https://www.cjc-ccm.gc.ca.

94 See "Constitutional Conventions," Library of Parliament Paper TIPS-1E, 11 July 2006, Parliament of Canada, and also Heard, "Constitutional Conventions and Parliament."

95 Re: Resolution to amend the Constitution (Patriation Reference), [1981] 1 SCR 753, paras 774-775.

96 Ibid., para 880.

97 Ibid., para 905.

98 Secession, supra para 32.

99 Ibid., para 98; affirmed again in *Ontario English Catholic Teachers' Association v Ontario (Attorney General)*, [2001] 1 SCR 470.

100 *Schmidt v Canada (Attorney General)*, 2016 FC 269 [Schmidt]. Reasons for Judgment, 2 March 2016.

101 Prime Minister John Diefenbaker's Bill of Rights from 1960.

102 Canadian Bill of Rights, SC 1960, c 44, s 3(1).; and Department of Justice Act, RSC 1985, c J-2, s 4.1.

103 Schmidt, supra para 186.

104 Schmidt, supra para 189, referring to Hogg, *Constitutional Law of Canada*, 36.

105 Schmidt, supra para 275.

106 Schmidt, supra para 276.

107 Schmidt, supra para 279.

108 Bill C-14, Legislative Background: Medical Assistance in Dying, 1st Sess, 42nd Parl, 2016 (assented to 17 June 2016), SC 2016, c 3.

109 In *Carter v Canada (Attorney General)*, [2015] 1 SCR 331., the Court held the total criminal prohibition on assisted dying unjustifiably infringed the section 7 Charter right to life, liberty and security of the person.

110 Though some government lawyers worry that the minister may plan to publicly disclose in some manner the legal opinions she gets from her departmental lawyers.

111 Where accountability was the catchword in the 2006 election and resulted in a change of Government, transparency was the equivalent in the 2015 election and led to a change of Government.

112 See House of Commons Debates, 42nd Parl, 1st Sess, No 45 (22 April 2016) at 1005 and 1030.

113 The addendum quotes this from *R v Mills*, [1999] 3 SCR 668, at para 55.

114 Ibid., para 58.

115 Smith, "A Question of Trust," 25.

116 Some also consider the chief commissioner of the Human Rights Commission and the public service commissioner to be officers of Parliament but this is not officially recognized. Some have also expressed the view that the parliamentary budget officer should be an officer of Parliament but that's another story.

117 On the Office of the Auditor General of Canada, see Dubois, "Accountability in Parliament," and Parliament of Canada Library of Parliament Background Paper No. 2011-71-E, "The Office of the Auditor General of Canada: Beyond Bean Counting," last updated 9 July 2014, http://www.lop.parl.gc.ca/content/lop/ResearchPublications/2011-71-e.htm. See also Auditor General Act, RSC 1985, c A-17.

118 Government of Canada, "Relations Between Parliamentary Agencies and the Public Service."

119 *Canada (Auditor General) v Canada (Minister of Energy, Mines & Resources)*, [1989] 2 SCR 49.

120 Conflict of Interest Act, SC 2006, c 9, s 2.

CHAPTER THREE

1 McKay, *Erskine May's Treatise on the Law*, 75; O'Brien and Bosc, *Procedure and Practice*, 60.

2 Constitution Act, 1867, s 18.

3 Parliament of Canada Act, RSC 1985, c P-1, s 4 and 5.

4 Erskine May, *Treatise on the Law* (1844), 1st ed., 48–9.

5 Constitution Act, 1867, s 18.; See Parliament of Canada Act, *supra*, s 4.

6 House of Commons Debates, 41st Parl, 1st Sess, No 232 (15 April 2013) at 1520 (Michael Chong).

7 Re Ouellet (No. 1), (1976) DLR (3d) 73 (Quebec SC). Freedom of speech in the House was also upheld in Canadian courts in *Stopforth v Goyer* (1978) 20 OR (2d) 262., (reversed on other grounds) and in *Janssen-Ortho Inc v Amgen Canada Inc* [2004] OJ No 2523. See also paragraphs 73–8 on appeal: *Janssen-Ortho Inc v Amgen Canada Inc* (2005), 256 DLR (4th) 407.

8 O'Brien and Bosc, *Procedure and Practice*, 59–159.

9 House of Commons Debates, 34th Parl, 3rd Sess, Vol. 4 (31 October 1991) at pp. 4309-10 (Ian Waddell) and House of Commons Debates (online), 37th Parl, 1st Sess, No 175 (24 April 2002) at 1505 (Keith Martin).

10 See O'Brien and Bosc, *Procedure and Practice*, 134–5. Also, the seat of a member convicted of an indictable offence and sentenced to imprisonment for two years or more is automatically vacated: Criminal Code of Canada, RSC 1986, c C-46, s 750(2).

11 In 1991, the year I came to the House, the House administration issued a policy on harassment for its staff (excluding members and members' staff).

12 Parliament of Canada, Code of Conduct for members of the House of Commons: Sexual Harassment, Ottawa: Standing Committee on Procedure and House Affairs.; House of Commons Debates, 41st Parl, 2nd Sess, No 226 (8 June 2016). Concurred in by the House 9 June 2015; see Standing Orders, Appendix II: Code of Conduct for Members of the House of Commons: Sexual Harassment.

13 Presumably, this means the code applies only where criminal charges have not been laid though they could be at some point as the Criminal Code covers sexual harassment: see section 264 (criminal harassment), section 265 (assault), and section 271 (sexual assault).

14 Erskine May, *Treatise on the Law* (1844), 1st ed., 56.

15 *Burdett v Abbot* [1814–23] All England Reports 101 at p 105.

16 See discussion in chapter 1, at p 33–4, infra.

17 See chapter 1, at p 34–5, infra.

18 See chapter 5, at p 153, infra.

19 See *Burdett v Abbott*; *Burdett v Coleman* (1811) K.B. 14 East 1-2, reproduced in Pollock, Campbell, and Saunders, eds. *Revised Reports of Cases in English Courts of Common Law and Equity from the Year 1785 as are still of practical utility*, at p 12: 450.

20 Supra, note 14.

21 He was found guilty of contempt by the House and was imprisoned for four months, until the end of the session. *Journals*, 14 February 1913 at p 249; 17 February 1913 at p 254; 18 February 1913 at p 266–7; 20 February 1913 at p 274–8.

22 One of the members (30 October 1991), angry at having missed a vote, tried to take hold of the mace as it was being carried out of the chamber by the sergeant-at-arms when the House adjourned for the day. The other member (7 April 2002), angry at Government members for defeating his bill, went to the table, picked up the mace, and shouted at the Speaker, "We don't live in a democracy anymore!"

23 House of Common Debates, 34th Parl, 3rd Sess, Vol 4 (31 October 1991) at p 4309 (Speaker John Fraser). For the arguments made by members with respect to the actions of the two members, see House of Commons Debates, 34th Parl, 3rd Sess, Vol 4 (31 October 1991) at p 4271–85 and House of Commons Debates, 37th Parl, 1st Sess, No 175 (24 April 2002) at p 1064–70.

24 *R v Pitt* (1762), 3 Burr. 1336; Maingot, *Parliamentary Privilege*, 179.

25 Standing Committee on Agriculture and Agri-food, 37th Parl, 3rd Sess, Meetings No. 2, 4, 7, 9, 10, 11, 13, 19, 21, and 22 (16 February–12 May, 2004).

26 Third Report, Standing Committee on Agriculture and Agri-food, tabled in the House and concurred in: see House of Commons, 37th Parl, 3rd Sess (6 May 2004).

27 Fourth Report, Standing Committee on Agriculture and Agri-food, tabled in the House: House of Commons, 37th Parl, 3rd Sess (13 May 2004).

28 *Landers v Woodworth*, (1878) 2 SCR 158., cited with approval in *Canada*

(*House of Commons*) *v Vaid*, 2005 SCC 30 at para 29 (sub-paragraph 11), [2005] 1 SCR 667.

29 *New Brunswick Broadcasting Co. v Nova Scotia (speaker of the House of Assembly)* [1993] 1 SCR 319 [New Brunswick]. As I was responsible only for legislative counsel services at the House at this time, I was not personally involved in the management of this case on behalf of the House.

30 *Canada (House of Commons) v Vaid*, 2005 SCC 30, [2005] 1 SCR 667 [Vaid].

31 Supra, note 29, at para 95.

32 Supra, note 30, at para 47.

33 Supra, note 30, at para 56.

34 Quoted with approval in *Vaid*, para 41.

35 Supra, note 30, at para 29, quoting *New Brunswick*, 343.

36 Supra, note 30, at para 29.

37 Supra, note 30, at para 39.

38 Supra, note 30, at para 46.

39 The Commission of Inquiry into the Sponsorship Program and Advertising Activities, Mr Justice John Gomery, commissioner, established by Order of the Governor-in-Council 2004-110 on 19 February 2004 pursuant to the Inquiries Act, RSC 1985, c I-11, Part I.

40 This may seem to some readers plenty of time, except that proceedings of the House and of committees do not happen quickly. Committees as a rule meet only on Tuesdays and Thursdays. Second, the two committees in this case (PAC and PROC) had to be consulted, one *after* the other. Third, committees act only through reports to the House. They do not resolve matters and report the same day. At the end of the first committee meeting on Tuesday (PAC), committee staff had to prepare a draft report for consideration at the next meeting of the committee (Thursday) where, it was hoped, a final report would be approved and the chair instructed to table it in the House (possibly not until Friday morning). Fourth, the House had to vote on the first report (PAC) before it was sent to the second committee (PROC). This had to be done no later than the following Monday. The same time-consuming process occurred with the second committee (PROC) before its report was tabled and the House voted on it, which could be no later than Friday as we had to report to the commission by the following Monday. Thus each committee-House stage needs a week IF everything works as hoped,

which in this case it did. There was no time for procedural delays, which are easily caused.

41 Gomery Inquiry Transcripts (Ottawa: Federal Government, 22 November 2004) vol 37, at 6332–44. (Online at Library and Archives Canada website, electronic collections).

42 Unlike the O'Connor Walkerton Commission Inquiry in Ontario in 200–02, where committee testimony was used without anyone rising to object.

43 *Gagliano v Canada (Attorney General)*, 2005 FC 576.

44 Ibid., at para 28.

45 Ibid., at para 77.

46 *Royal Canadian Mounted Police Deputy Commissioner v Canada (Attorney General)*, 2007 FC 564, 158 ACWS (3d) 656.

47 Ibid., at para 44.

48 Ibid., at para 58.

49 Ibid., at paras 63, 64.

50 *Knopf v Canada (speaker of the House of Commons)*, 2006 FC 808, 149 ACWS (3d) 1134.

51 Ibid., at para 53.

52 Fédération franco-ténoise c Canada (Procureur général), 2008 NWTCA 8 [Fédération Franco-Ténoise]. The NWT Official Languages Act, RSC 1985, c 31 (4th Supp.) applied to all "government institutions," which are defined in the Act to include the NWT Legislative Assembly.

53 The Legislative Assembly and Executive Council Act (Nunavut), RSNWT 1988, c L-5, s 12(1)., vests the NWT Legislative Assembly with "the same rights, privileges, immunities and powers" as those held by the House of Commons and requires that the courts take judicial notice of these.

54 Fédération Franco-Ténoise, supra at para 297.

55 Fédération Franco-Ténoise, supra at para 287.

56 Evidence, Meeting No. 29, Standing Committee on Public Accounts, House of Commons, 40th Parl, 2nd Sess (18 June 2009) at 1605 (Rob Walsh).

57 See speaker's ruling in the House of Commons Debates, 37th Parl, 2nd Sess, No 78 (26 May 2003) at 1205.

58 The use of forty days for a prescribed period of time goes back as far as

the Magna Carta in 1225 and finds its beginnings in the Bible (Christ's time in the desert).

59 There are exceptions. I recall the member from the Yukon telling me that if he left Ottawa following House adjournment on Friday and was back for Monday morning opening of the House, he only had time for a coffee at the Whitehorse airport. It took the member fourteen hours and three airlines each way. Many members from distant ridings are allowed by their whips to leave Ottawa on Thursday so they can fly back on Sunday, which explains why Friday is often a non-event day (no votes).

60 For example, see *R v Brown* 2001 PESCTD 6 (CanLII) at https://www.canlii.org/en/pe/pesctd/doc/2001/2001pesctd6/2001pesctd6.html.

61 *Ainsworth Lumber Co v Canada (Attorney General)* [2003] BCCA 239, 121 ACWS (3d) 836.

62 *Samson Indian Nation and Band v Canada*, 2003 FC 975.

63 Supra, note 29.

64 *Telezone Inc v Canada (Attorney General)* [2003] OJ No 2543.

65 *Manley v Telezone Inc & Canada* (2004), 69 OR (3d) 161.

66 Ibid., at para 39.

67 Ibid., at paras 41–4.

68 Ibid., at para 51.

69 The practice of referring to the Senate as "the other place" is a carry-over from the British Parliament where members in the Commons referred to the House of Lords only as "the other place." The historic origins of this practice are not clear although a British House of Commons Select Committee Report in 1998 thought the practice was meant to prevent members from saying anything derogatory about the House of Lords, which was not allowed: see paragraph 35, Fourth Report (4 March 1998), Select Committee on Modernisation of the House of Commons, available on the UK parliamentary website at www.publications.parliament.uk.

70 House of Commons Debates, 37th Parl, 2nd Sess, No 105 (26 May 2003) at 1205 (Speaker Peter Milliken).

71 Eighth Report, Standing Committee on Procedure and House Affairs, House of Commons, 37th Parl, 3rd Sess (8 March 2004).

72 Following the shooting incident on Parliament Hill on October 22, 2014, the Government proposed that the RCMP assume responsibility

for security within the parliamentary precincts. This was legislated by clause 98 of Bill C-59, Economic Action Plan 2015 Act, No 1, 2nd Sess, 41st Parl, 2015 (assented to 23 June 2015), SC 2015, c 36. This regime will be subject to direction by the Speakers, which is consistent with the privileges of the House.

73 *Zündel v Boudria* (1999), 46 OR (3d) 410, para 18. see also *R v Behrens*, 2004 ONCJ 327., where the court accepted that the Ontario speaker's authority applied to the grounds around the parliamentary building and his actions were an exercise of privilege and beyond the court's jurisdiction.

74 *Zündel v Liberal Party of Canada* [1999] SCCA No 593., per Chadwick, J., court file No. 98-CV-7845, January 22, 1999.

75 *Payson v Hubert* (1904) 34 SCR 400.

76 Supra, note 7, 87.

77 *Ainsworth Lumber Co v Canada (Attorney General)* [2003] BCCA 239, 121 ACWS (3d) 836. When the House adjourns for the six-week Christmas break, the two-week Easter break or the eleven-week summer break, it nonetheless remains in session and the privilege applies during these adjournment periods. This leaves only the period following a prorogation or a dissolution which, when one applies the forty-day shoulder periods, leaves little opportunity for serving a subpoena on a member within the precincts.

78 Letter from Carolyn Kobernick, assistant deputy minister, Department of Justice, dated 9 December 2009, to me as law clerk and parliamentary counsel, House of Commons, provided to the Special Committee on the Canadian Mission in Afghanistan.

79 At the time of writing, there have been reports that the Government will be proposing amendments to the Access to Information Act, RSC 1985, c A-1., which does not apply to the House, to make it apply with respect to members' expenses. Whether disclosure of other House financial information will be included has not been indicated. In my view, legislated public disclosure of House expenditures, in whole or in part, would not be an encroachment on the privileges of the House, in particular, its privilege of exclusive control of its internal affairs, although board meetings on financial matters may, at least in part, be privileged and protected from disclosure.

CHAPTER FOUR

1 See Monahan and Shaw, *Constitutional Law*, 262–85.

2 Constitution Act, 1867, s 93 and 95.

3 Constitution Act, 1867, s 92A and 94A.

4 Sections 2, 8 and 9, Canadian Charter of Rights and Freedoms, Part I of the Constitution Act. 1982, being Schedule B to the Canada Act 1982 (UK), 1982, c 11, s 2, 8, and 9.

5 Canadian Charter of Rights and Freedoms, Part I of the Constitution Act. 1982, being Schedule B to the Canada Act 1982 (UK), 1982, c 11, s 7, 10-14.

6 Canadian Charter of Rights and Freedoms, Part I of the Constitution Act. 1982, being Schedule B to the Canada Act 1982 (UK), 1982, c 11, s 15.

7 Canadian Charter of Rights and Freedoms, Part I of the Constitution Act. 1982, being Schedule B to the Canada Act 1982 (UK), 1982, c 11, s 1.

8 Canadian Charter of Rights and Freedoms, Part I of the Constitution Act. 1982, being Schedule B to the Canada Act 1982 (UK), 1982, c 11, s 33.

9 Private member bills are not to be confused with private bills. Both government bills and private member bills are public bills, that is, bills that deal with matters of general application. Private bills relate to matters of interest to the individual or corporation named in the bill and are the descendants of the ancient practice in which petitions were made to the king on a legal issue for which there was no relief in the courts under the common law. Today, private bills account for only a "miniscule percentage" of House business: see O'Brien and Bosc, *Procedure and Practice*, 1177.

10 See Chapter 2 discussion of Schmidt.

11 Bill C-52, An Act to implement certain provisions of the budget tabled in Parliament on March 19, 2007, 1st Sess, 39th Parl, 2007, s 85 (assented to 22 June 2007), SC 2007, c 29.

12 See Senate Bill S-236, An Act to amend the Financial Administration Act (borrowing of money), 2nd Sess, 39th Parl, 2008, (second reading 10 June 2008, died on the Order Paper with dissolution on 7 September 2008) and Bill S-217, An Act to amend the Financial Administration Act (borrowing of money), 1st Sess, 41st Parl, 2013, (second reading 21 May 2013, died on the Order Paper with dissolution on 13 September 2013), reintroduced as Bill S-204, An Act to amend the Financial Administration Act (borrowing of money), 2nd Sess, 41st Parl, 2013,

(second reading and referred to committee on 6 March 2014), and not heard from since.

13 Since 2007, the federal government's debt has increased from $457 billion in fiscal 2007–08 to $612 billion in fiscal 2013–14, a 33% increase. See Scott Clark and Peter Devries, "Mr. Flaherty's Blank Cheque," 18 June 2013, at www.ipolitics.ca.

14 See discussion on proposals for miscellaneous statute law amendments before the Standing Committee on Justice and Human Rights, 2nd Sess, 41st Parl, Meeting No. 45 (7 October 2014), and Meeting No. 53, (20 November 2014); see Bill C-47, Miscellaneous Statute Law Amendment Act, 2014, 2nd Sess, 41st Parl, 2015 (assented to 26 February 2015), SC 2015, c 3.

15 See Massicotte, "Omnibus Bills in Theory and Practice"; O'Brien and Bosc, *Procedure and Practice*, 724–5; see legal analysis in Dodek, "Omnibus Bills: Constitutional and Legislative Liberations," infra.

16 See O'Brien and Bosc, *Procedure and Practice*, 724.

17 Bill C-38, An Act to implement certain provisions of the budget tabled in Parliament on March 29, 2012 and other measures, 1st Sess, 41st Parl, 2012 (tabled 26 April 2012). For members' objections, see House of Commons Debates, 41st Parl, 1st Sess, No 133 (4 June 2012) at 1200, No 137 (8 June 2012) at 1010 and No 138 (11 June 2012) at 1510. Note: a bill has "clauses" that become "sections" once the bill is enacted as an Act of Parliament.

18 The three acts were Canadian Environmental Assessment Act 2012, SC 2012, c 19, s 52., (129 sections), Integrated Cross-border Law Enforcement Operations Act, SC 2012, c 19, s 368., (16 sections) and Shared Services Canada Act, SC 2012, c 19, s 711., (20 sections). In 2015 an omnibus bill to implement the Government's 2015 budget included two new acts: Federal Balanced Budget Act, SC 2015, c 36, s 41., and the Prevention of Terrorist Travel Act, SC 2015, c 36, s 42., as well as provisions relating to security on the Hill and legalizing RCMP actions under the Access to Information Act, RSC 1985, c A-1.

19 As quoted by Leslie MacKinnon, "Powering up the Speaker of the House."

20 House of Commons Debates, 35th Parl, 1st Sess, No 45 (25 March 1994) at 1005 (Stephen Harper).

21 The Liberal Government elected in 2015 introduced an omnibus budget bill, Bill C-44, An Act to implement certain provisions of the budget

tabled in Parliament on 22 March 2017 and other measures: House of
Commons Debates, 42nd Parl, 1st Sess, No. 164 (11 April 2017) at 1545
(Bill Morneau).

22 For example, see the change in public opinion on Bill C-51, which
became the Anti-terrorism Act, 2015, between its introduction in the
House on 30 January 2015 and approval by the House on 6 May 2015
and while the bill was in the Senate until enactment on 18 June 2015.

23 House of Commons, Standing Orders of the House of Commons, s 78
(November 2016). See O'Brien and Bosc, *Procedure and Practice*, 660–70.

24 House of Commons, Standing Orders of the House of Commons, s
71(November 2016). The term "reading" originates from "ancient Parliamentary practice" in England when bills could not be reproduced readily
for members and the clerk had to read the bill out to members at each
stage in the process: see O'Brien and Bosc, *Procedure and Practice*, 735.

25 O'Brien and Bosc, *Procedure and Practice*, 744.

26 This contrasts with the American legislative process in the US Congress,
which allows the legislative houses to "tack on" unrelated items to a bill.

27 In most cases, the bill, as amended by the committee, is reprinted to facilitate the preparation of amendments to the committee-amended bill.

28 In the mid-1990s, the rules for amendments at report stage were
changed to prevent opposition parties from proposing hundreds of
amendments – in one or two cases over a thousand – in an attempt to
slow down, if not obstruct, the legislative process. See report stage proceedings on bill C-68, An Act respecting firearms and other weapons
(gun control), 1st Sess, 35th Parl. *House of Commons Debates*, 35th Parl,
1st Sess, No 216 (12 June 1995). Bill C-9, An Act to give effect to the
Nisga'a Final Agreement, 2nd Sess, 36th Parl. *House of Commons Debates*,
36th Parl, 2nd Sess, No 33 (2 December 1999), and *House of Commons
Debates*, 36th Parl, 2nd Sess, No 35 (6 December 1999), and Bill C-20,
An Act to give effect to the requirement for clarity as set out in the
opinion of the Supreme Court of Canada in the Quebec Secession Reference (Clarity Bill), 2nd Sess, 36th Parl, 2000 (assented to 29 June
2000), SC 2000, c 26., *House of Commons Debates*, 36th Parl, 2nd Sess, No
62 (3 March 2000) at 1255 (Daniel Turp) and No 63 (13 March 2000) at
1155 (Suzanne Tremblay).

29 See Standing Orders, chapter 40.

30 Items at the bottom of the Order of Precedence take at least six weeks

to get to the top and probably longer when one takes into account last minute cancellations during the Private Members' Business hour due to unavailability of the sponsoring member or changes in the House's daily program as well as the scheduled week-long breaks in the House's sitting schedule.

31 House of Commons, Standing Orders of the House of Commons, s 97.1 (November 2016).

32 See Third Report, Special Committee on the Modernization and Improvement of the Procedures of the House of Commons, 37th Parl, 2nd Sess (28 February 2003), concurred in by the House on 17 March 2003 and the 49th Report, Standing Committee on Procedure and House Affairs, House of Commons, 39th Parl, 1st Sess (7 May 2007).

33 By comparison, in this eighteen-month period, fifty-seven government bills were introduced in the House, of which thirty-six advanced through the House and the Senate and received royal assent by 22 April 2015.

34 Bill C-247, An Act to expand the Mandate of Service Canada in respect of the death of a Canadian citizen or Canadian resident, 2nd Sess, 41st Parl, 2013–2015 (assented to 18 June 2015), SC 2015, c 15.

35 Bill-217, An Act to amend the Criminal Code (mischief relating to war memorials), 2nd Sess, 41st Parl, 2013-2015 (assented to 6 June 2014), SC 2014, c 9.

36 House of Commons, Standing Orders of the House of Commons, s 91.1 (November 2016).

37 Bill C-425, An Act to amend the Citizenship Act (honouring the Canadian Armed Forces), 2nd Sess, 41st Parl, 2013-2015.

38 Eighth Report, Standing Committee on Citizenship and Immigration, House of Commons, 41st Parl, 1st Sess (23 April 2013) at 1005.

39 House of Commons Debates, 41st Parl, 1st Sess, No 238 (25 April 2013) at 1510 (Bob Rae).

40 House of Commons Debates, 41st Parl, 1st Sess, No 252 (21 May 2013) at 1335 (Speaker Milliken).

41 Section 54 is repeated in Standing Orders of the House of Commons, s 79(1). See also Speaker's ruling on Bill C-363, An Act to amend the Canada Mortgage and Housing Corporation Act (profits distributed to provinces), 1st Sess, 38th Parl, 2004-2005 at House of Commons Debates, 38th Parl, 1st Sess, No 130 (3 October 2005) at 1100 (Deputy Speaker Blaikie) and also the speaker's ruling on Bill C-279, An Act to

amend the DNA Identification Act (establishment of indexes), 1st Sess, 39th Parl, 2006-2007 at House of Commons Debates, 39th Parl, 1st Sess, No 79 (8 November 2006) at 1515 (Speaker Milliken).

42 Bill C-216, An Act to amend the Unemployment Insurance Act (jury service), 1st Sess, 35th Parl, 1994-1996 (assented to 26 March 1995), SC 1995, c 7.

43 See Speaker's rulings, House of Commons Debates, 38th Parl, 1st Sess, No 27 (18 November 2004) at 1500 (Speaker Milliken) and House of Commons Debates, 39th Parl, 1st Sess, No 30 (31 May 2006) at 1540 (Speaker Milliken).

44 By virtue of the Interpretation Act, RSC 1985 c I-11, s 23(4), the power to appoint a person to a public office includes the power to pay the person appointed.

45 *House of Commons Debates*, 38th Parl, 1st Sess, No 52 (8 February 2005) at 1810 (Acting Speaker Marcel Proulx). As of 1 January 2009, all amounts received or paid out under the Employment Insurance Act, SC1996, c 23, have been assigned to a separate account, the Employment Insurance Operating Account. If the royal recommendation requirement is limited to charges made upon the Consolidated Revenue Fund, it may be that bills increasing employment insurance benefits may no longer require a royal recommendation.

46 Bill C-331, Ukrainian Canadian Restitution Act, 1st Sess, 37th Parl, 2001-2002. See House of Commons Debates, 38th Parl, 1st Sess, No 71 (21 March 2005) at 1500 (Speaker Milliken).

47 The Speaker applied the same reasoning on bill C-333, Chinese Canadian Recognition and Redress Act, 1st Sess, 38th Parl, 2004–2005. See House of Commons Debates, 39th Parl, 1st Sess, No 71 (21 March 2005) at 1500 (Speaker Milliken).

48 House of Commons Debates, 39th Parl, 1st Sess, No 52 (25 September 2006) at 1515 (Speaker Milliken).

49 Bill C-259, An Act to amend the Excise Tax Act (elimination of excise tax on jewellery), 1st Sess, 38th Parl, 2004-2005.

50 Evidence, Meeting No. 60, Standing Committee on Finance, House of Commons, 38th Parl, 1st Sess (17 May 2005), testimony of Mr Geoff Trueman, Senior Tax Policy Officer, Sales Tax Division, Tax Policy Branch, Department of Finance.

51 The House gave its final approval to Bill C-259, supra, on 14 June 2005. The bill was later adopted in the Senate and received royal assent and

became law on Friday, 25 November 2005 – just-in-time delivery: on the next sitting day, Monday, 28 November 2005, Parliament was dissolved for the election of 23 January 2006.

52 See Speaker's ruling on Bill C-474, National Sustainable Development Act, 2nd Sess, 39th Parl, 2007-2008 at House of Commons Debates, 39th Parl, 2nd Sess, No 48 (11 February 2008) at 1100 (Speaker Milliken).

53 See Speaker's ruling on financial control of the Government: Bill C-23, An Act to establish the Department of Human Resources and Skills Development and to amend and repeal certain related Acts, 1st Sess, 38th Parl, 2004-2005. See House of Commons Debates, 38th Parl, 1st Sess, No 64 (24 February 2005) at 1505 (Speaker Milliken); see O'Brien and Bosc, *Procedure and Practice*, 833.

54 Financial Administration Act, RSC 1985, c F-11, s 26., provides that "no payments shall be made out of the Consolidated Revenue Fund without the authority of Parliament."

55 The fiscal year is legally defined by the Financial Administration Act, *supra*, s 2.

56 As the main estimates for the fiscal year are not approved until three months after the start of the fiscal year, the rules provide for the Government to table interim estimates before the start of the fiscal year, which are designed to enable the government to function until the main estimates are approved in June.

57 House of Commons, Standing Orders of the House of Commons, s 81(4) (November 2016)

58 Unlike committee reports generally, committee reports on estimates do not receive a debate to obtain concurrence in the House unless a concurrence motion is made on an opposition day: House of Commons, Standing Orders of the House of Commons, s 81(9) (November 2016)

59 Available on the Parliament of Canada website.

60 For a detailed procedural account, see O'Brien and Bosc, *Procedure and Practice*, 860–81.

61 See O'Brien and Bosc, *Procedure and Practice*, 893, fn 407.

62 House of Commons, Standing Orders of the House of Commons, s 83 & 84 (November 2016); O'Brien and Bosc, *Procedure and Practice*, 887, 893.

63 O'Brien and Bosc, *Procedure and Practice*, 888.

64 Ibid., 901–2.

65 House of Commons, *Standing Orders of the House of Commons*, s 52 (November 2016).

66 See O'Brien and Bosc, *Procedure and Practice*, 693–4.

67 O'Brien and Bosc, *Procedure and Practice*, 690.

68 House of Commons, *Standing Orders of the House of Commons*, s 53.1 (November 2016).

CHAPTER FIVE

1 Government of Canada, Privy Council Office, "Accountable Government: A Guide for Ministers and Ministers of State," 2011, available online on Privy Council Office website.

2 Tenth Report, "Governance in the Public Service of Canada: Ministerial and Deputy Ministerial Accountability," Standing Committee on Public Accounts, 38th Parl, 1st Sess, tabled in the House on 10 May 2005, concurred in by the House on 22 November 2005; Government Response tabled in the House on 17 August 2005. See testimony of C.E.S. Franks, professor emeritus of political science, Queen's University, before the Public Accounts Committee, 38th Parl, 1st Sess, Meeting No. 13 (14 December 2004) at 1555.

3 An Act providing for conflict of interest rules, restrictions on election financing and measures respecting administrative transparency, oversight and accountability (Federal Accountability Act), SC 2006, c 9 (Conflict of Interest Act, SC 2006, c 9, s 2.)

4 After the question is asked, a page may go to the member to get the member's written question for the Debates editors as the noise in the chamber during QP can sometimes make a member's question partially inaudible in the audio recording on which the editors rely.

5 See O'Brien and Bosc, *Procedure and Practice*, 501–4.

6 For example: "if the Government has the guts to ..." House of Commons Debates, 37th Parl, 1st Sess, No 126 (6 December 2001) at 1425 (Alexa McDonough); "Will the minister admit that ... she lied to the House and to Canadians?" House of Commons Debates, 39th Parl, 1st Sess, No 65 (19 October 2006) at 1445 (Nathan Cullen).

7 See House of Commons Debates, 41st Parl, 2nd Sess, No 196 (20 April 2015) at 1425 (Speaker Milliken).

8 House of Commons Debates 41st Parl, 2nd Sess, No 36 (28 January 2014) at 1010 (Speaker Milliken).

9 House of Commons Debates, 41st Parl, 2nd Sess, No 114 (23 September 2014) at 1415 (Thomas Mulcair).

10 At the end of the week, the parliamentary secretary rose in the House to apologize for his non-answer but went on to say that it would not be the last time that he would not "effectively respond" to a question: House of Commons Debates, 41st Parl, 2nd Sess, No 117 (26 September 2014) at 1205 (Paul Calandra).

11 House of Commons Debates, 41st Parl, 2nd Sess, No 115 (24 September 2014) at 1420 (Speaker Milliken).

12 The 1997 election resulted in the 36th Parliament, which had 171 Liberal, 66 Canadian Reform Conservative Alliance, 38 Bloc Québécois, 13 New Democratic Party, and 12 Progressive Conservative members.

13 A table officer uses a stopwatch for a thirty-five-second countdown that is visible to the Speaker on the computer screen at his or her feet.

14 See House of Commons Debates, 41st Parl, 1st Sess, No 232 (15 April 2013) at 1525 (Michael Chong).

15 See Chapter 1, infra, Members' Statements.

16 See House of Commons Debates, 41st Parl, 1st Sess, No. 238 (23 April 2013) at 1505 (Speaker Scheer).

17 See discussion of questions on the Order Paper in chapter 4 and House of Commons, Standing Orders of the House of Commons, s 39 (November 2016): not more than four written questions at any one time.

18 O'Brien and Bosc, *Procedure and Practice*, 520.

19 Ibid., 522; see Standing Orders of the House of Commons, s 39(1) (November 2016).

20 House of Commons Debates, 41st Parl, 1st Sess, No 105 (3 April 2012) at 1500 (Question #410).

21 House of Commons Debates, 41st Parl, 2nd Sess, No 234 (18 June 2015) at 1600 (Irwin Cotler). As the House adjourned for its summer break the next day, there was no time for a ruling by the Speaker before the adjournment. Parliament was dissolved on 2 August 2015 for an election on 19 October 2015.

22 Pursuant to Financial Administration Act, RSC 1985, c F-11, s 63(1) and Auditor General Act, RSC 1985, c A-17, s 6. See also O'Brien and Bosc, *Procedure and Practice*, 907–11.

23 Introduction, 11th Report, "Public Accounts of Canada 2014," Standing

Committee on Public Accounts, House of Commons, 41st Parl, 2nd Sess (1 December 2014). The public accounts for 2013–14 were tabled in the House on 29 October 2014. Public Accounts of Canada can be found on the Government of Canada website at https://www.tpsgc-pwgsc.gc .ca/recgen/cpc-pac/2016/index-eng.html.

24 House of Commons, Standing Orders of the House of Commons, s 108(3)(g) (November 2016).

25 Minutes of Proceedings, Meeting No. 37, Standing Committee on Public Accounts, House of Commons, 41st Parl, 2nd Sess (6 November 2014) available on the Parliament of Canada website at www.parl.gc.ca.

26 Auditor General Act, RSC 1985, c. A-17, s. 7.

27 Auditor General Act, supra, s 7(2).

28 Report of the Auditor General to the House of Commons: Matters of Special Importance, chapter 3, The Sponsorship Program, November 2003, tabled in the House, House of Commons Debates, 37th Parl, 3rd Sess, No. 7 (10 February 2004) at 1355, available on the Auditor General of Canada website at http://www.oag-bvg.gc.ca.

29 The Government's sponsorship program, which ran from 1997 to 2001, was intended to raise the profile of Canada in Quebec through advertising and other promotional initiatives to counter the Quebec provincial government's promotion of Quebec independence or sovereignty.

30 Available online at http://www.publicsafety.gc.ca/cnt/rsrcs/pblctns /gvrnmnt-rspns-rstrng-hnr-eng.aspx.

31 Online access to PAC proceedings and reports and Government responses can be had at the Parliament of Canada website at http://www.parl.gc.ca.

32 House of Commons, Standing Orders of the House of Commons, s 108(1)(a) (November 2016).

33 22nd Report, "Power of Committees to Order the Production of Documents," Standing Committee on Public Accounts, House of Commons, 40th Parl, 2nd Sess, adopted by the committee on 18 November 2009, tabled in the House on 3 December 2009, Government Response tabled in the House on 12 April 2010, available on the Parliament of Canada website at www.parl.gc.ca.

34 See "Introduction" in the Appendix to the Government's Response to the 22nd Report of Public Accounts Committee, supra, House of Com-

mons Debates, 40th Parl, 3rd Sess, No 21 (31 March 2010) available at the Parliament of Canada website at http://www.parl.gc.ca.

35 Ibid.

36 Federal Accountability Act, SC 2006, c 9.

37 House of Commons Debates, 40th Parl, 2nd Sess, No 116 (24 November 2009) at 1420 (Stephen Harper).

38 House of Commons Debates, 40th Parl, 2nd Sess, No 120 (30 November 2009) at 1425 (Peter MacKay).

39 House of Commons Debates, 40th Parl, 2nd Sess, No 121 (1 December 2009) at 1415 (John Baird).

40 Canada Evidence Act, RSC 1985, c C-5, s 38., defines sensitive information as "information relating to international relations or national defence or national security that is in the possession of the government of Canada, whether originating from inside or outside Canada, and is of a type that the government of Canada is taking measures to safeguard" and "potentially injurious information" as "information of a type that, if it were disclosed to the public, could injure international relations or national defence or national security." Also, the Security of Information Act, RSC 1985, c O-5, s 13 & 14., makes an unauthorized disclosure of "special operational information" (as defined in s 8) an indictable offence. However, section 15 allows such disclosure where it relates to a legal offence committed or about to be committed and the public interest in disclosure outweighs the public interest in non-disclosure.

41 Journals, House of Commons, 40th Parl, 2nd Sess (10 December 2009) (Business of Supply).

42 House of Commons Debates, 40th Parl, 2nd Sess, No 128 (10 December 2009) at 1030 (Rob Nicholson).

43 See House of Commons Debates, 40th Parl, 2nd Sess, No 128 (10 December 2009) at 1035 (Ujjal Dosanjh).

44 House of Commons Debates, 40th Parl, 2nd Sess, No 128 (10 December 2009). The motion carried, with 146 for and 143 against.

45 After the Christmas break, the House did not resume sitting until March as the session was prorogued by the prime minister, ostensibly to allow Canadians to enjoy the winter Olympics in Vancouver in February 2010.

46 See Question Period, House of Commons Debates, 40th Parl, 3rd Sess, No 2 (4 March 2010) at 1420 (Stephen Harper).

47 See Canada Evidence Act, RSC 1985, c C-5, s 38.03.

48 House of Commons Debates, 40th Parl, 3rd Sess, No 12 (18 March 2010) at 1015 (Derek Lee).

49 Letter dated 9 December 2009 from the assistant deputy minister, Public Law Sector, Department of Justice, to the law clerk of the House, tabled in the House on 18 March 2010: House of Commons Debates, 40th Parl, 3rd Sess, No 12 (18 March 2010) at 1030 (Derek Lee).

50 Ibid.

51 Ibid.

52 House of Commons Debates, 40th Parl, 3rd Sess, No 21 (31 March 2010) at 1540 (Rob Nicholson).

53 Ibid.

54 Ibid. The test, one has to assume, is the meaning to be given to "as possible."

55 Ibid.

56 House of Commons Debates, 40th Parl, 3rd Sess, No 34 (27 April 2010) at 1505 (Speaker Milliken). The Speaker rules only on whether there has been a prima facie breach of privilege. If so, the matter is either considered further by the full House or, as is usually the case, referred to the Standing Committee on Procedure and House Affairs for further study and a report back to the House. The House then decides on whether any further action should be taken.

57 Ibid.

58 Ibid., at 1525, citing Bourinot, *Parliamentary Procedure and Practice in the Dominion of Canada*.

59 House of Commons Debates, 40th Parl, 3rd Sess, No 34 (27 April 2010) at 1530 (Speaker Milliken).

60 Ibid.

61 Ibid.

62 Routine Proceedings, Documents Regarding Mission in Afghanistan, House of Commons Debates, 40th Parl, 3rd Sess, No 63 (15 June 2010) at 1000 (Jay Hill).

63 See Schneiderman, *Red, White, and Kind of Blue?*, 148–58.

64 One of the opposition parties did not agree with this disclosure process.

65 The committee demanded that the Government, within ten days, indicate the adjustments to the fiscal framework required to incorporate the costs of nine government justice bills listed in the motion and then

before the House: Minutes of Proceedings, Meeting No. 33, Standing
Committee on Finance, 40th Parl, 3rd Sess (6 October 2010) available
on the Parliament of Canada website at www.parl.gc.ca.

66 The Government always has the option of disclosing information that
    might be a cabinet confidence. In 2004, the Martin Government
    expressly waived cabinet confidentiality when it gave the Public
    Accounts Committee cabinet documents relating to the sponsor-
    ship program.

67 Tenth Report, "Question of Privilege–Production of Documents," Stand-
    ing Committee on Finance, *House of Commons*, 40th Parl, 3rd Sess (7
    February 2011), available at the Parliament of Canada website at
    http://www.parl.gc.ca.

68 House of Commons Debates, 40th Parl, 3rd Sess, No 142 (9 March
    2011) at 1540 (Speaker Milliken).

69 27th Report, "Question of Privilege Relating to the Failure of the Gov-
    ernment to Fully Provide the Documents as Ordered by the House,"
    Standing Committee on Procedure and House Affairs, *House of Com-
    mons*, 40th Parl, 3rd Sess, No 145 (21 March 2011), available at the Par-
    liament of Canada website at http://www.parl.gc.ca.

70 The non-confidence motion carried 156 to 145. The Government had
    at last fallen and on a Friday, which is usually the least eventful day of
    the week.

71 The Access to Information Act, RSC 1985, c A-1., does not apply to the
    House of Commons. Thus government documents in the possession of
    a House committee are not subject to disclosure on an application
    under that Act. See 42nd Report, "Access to Information Requests and
    Parliamentary Privilege," Standing Committee on Procedure and House
    Affairs, House of Commons Debates, 41st Parl, 1st Sess, No 221 (7
    March 2013) and the Government's response tabled ("back door") on
    17 July 2013.

72 National Security and Intelligence Committee of Parliamentarians Act,
    SC 2017, c. 15.

73 Ibid., clause 10; see the Schedule to the Bill for the text of the oath.

74 Ibid., clause 12.

75 Ibid., clause 8.

76 Ibid., clause 16.

77 O'Brien and Bosc, *Procedure and Practice*, 468–75.

78 Ibid., 468–75.

79 Ibid., 473–4.

CHAPTER SIX

1 Parliament of Canada Act, RSC 1985, c P-1, s 52.4.

2 See Government Estimates 2016–17, online at tbs-sct.gc.ca.

3 The salaries, or "sessional allowances," of members are set under the Parliament of Canada Act, supra. House officers (the speaker, leader of the official opposition, the leaders of recognized parties, recognized party House leaders, and whips) receive additional salaries or allowances. See Parliament of Canada Act, RSC 1985, c P-1, s 62.1-62.3., or the parliamentary website for a full list of the additional allowances.

4 For a detailed breakdown of House finances see House of Commons Report to Canadians 2016, 32-33, available online at http://www.parl.gc.ca/About/House/ReportToCanadians/2016/rtc2016-e.pdf.

5 Parliament of Canada Act, supra, s 50.

6 Ibid., s 52.2, s 52.6 and s 52.3, respectively. The courts have determined that the board's exclusive authority under the act does not remove it from the jurisdiction of the courts for all purposes: See *Ontario v Bernier* 70 OAC 400 (29 March 1994: Ontario Court of Appeal), *R v Fontaine* [1995] AQ No. 295 (24 March 1995: Quebec Court of Appeal) and *Pankiw v Canadian Human Rights Commission*, 2006 FC 601, 2007 FCA 386.

7 Ibid., s 52.5. Note: On administrative and financial matters, the House is not governed by the Financial Administration Act, supra, which applies to government departments and agencies only.

8 Parliament of Canada Act, supra, s 50.

9 Ibid., s 52: if the Speaker is unavailable, quorum may be based on five board members, one of whom must be a minister.

10 In the 42nd Parliament for fiscal year 2016–17 the office budget for the Speaker was approximately $1.2 million, the deputy speaker $91,000, and the other chair occupants approximately $40,000 each. The offices of the leader of the official opposition (Conservative Party of Canada, ninety-six members) received approximately $4.4 million and the leader of the second party in opposition (New Democratic Party, forty-four members) approximately $2 million. The board does not fund the Prime Minister's

Office. The budgets for the offices of the Government whip, official opposition whip, and second opposition party whip were approximately $900,000, $600,000, and $340,000, respectively. The research budgets for the three caucuses were approximately $3 million, $2.7 million, and $1.7 million, respectively. Further information on House office budgets is available at the parliamentary website at www.parl.gc.ca.

11 In the 42nd Parliament, for fiscal year 2016–17, the office budget for each member was $349,100 plus reimbursable expenses for miscellaneous expenditures (three per cent of budget), advertising (ten per cent of budget) and travel ($30,000), plus supplements for ridings with more than 150,000 electors and/or a geographic area of more than 500,000 square kilometres. Further information on members' office budgets is available at the parliamentary website at www.parl.gc.ca.

12 Parliament of Canada Act, supra, s 50.

13 See Order Paper, 41st Parl, 2nd Sess, Government Business No. 2, paragraph (b), 21 October 2013, at www.parl.gc.ca.

14 Budget Implementation Act, 2017, No. 1 SC 2017, c. 20, ss. 123.

15 Vaid, infra, para 46.

16 At the time of writing, the issue of whether parliamentary privilege applies to the board is before the courts in a legal action brought by some NDP members against the board relating to board demands for repayment of funds allegedly wrongly used by the members: Boulerice et al v Board of Internal Economy et al, Federal Court of Canada, File No. T-1526-14.

17 Budget Implementation Act, 2017, No. 1 SC 2017, c. 20, s. 124. It's not clear whether this amendment will retroactively provide a defence of parliamentary privilege to the board in Boulerice, supra.

18 Board of Internal Economy Bylaws, Members' Bylaw, s 1(1).

19 Ibid., s 19(b).

20 Ibid., s 4(2)., and see definition of "parliamentary functions" in Members' Bylaw, s 1(1), supra.

21 Ibid., s 4(3).

22 House of Commons, Standing Orders of the House of Commons, s 151 (November 2016). There have been thirteen clerks since Confederation.

23 Parliament of Canada Act, supra, s 51.

24 See Evidence, Meeting No. 4, Standing Committee on Procedure and House Affairs, House of Commons, 41st Parl, 2nd Sess (5 November

2013) at 1100 (testimony of Audrey O'Brien, clerk of the House, on the history of the Board of Internal Economy and the clerk's administrative role as Secretary to the board), available online at the Parliament of Canada website at www.parl.gc.ca.

25 A few times the deputy speaker joined the meeting but this was frowned upon as it constrained the clerks in their reports about business in the chamber, not to mention their reports on rumours and jokes.

26 Wicksteed, *Waifs in Verse,* with appendix and notes ("Apology").

27 Report of the Commission to Investigate and Report upon the Working of the Law Branch of the House of Commons of Canada, 7 May 1912.

28 House of Commons, Standing Orders of the House of Commons, s 156 (November 2016)., authorizes the law clerk to make "non-substantive" changes to the texts of bills.

29 Lawyers might be interested to know that Law Clerk O'Brien was the author of *O'Brien's Conveyancer* (1893), a compendium of legal forms for real estate conveyances, as well as several other compendia of legal forms and legal digests that have been brought together as *O'Brien's Encyclopedia of Forms* (11th ed., Canada Law Book, 2006), which is available online at obriensforms.com.

30 Letter from House Clerk W.B. Northrup to the secretary of the Civil Service Commission, 25 November 1924.

31 Marleau and Montpetit, eds. *House of Commons Procedure and Practice,* 612.

32 This is the formality where, on 18 May 2016, Prime Minister Justin Trudeau, waiting for the vote to begin, left his seat, marched down the floor of the chamber to where several members were making it difficult for the opposition whip to get to the clerk's table. He took the whip by the arm, some thought forcibly, and escorted him toward the table. The PM's action gave rise to objections from opposition members and the PM apologized unreservedly: House of Commons Debates, 42nd Parl, 1st Sess, No 58 (18 May 2016) at 1510 (Justin Trudeau) and House of Commons Debates, 42nd Parl, 1st Sess, No 59 (19 May 2016) at 1030 (Justin Trudeau).

33 Soon after the bells incident, the bells were replaced with a more muted beeping sound.

34 For a detailed account of this incident, particularly the ineffectual role of the speaker, see Robert, "Ringing in Reform," 46.

35 Bill C-20, An Act to give effect to the requirement for clarity as set out

in the opinion of the Supreme Court of Canada in the Quebec Secession Reference, 2nd Sess, 36th Parl, 2000 (assented to 29 June 2000), SC
2000, c 26.

36 House of Commons Debates, 36th Parl, 2nd Sess, No 65 (16 March
2000) at 1115 (Gilles Duceppe).

37 34th Report, Standing Committee on Procedure and House Affairs,
House of Commons, 36th Parl, 2nd Sess (9 June 2000), available online at
the Parliament of Canada website at www.parl.gc.ca.

38 Ibid.

39 Meeting No. 49, Standing Committee on Procedure and House Affairs,
House of Commons, 36th Parl, 2nd Sess (15 June 2000), available online
at the Parliament of Canada website at www.parl.gc.ca.

40 www.parl.gc.ca and http://intraparl.parl.gc.ca.

41 The number of Blackberries at the House increased from 300 in 2004 to
over 1,500 in 2008 (a 500 per cent increase) and the number of laptops
increased from 200 to 1,200 (a 600 per cent increase).

42 House of Commons Report to Canadians 2016, 26, supra, endnote 4.

43 House of Commons Report to Canadians 2016, 25, supra, endnote 4.

44 See Evidence, Standing Committee on Procedure and House Affairs,
House of Commons, 41st Parl, 2nd Sess (5 November 2013) (Mark G Wat-
ters, House chief financial officer), available online at the Parliament of
Canada website at www.parl.gc.ca.

45 Ibid. See also Board of Internal Economy Bylaws, Rules of Practice and
Procedure of the Board of Internal Economy, s 9.

46 Staffing of the federal Public Service is governed by the Public Service
Employment Act, SC 2003, c 22, s. 12 and 13. The Treasury Board of the
Government of Canada is the employer of federal public servants under
the Financial Administration Act, RSC 1985, c F-11.

EPILOGUE

1 M-517, see House of Commons Debates, 40th Parl, 3rd Sess, No 50
(27 May 2010) at 1730 (Michael Chong). The motion was carried
235–44.

2 See Evidence, Meeting No. 28, Standing Committee on Procedure and
House Affairs, House of Commons Debates, 40th Parl, 3rd Sess, No 89
(28 October 2010).

3 Bill C-38, Jobs, Growth and Long-term Prosperity Act, 1st Sess, 41st
   Parl, 2012 (assented to 29 June 2012), SC 2012, c 19., Bill C-59, Economic Action Plan 2015 Act, No 1, 2nd Sess, 41st Parl, 2015 (assented to 23
   June 2015), SC 2015, c 36 and Bill C-44, An Act to implement certain
   provisions of the budget tabled in Parliament on 22 March 2017 and
   other measures, 42nd Parl, 1st Sess, First Reading, House of Commons
   Debates, No. 164 (11 April 2017) at 1545.

4 At present, under the Standing Orders of the House of Commons, s
   108(1)(a), dissenting minority views may only be appended to a committee report by majority vote of the committee, which means not
   often when the Government side has a majority.

5 Budget Implementation Act, 2017, No. 1, SC 2017, c. 20, s. 123.

6 See chapter 1, endnote 41.

7 The member's initiative began as Bill C-559, An Act to amend the Canada Elections Act and the Parliament of Canada Act (reforms), 2nd Sess,
   41st Parl, 2013 (first reading on 3 December 2013). It was abandoned by
   the member and a variant bill introduced as Bill C-586, An Act to amend
   the Canada Elections Act and the Parliament of Canada Act (candidacy
   and caucus reforms), 2nd Sess, 41st Parl, 2014 (assented to 23 June 2015).

8 Statement to Maclean's Online, "Video: The Reform Act in 60 Seconds,"
   2013: www.macleans.ca.

9 See An Act to amend the Canada Elections Act and the Parliament of
   Canada Act (candidacy and caucus reforms), SC 2015, c 37, s 4 amending the Parliament of Canada Act, RSC, c P-1, adding s. 49.8. See 29th
   Report, Standing Committee on Procedure and House Affairs, 41st Parl,
   2nd Sess, tabled 26 January 2015, concurred in by the House on 3 February 2015.

10 House of Commons Debates, 41st Parl, 2nd Sess, No 168 (3 February
   2015) at 1815. It seems rather ironic that the Reform Act, 2014, SC
   2015, c 37., or what was left of it, received final House approval on the
   day the House was commemorating the destruction of the Parliament
   buildings by fire in 1916.

11 The vote of 260–17 on Bill C-586 after third and final reading in the
   House on 25 February 2015 can only be explained by the fact that the
   bill as amended posed no threat to the powers of the party leaders, especially the prime minister: House of Commons Debates, 41st Parl, 2nd
   Sess, No 179 (25 February 2015) at 1515.

12 Bill C-586 was passed by the Senate on 22 June 2015 and received royal assent and became law on 23 June 2015: Reform Act, 2014, SC 2015, c 37.

13 While subsection 48.9(5) in Bill C-586 requires the chairs of each caucus to "inform the Speaker of the outcome of each vote," the legislation does not require that this be done publicly or on the floor of the House.

Bibliography

Axworthy, Thomas S. *Everything Old Is New Again: Observations on Parliamentary Reform*. Kingston, ON: Centre for the Study of Democracy, Queen's University, 2008.

Baker, Dennis. "'The Real Protection of the People': The Royal Recommendation and Responsible Government." *Journal of Parliamentary and Political Law* 4:197 (2010).

Banks, Margaret A. *Sir John George Bourinot, Victorian Canadian: His Life, Times and Legacy*. Montreal, QC: McGill-Queen's University Press, 2001.

Bédard, Michel, and Philippe Lagassé, eds. *The Crown and Parliament*. Montreal, QC: Éditions Yvon Blais, 2015.

Bejermi, John. *How Parliament Works*. Ottawa, ON: Borealis Press, 2005.

Bingham, Tom. *The Rule of Law*. London, England: Penguin Books, 2010.

Birch, A.H. *Representative and Responsible Government: An Essay on the British Constitution*. London, England: Unwin University Books, 1964.

Blackburn, Robert. "The Prerogative Power of Dissolution of Parliament: Law, Practice, and Reform." *Public Law* 766 (2009).

Blowden, James. "Dawson and Forsey Clash on the Prorogation of 2008 and Over Responsible government," *Parliamentum*, posted 20 February 2012, available online at http://parliamentum.org/2012/02/20/dawson-and-forsey-clash-on-the-prorogation-of-2008/.

Bourinot, J.G. *Parliamentary Procedure and Practice in the Dominion of Canada*, 4th ed. Montreal, QC: Dawson Brothers, 1916.

Bowen, Catherine Drinker. *The Lion and the Throne: The Life and Times of Sir Edward Coke 1552–1634*. London, England: Hamish Hamilton, 1957.

Butt, Ronald. *The Power of Parliament.* New York, NY: Walker and Company, 1967.

– *A History of Parliament: The Middle Ages.* London, England: Constable, 1989.

Careless, J.M.S. *The Union of the Canadas: The Growth of Canadian Institutions 1841–1857.* Toronto. ON: McClelland & Stewart, 1967.

Clark, Scott, and Peter Devries, "Mr. Flaherty's Blank Cheque," 18 June 2013, at www.iPolitics.ca.

De Smith, S.A. "Parliamentary Privilege and the Bill of Rights." *Modern Law Review* 21:5 (1958): 465.

Dodek, Adam M., "Omnibus Bills: Constitutional and Legislative Liberations," *Ottawa Law Review* 48:1 (2017) 1–42, available online at www.commonlaw.uottawa.ca.

Doody, Peter K. "Should Persons Affected by Parliamentary Committees Be Treated Fairly?" *Journal of Parliamentary and Political Law* 4 (2011): 263–74.

Driedger, Elmer A, "Money Bills and the Senate." *Ottawa Law Review* 3:1 (1968): 25, available online at www.commonlaw.uottawa.ca.

Dubois, Raymond. "Accountability in Parliament: The Role of the Auditor General," *Canadian Parliamentary Review* 13:1 (1990), available online at www.revparl.ca.

Ehrlich, J.W. *Ehrlich's Blackstone.* San Carlos, CA: Nourse Publishing Company, 1959.

Field, John. *The Story of Parliament: In the Palace of Westminster.* London: UK: James & James Publishers, 2002.

Flinders, Matthew. "In Defence of Politics." *Political Quarterly* 81:3 (2010): 309.

Forsey, Eugene. "Mr. King and Parliamentary Government." *Canadian Journal of Economic and Political Science* 17:4 (1951): 451.

– "The Dissolution of Parliament in Canada." *The Parliamentarian* 58:1 (1977): 5.

Fox-Decent, Evan. "Parliamentary Privilege, Rule of Law and the Charter After the Vaid Case." *Canadian Parliamentary Review* 30:3 (2007): 27, available online at www.revparl.ca.

Global Centre for ICT in Parliament: http://www.ictparliament.org

Gomery Commission of Inquiry and Sponsorship Scandal: http://mapleleaf web.com/features/gomery-commission-inquiry-sponsorship-scandal

Government of Canada, "Relations Between Parliamentary Agencies and the Public Service: New Perspectives." Canadian Centre for Management Development (2002): 5.

Harrison, Brian. *The Transformation of British Politics 1860–1995*. Oxford, UK: Oxford University Press, 1996.

Heard, Andrew. *Canadian Constitutional Conventions: The Marriage of Law and Politics*, 2nd edition. Toronto, ON: Oxford University Press Canada, 2014.

"Constitutional Conventions and Parliament," *Canadian Parliamentary Review* 28:2 (2005), available online at www.revparl.ca.

Hicks, Bruce. "The Crown's 'Democratic' Reserve Powers." *Journal of Canadian Studies* 44:2 (2010): 5.

Hill, Christopher. *The Century of Revolution (1603–1714)*. New York, NY: Norton Library, 1961.

– *Intellectual Origins of the English Revolution*. Oxford, UK: Oxford University Press, 1965.

– *The World Turned Upside Down: Radical Ideas During the English Revolution*. New York, NY: Penguin Books, 1975.

Hindley, Geoffrey. *The Magna Carta: The Story of the Origins of Liberty*. London, UK: Constable & Robinson, 2008.

Hogg, Peter. *Constitutional Law of Canada*, 5th Edition. Toronto, ON: Carswell, 2007.

House of Commons, Standing Orders of the House of Commons (November 2016).

Hubbard, Robert W., Susan Magotiaux, and Suzanne M Duncan. *The Law of Privilege in Canada*. Toronto, ON: Canada Law Book, 2006.

Keyes, John Mark. "When Bills and Amendments Require the Royal Recommendation: A Discussion Paper and Guidelines." *Canadian Parliamentary Review* 20:4 (1997), available online at www.revparl.ca.

– "The Royal Recommendation: An Update." *Canadian Parliamentary Review* 22:2 (1999), available online at www.revparl.ca.

Laundy, Philip. *The Office of Speaker*. London, UK: Cassell & Company Ltd., 1964.

Leacock, Stephen. *Baldwin Lafontaine Hinks: Responsible Government*. Volume 14, *The Makers of Canada*. Toronto: Morand & Co., 1907.

Lee, Derek. *The Power of Parliamentary Houses to Send for Persons, Papers and Records: A Sourcebook on the Law and Precedent of Parliamentary Subpoena*

Powers for Canadian and Other Houses. Toronto, ON: University of Toronto Press Incorporated, 1999.

Library of Parliament: http://www.lop.parl.gc.ca/About/Library/Virtual Library/index-e.asp (1985).

Lock, G.F. "Parliamentary Privilege and the Courts: The Avoidance of Conflict." *Public Law* (1985): 64.

Lukyniuk, Michael. "Spending Proposals: When Is a Royal Recommendation Needed?" *Canadian Parliamentary Review* 33:1 (2010), available online at www.revparl.ca.

Lyon, Ann. *Constitutional History of the United Kingdom.* London, UK: Cavendish Publishing, 2003.

MacKinnon, Leslie. "Powering up the Speaker of the House," *CBC News*, 28 December 2012, www.cbc.ca/news/politics/powering-up-the-speaker-of-the-house-1.1279680.

Madgwick, Peter James, and Diana Woodhouse. *The Law and Politics of the Constitution of the United Kingdom*. New York, NY: Harvester Wheatsheaf, 1995.

Maingot, Joseph. *Parliamentary Privilege in Canada*, 2nd Edition. Ottawa, ON: House of Commons and McGill-Queen's University Press, 1997.

Massicotte, Louis. "Omnibus Bills in Theory and Practice." *Canadian Parliamentary Review* 36:1 (2013): 13–17; available online at www.revparl.ca.

McKay, Sir William, ed. *Erskine May's Treatise on the Law, Privileges, Proceedings and Usage of Parliament*, 23rd edition. London, UK: LexisNexis UK, 2004.

McLachlin, Beverley, Rt. Hon. "Judges of the Court: Remarks given at the 2005 Lord Cooke Lecture in Wellington, New Zealand" (2005): available online at http://www.fact.on.ca/judiciary/NewZeal.pdf.

– "Unwritten Constitutional Principles: What Is Going On?" Robin Cooke Lecture at the University of Wellington for the Faculty of Law, Wellington, New Zealand, 1 December 2005.

Mill, John Stuart. *Considerations on Representative Government*, 1861, 58. 29n. Accessed 29 January 2017, available online at http://pinkmonkey.com/dl /library1/jsto2.pdf.

Monahan, Patrick J., and Byron Shaw. *Constitutional Law*, 2nd edition. Toronto, ON: Irwin Law Inc., 2013.

Munro, Colin R. *Studies in Constitutional Law*, 2nd Edition. Oxford, UK: Oxford University Press, 1999.

- "Reflections on the Autonomy of Parliament." *Canadian Parliamentary Review* 27:1 (2004): 4, available online at www.revparl.ca.
Newman, Warren J. "The Principles of the Rule of Law and Parliamentary Sovereignty in Constitutional Theory and Litigation." *National Journal of Constitutional Law* 16:2 (2005): 175.
- "Parliamentary Privilege, the Canadian Constitution and the Courts." *Ottawa Law Review* 39:3 (2007): 575, available online at www.common law.uottawa.ca.
- "Of Dissolution, Prorogation, and Constitutional Law, Principle and Convention: Maintaining Fundamental Distinctions During a Parliamentary Crisis." *National Journal of Constitutional Law* 27 (2010): 217.
O'Brien, Audrey, and Marc Bosc, eds. *House of Commons Procedure and Practice*, 2nd ed. House of Commons and Éditions Yvon Blais, 2009, available online on Parliament of Canada website at www.parl.gc.ca.
Oliver, Dawn, and Gavin Drewry, eds. *The Law and Parliament*. Cambridge, UK: Cambridge University Press, 1998.
Open Parliament: https://openparliament.ca
Page, Kevin. *Unaccountable: Truth and Lies on Parliament Hill*. Toronto, ON: Viking, 2015.
Parliament of Canada: http://www.parl.gc.ca/Default.aspx?Language=E
Pepall, John. *Against Reform*. Toronto, ON: University of Toronto Centre for Public Management, 2010.
Philip, Mark. "Delimiting Democratic Accountability." *Political Studies* 57:1 (2009): 28.
Pincus, Steven. *1688: The First Modern Revolution*. New Haven, CT: Yale University Press, 2009.
Plante, Francois. "The Curtailment of Debate in the House of Commons: An Historical Perspective'" *Canadian Parliamentary Review* 36:1 (2013), available online at www.revparl.ca.
Pollock, Frederick, R. Campbell, and O.A. Saunders, eds. *Revised Reports of Cases in English Courts of Common Law and Equity from the Year 1785 as are still of practical utility*. Vol. 12, 1811–13. London: Sweet & Maxwell, 1893.
Privy Council Office, Government of Canada: http://www.pco-bcp.gc.ca /index.asp?lang=eng
Public Services and Procurement Canada: http://www.tpsgc-pwgsc.gc.ca /comm/index-eng.html
Robert, Charles. "Ringing in Reform: An Account of the Canadian Bells

Episode of March 1982." *The Table: The Journal of the Society of Clerks-at-the-Table in Commonwealth Parliaments* 51 (1983): 46.

Robert, Charles, and Vince MacNeil. "Shield or Sword? Parliamentary Privilege, Charter Rights and the Rule of Law." *The Table* 75 (2007): 17.

Royle, Trevor. *The British Civil War*. New York, NY: Palgrave Macmillan, 2004.

Russell, Peter H. "Does It Matter If Our Laws Are Passed Illegally?" *Globe and Mail*, 30 December 2011; http://www.theglobeandmail.com/opinion /does-it-matter-if-our-laws-are-passed-illegally/article4248266/.

Russell, Peter, and Cheryl Milne. "Adjusting to a New Era of Parliamentary Government." David Asper Centre for Constitutional Rights. Toronto, ON: University of Toronto, 2011.

Russell, Peter H., and Lorne Sossin, eds. *Parliamentary Democracy in Crisis*. Toronto, ON: University of Toronto Press, 2009.

Savoie, Donald J. *Court Government and the Collapse of Accountability in Canada and the United Kingdom.* Toronto, ON: University of Toronto Press, 2008.

Schmitt, Carl. *Constitutional Theory*. Translated and edited by Jeffrey Seitzer. Durham, NC: Duke University Press, 1988.

– *The Crisis of Parliamentary Democracy*. Translated by Ellen Kennedy. Cambridge, MA: MIT Press, 1988.

– *The Concept of the Political*. Translated with an introduction by George Schwab. Chicago, IL: University of Chicago Press, 1996.

– *Theory of the Partisan*. Translated by G.L. Ulmen. New York, NY: Telos Press Publishing, 2007.

Schneiderman, David. *Red, White, and Kind of Blue?: A Canadian Separation of Powers?* Toronto, ON: University of Toronto Press, 2015.

Small, Joan. "Money Bills and the Use of the Royal Recommendation in Canada: Practice versus Principle?" *Ottawa Law Review* 27:1 (1995): 33, available online at www.commonlaw.uottawa.ca.

Smith, David E. "Clarifying the Doctrine of Ministerial Responsibility as It Applies to the Government and the Parliament of Canada." Gomery Commission of Inquiry Research Paper, Government of Canada Publications, December 2004, available online at Privy Council website www.pco-bcp.gc.ca.

– "A Question of Trust: Parliamentary Democracy and Canadian Society."

Canadian Parliamentary Review 24–9: 1 (2004), available online at www.revparl.ca.

– *The People's House of Commons: Theories of Democracy in Contention*. Toronto, ON: University of Toronto Press, 2007.

Stanford, Geoffrey H. *Bourinot's Rules of Order*, 4th Edition. Toronto, ON: McClelland & Stewart Inc., 1995.

Statutes of Canada: http://laws-lois.justice.gc.ca/eng/acts/

Supreme Court of Canada: http://scc-csc.lexum.com/scc-csc/en/nav.do

Swinton, Katherine. "Challenging the Validity of an Act of Parliament: The Effect of Enrolment and Parliamentary Privilege." *Osgoode Hall Law Journal* 14:2 (1976): 345.

Tardi, Gregory. *The Theory and Practice of Political Law*. Toronto, ON: Carswell, 2011.

Todd, Alpheus. *On Parliamentary Government in England*. Vols 1, 2. London, UK: Longmans Green, 1887, 1889.

Veitch, G.S. *The Genesis of Parliamentary Reform*. London, UK: Constable, 1914, reissued with Introduction by Ian R. Christie (1965).

Vile, M.J.C. *Constitutionalism and the Separation of Powers*. Oxford, UK: Clarendon Press, 1967.

Walsh, Rob. "Some Thoughts on Section 54 and the Financial Initiative of the Crown." *Canadian Parliamentary Review* 17:2 (1994), available online at www.revparl.ca.

– "By the Numbers: A Statistical Survey of Private Member's Bills." *Canadian Parliamentary Review* 25:1 (2002), available online at www.revparl.ca.

– "Fairness in Committees." *Canadian Parliamentary Review* 31:2 (2008), available online at www.revparl.ca.

Wedgwood, C.V. *The Trial of Charles I*. London, UK: Reprint Society, 1966.

Weinrib, Lorraine E. "The Supreme Court of Canada in the Age of Rights: Constitutional Democracy, the Rule of Law and Fundamental Rights Under Canada's Constitution" *Canadian Bar Review* 80 (2001): 699.

Wicksteed, G.W. *Waifs in Verse*, Ottawa: A. Bureau & Frères, 1887.

Wilding, Norman, and Philip Laundy. *An Encyclopedia of Parliament*, 4th rev. ed. London, UK: Cassell, 1972.

Winetrobe, Barry K. "The Autonomy of Parliament." In Oliver and Drewry, eds., *The Law and Parliament*, 14.

Wollheim, Richard. "Democracy," *Journal of the History of Ideas* 19:2 (1958): 225.

Young, Carolyn A. *The Glory of Ottawa: Canada's First Parliament Buildings.* Montreal & Kingston: McGill-Queen's University Press, 1995.

Zagorin, Perez. *A History of Political Thought in the English Revolution.* London, UK: Routledge & Kegan Paul, 1954.

– *The English Revolution: Politics, Events, Ideas.* Ashgate, UK: Ashgate Publishing, 1998

Index